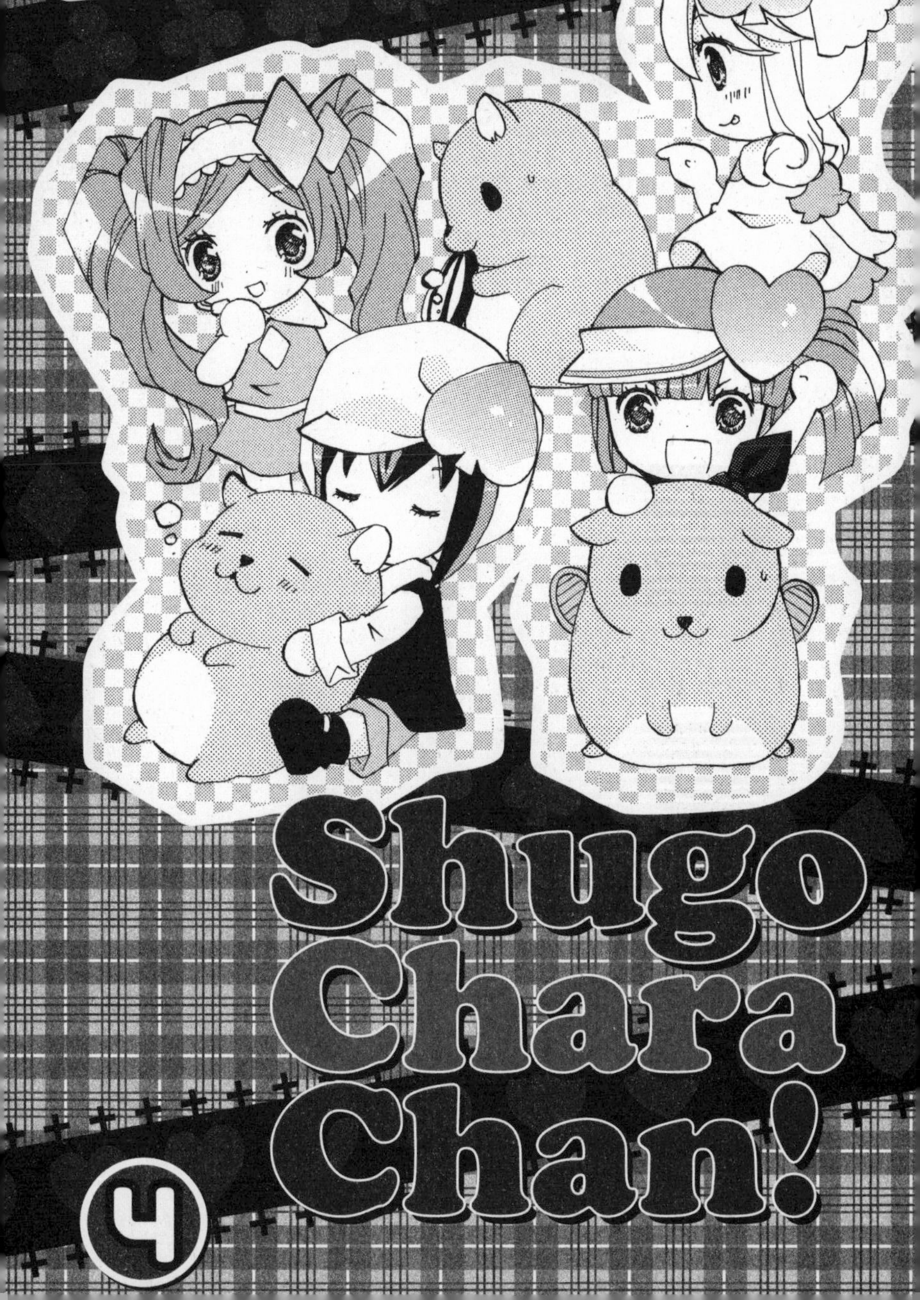
Shugo
Chara
Chan!
4

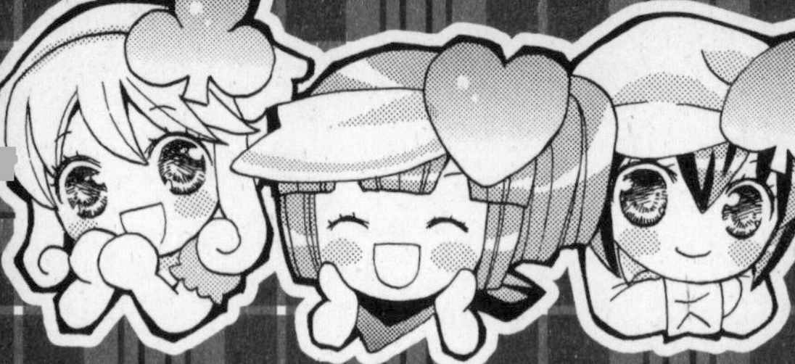

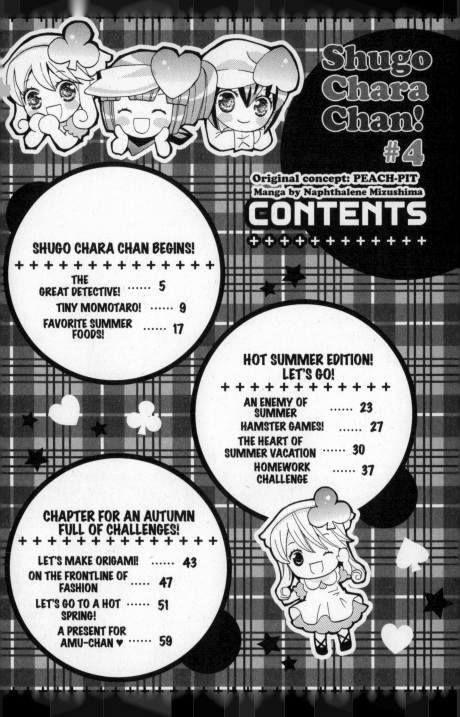

Shugo Chara Chan! #4

Original concept: PEACH-PIT
Manga by Naphthalene Mizushima

CONTENTS

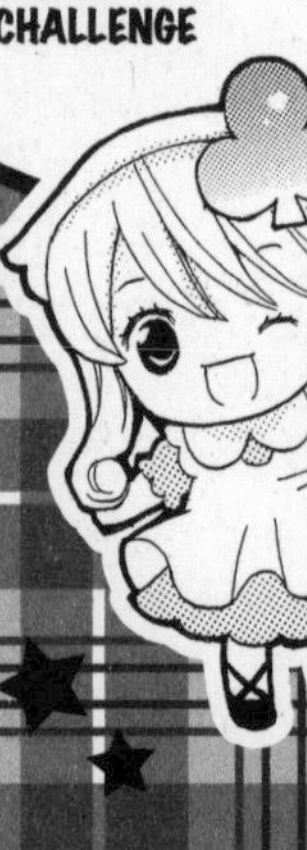

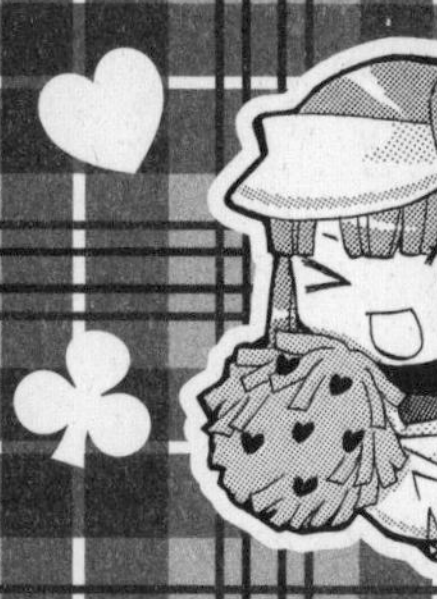

GETTING CLOSE TO THE END!

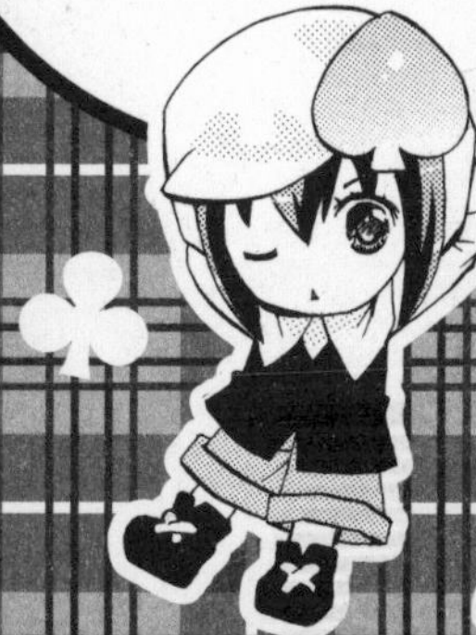

WINTER CHAPTER & GRANDE FINALE

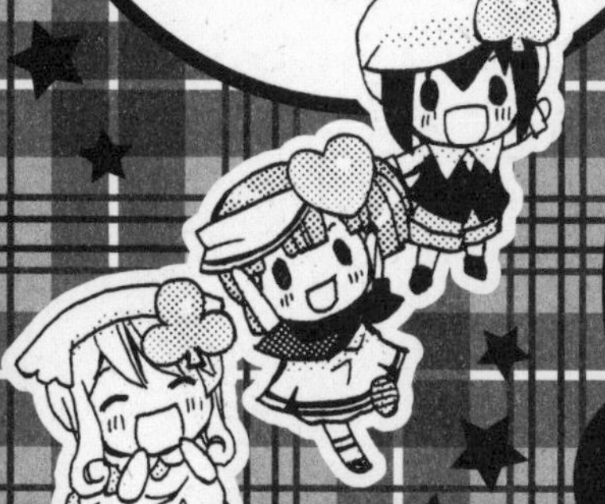

SPECIAL BONUS EPILOGUE SHUGO CHARA CHAN!

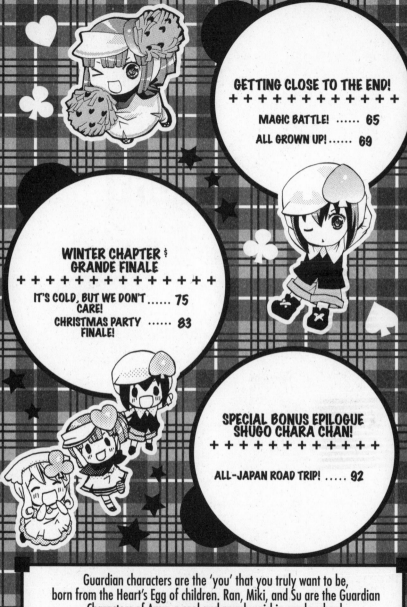

Guardian characters are the 'you' that you truly want to be, born from the Heart's Egg of children. Ran, Miki, and Su are the Guardian Characters of Amu, a cool and spunky girl in grade school. There's always something fun going on every day with these tiny, upbeat girls. Come take a look!

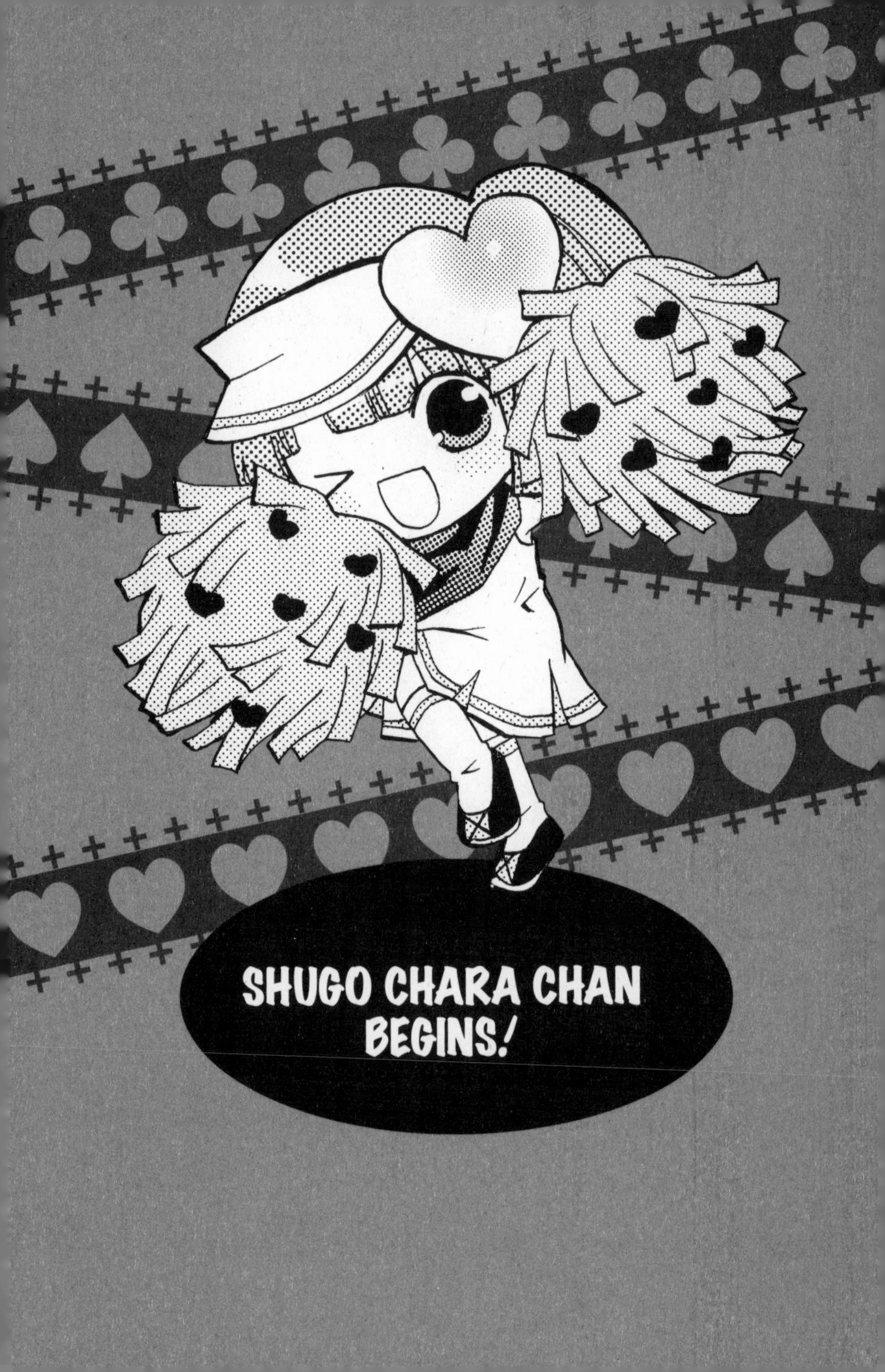
SHUGO CHARA CHAN
BEGINS!

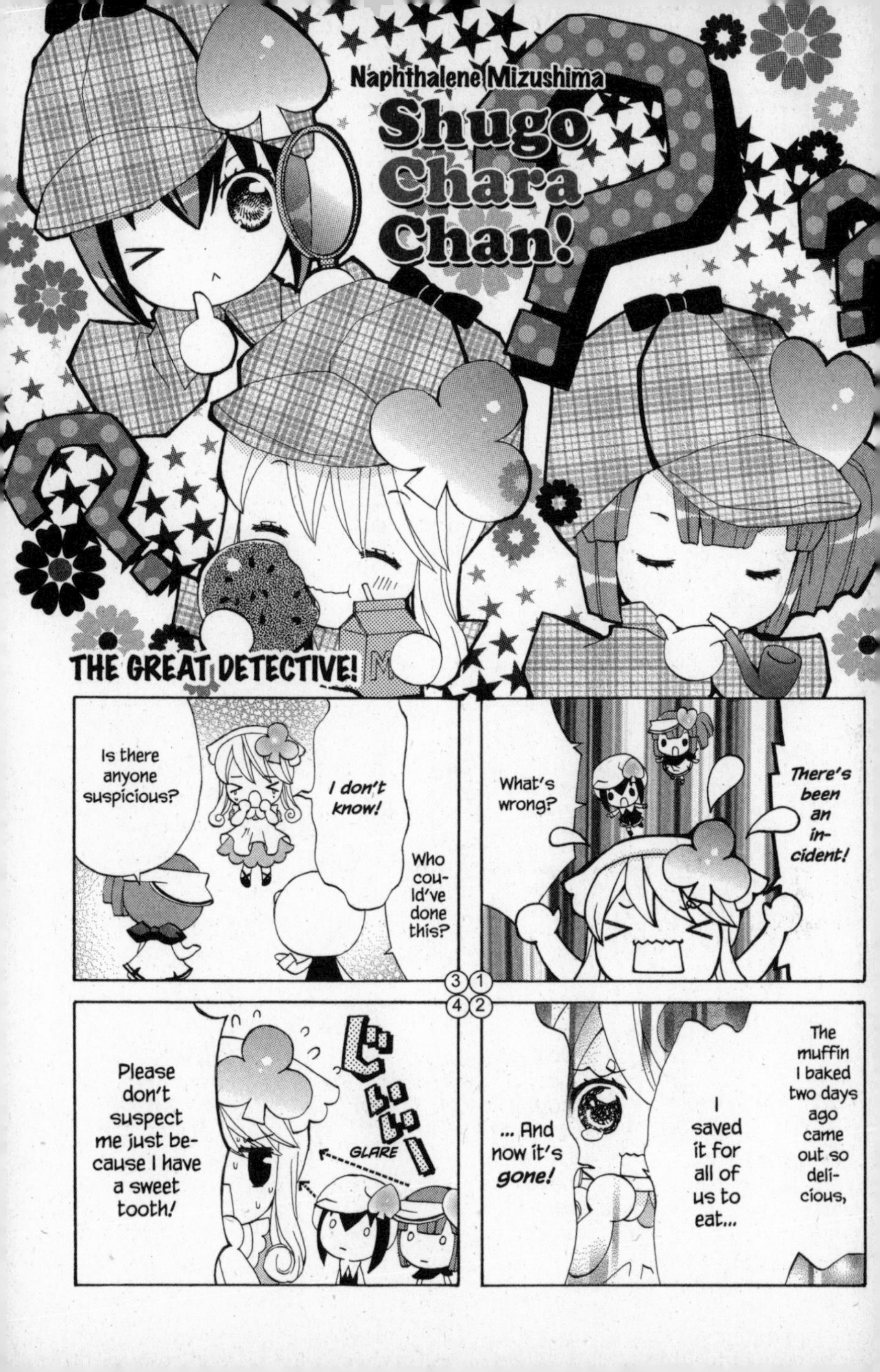
Naphthalene Mizushima
Shugo Chara Chan!
THE GREAT DETECTIVE!
There's been an incident!
What's wrong?
The muffin I baked two days ago came out so delicious,
I saved it for all of us to eat...
... And now it's gone!
Who could've done this?
Is there anyone suspicious?
I don't know!
GLARE
Please don't suspect me just because I have a sweet tooth!

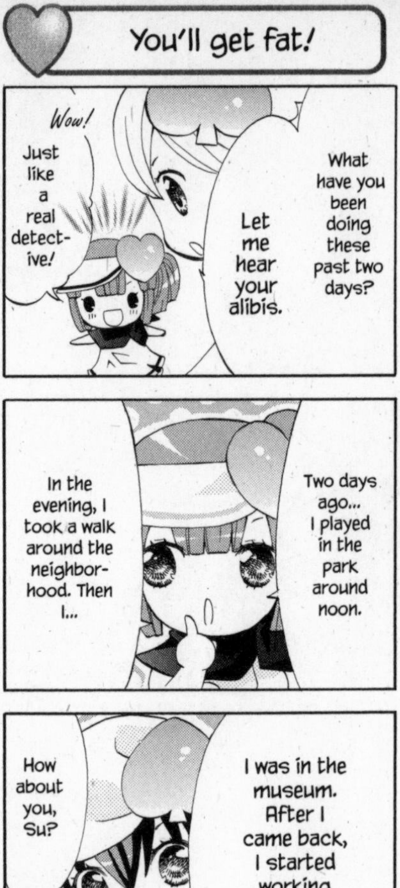
You'll get fat!
What have you been doing these past two days?
Let me hear your alibis.
Wow!
Just like a real detective!
Two days ago... I played in the park around noon.
In the evening, I took a walk around the neighborhood. Then I...
I was in the museum. After I came back, I started working on a painting.
How about you, Su?
After breakfast, I took a nap. Then I had a snack before lunch and then another nap. After my 3 o'clock snack, I...
You sleep and eat way too much!
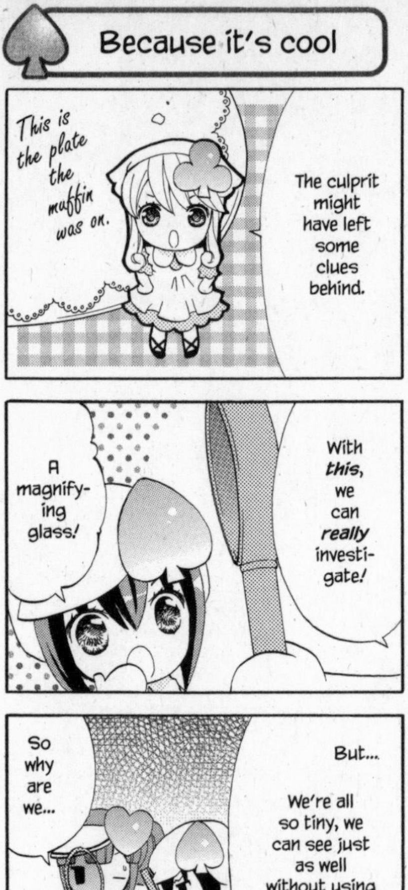
Because it's cool
The culprit might have left some clues behind.
This is the plate the muffin was on.
With this, we can really investigate!
A magnifying glass!
But...
We're all so tiny, we can see just as well without using these...
So why are we...
Because it's super cool this way, isn't that obvious?
Ahh...

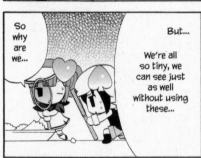

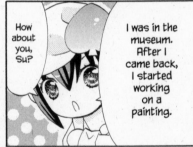

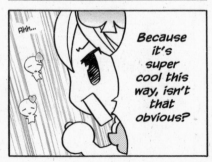

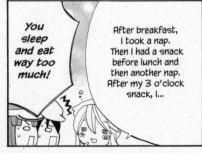

The decoy ★

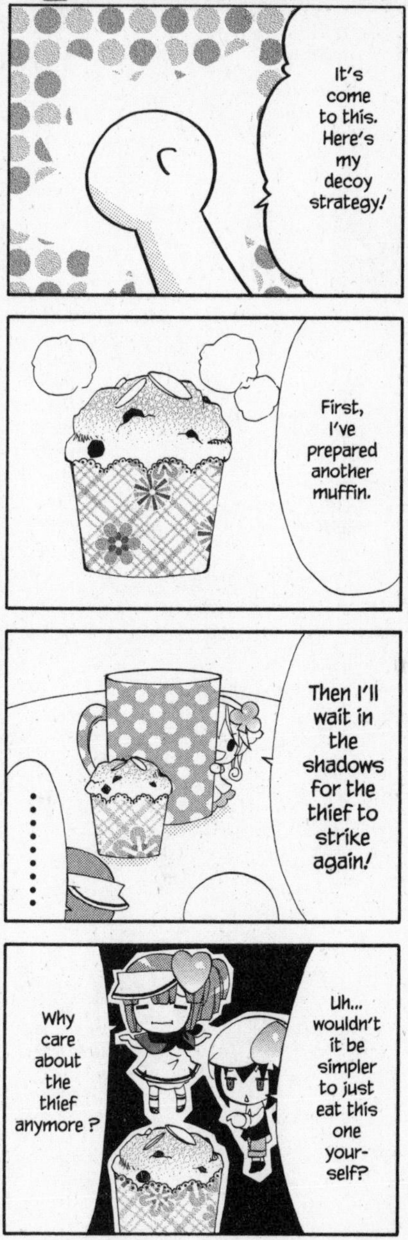
It's come to this. Here's my decoy strategy!
First, I've prepared another muffin.
Then I'll wait in the shadows for the thief to strike again!
……
Uh... wouldn't it be simpler to just eat this one your-self?
Why care about the thief anymore ?

Failure

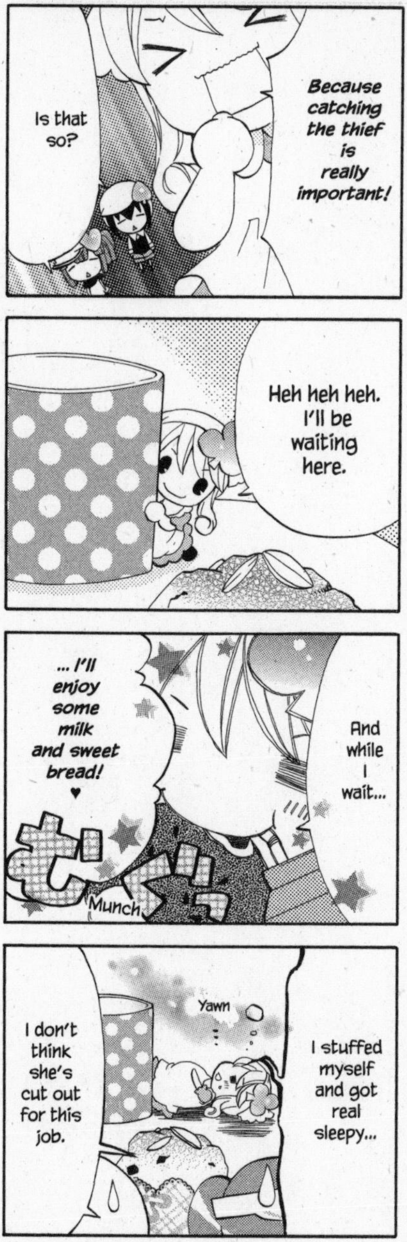
Because catching the thief is really important!
Is that so?
Heh heh heh. I'll be waiting here.
And while I wait...
... I'll enjoy some milk and sweet bread! ♥
Munch
I stuffed myself and got real sleepy...
Yawn
I don't think she's cut out for this job.

The suspect

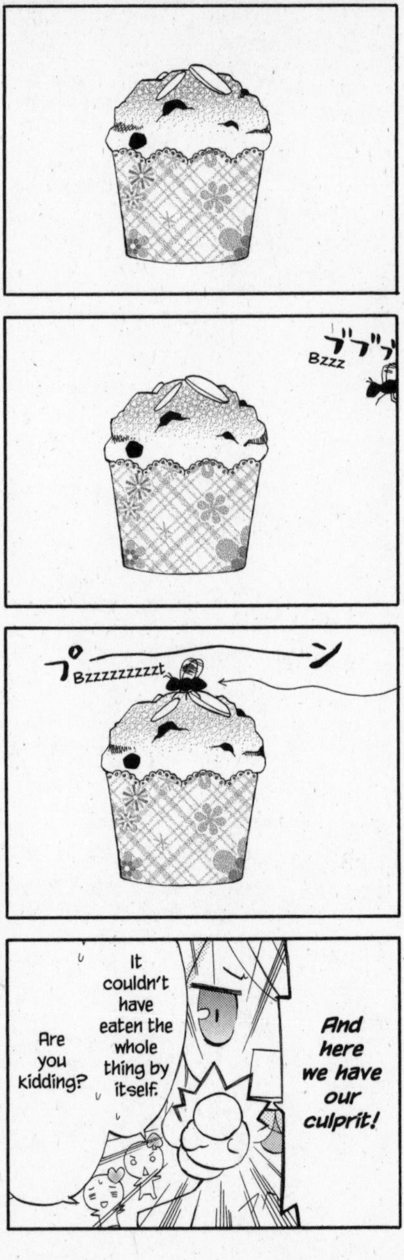

ブブブ
Bzzz
プ——ン
Bzzzzzzzzzt
And here we have our culprit!
It couldn't have eaten the whole thing by itself.
Are you kidding?

Resolution!

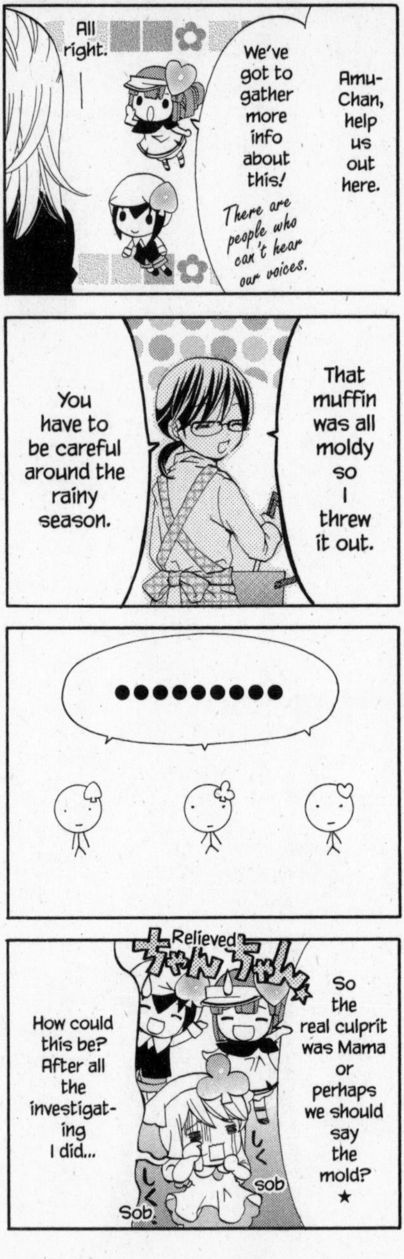

Amu-Chan, help us out here.
We've got to gather more info about this!
There are people who can't hear our voices.
All right.
That muffin was all moldy so I threw it out.
You have to be careful around the rainy season.
•••••••••
So the real culprit was Mama or perhaps we should say the mold? ★
ちゃんちゃん
Relieved
How could this be? After all the investigating I did...
しく
sob
しくしく
Sob.

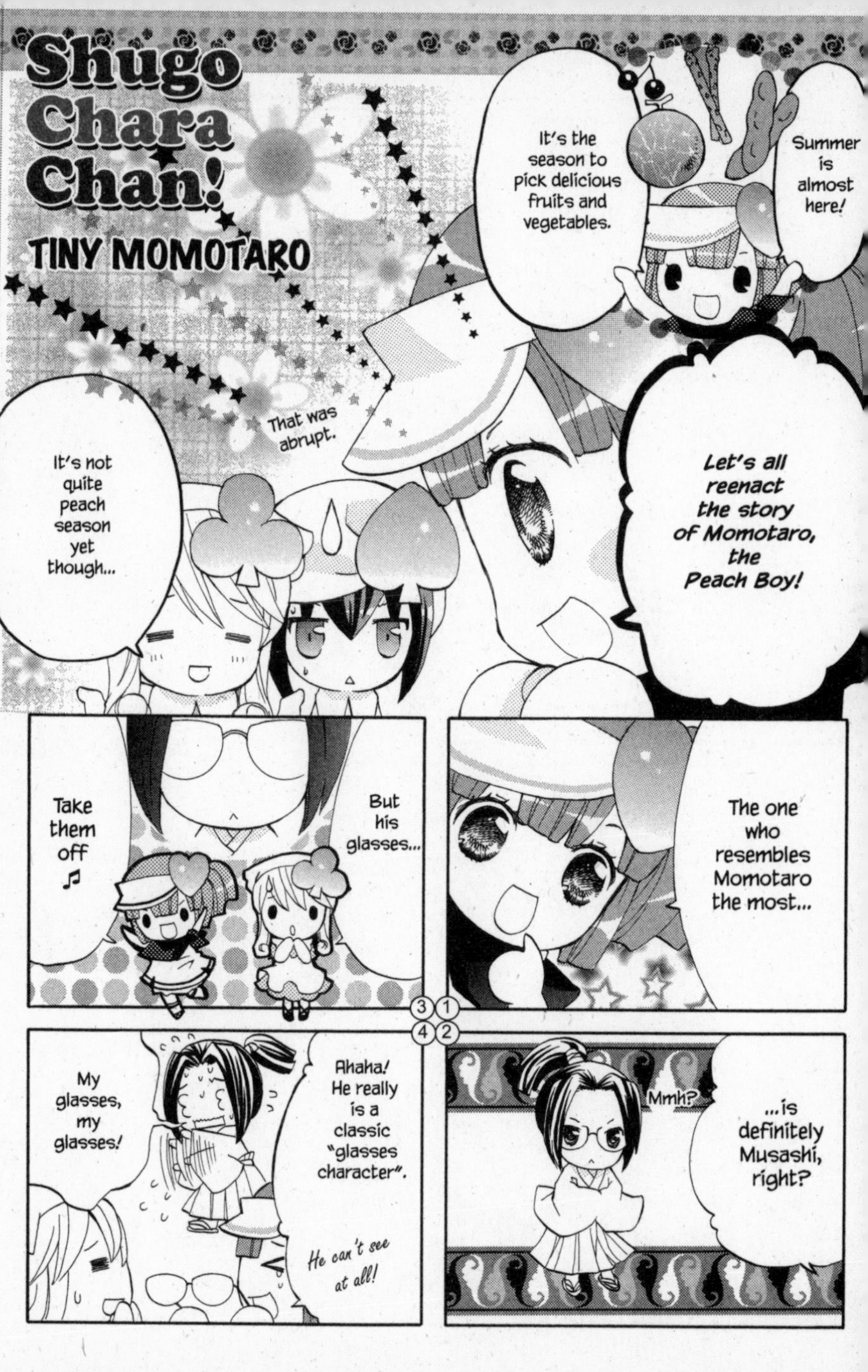

Shugo Chara Chan!
TINY MOMOTARO
Summer is almost here!
It's the season to pick delicious fruits and vegetables.
Let's all reenact the story of Momotaro, the Peach Boy!
That was abrupt.
It's not quite peach season yet though...
The one who resembles Momotaro the most...
...is definitely Musashi, right?
Mmh?
But his glasses...
Take them off ♫
Ahaha! He really is a classic "glasses character".
My glasses, my glasses!
He can't see at all!

Filling the roles

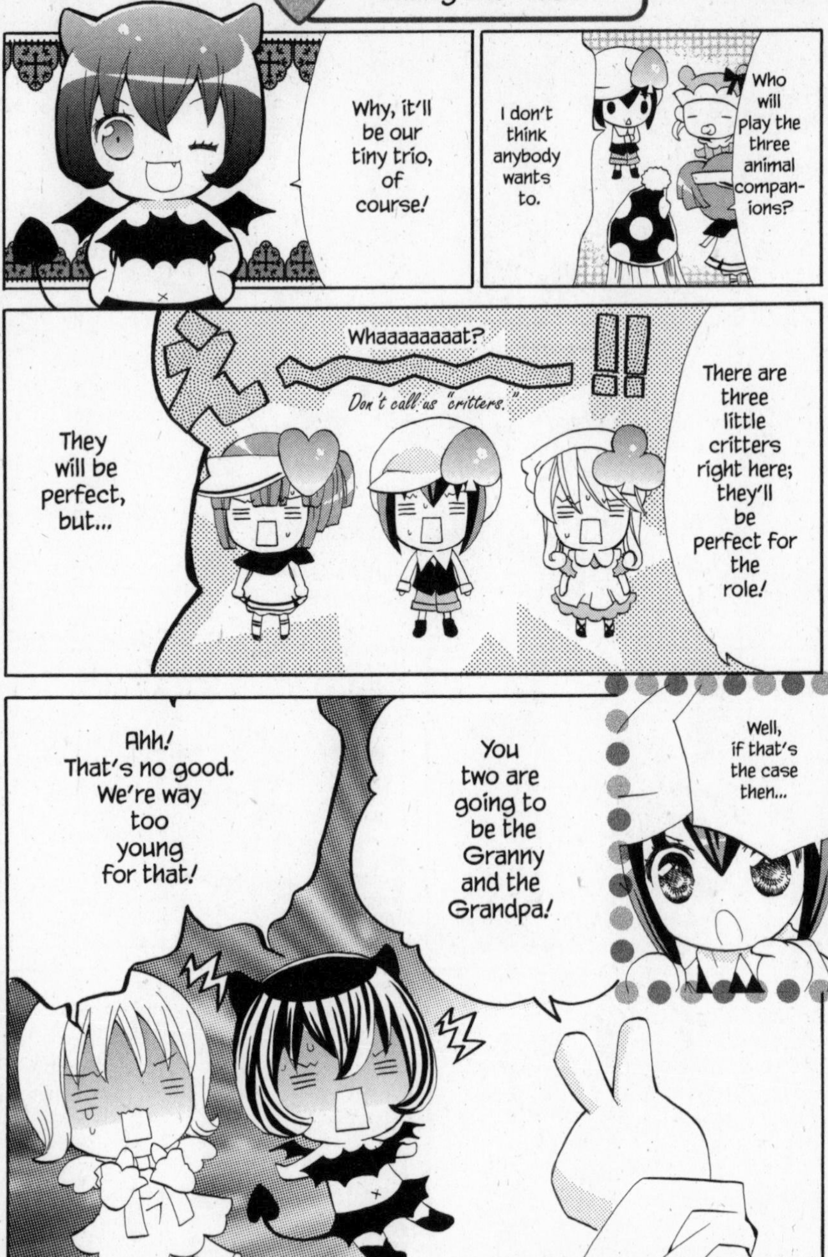
Who will play the three animal companions?
I don't think anybody wants to.
Why, it'll be our tiny trio, of course!
There are three little critters right here; they'll be perfect for the role!
Whaaaaaaaat?
Don't call us "critters."
They will be perfect, but...
Well, if that's the case then...
You two are going to be the Granny and the Grandpa!
Ahh! That's no good. We're way too young for that!

Image

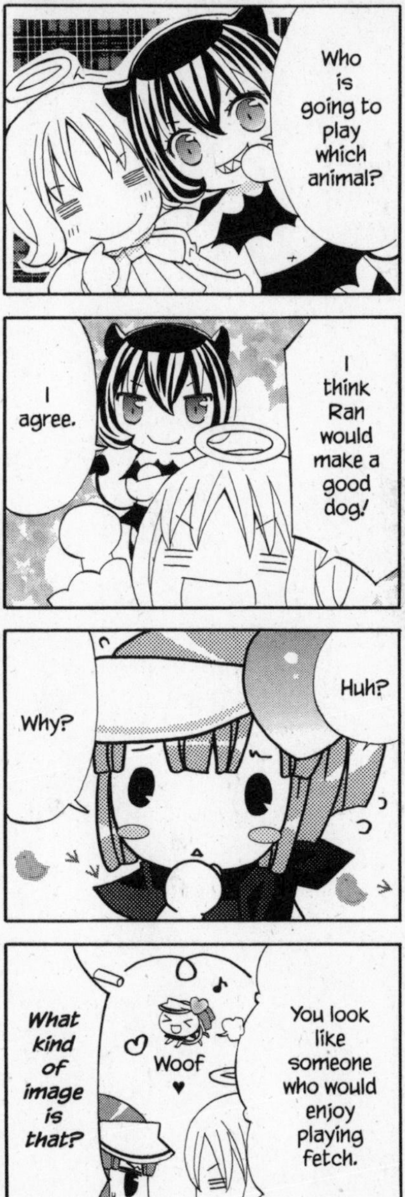
Who is going to play which animal?
I think Ran would make a good dog!
I agree.
Huh?
Why?
You look like someone who would enjoy playing fetch.
Woof ♥
What kind of image is that?

A new companion

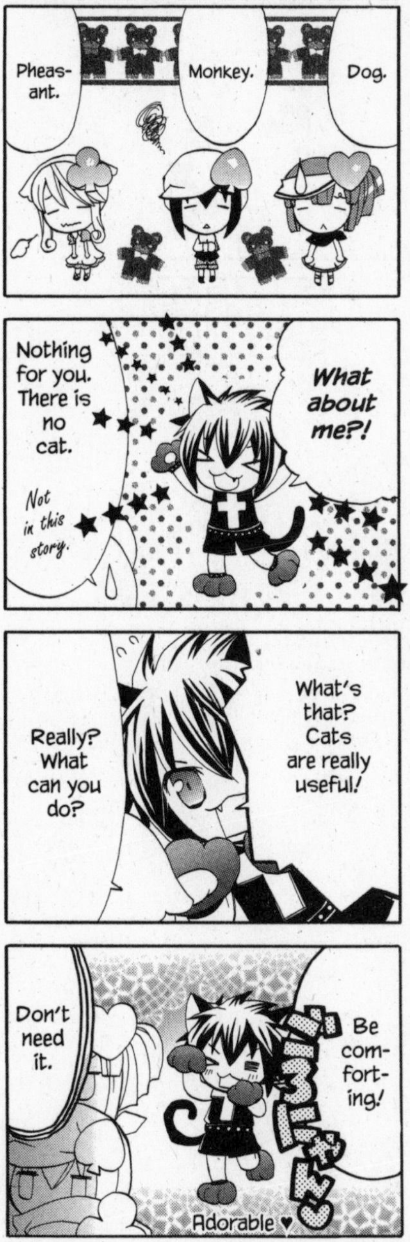
Dog.
Monkey.
Pheas-ant.
What about me?!
Nothing for you. There is no cat.
Not in this story.
What's that? Cats are really useful!
Really? What can you do?
Be com-fort-ing!
Don't need it.
Adorable ♥

A suitable replacement

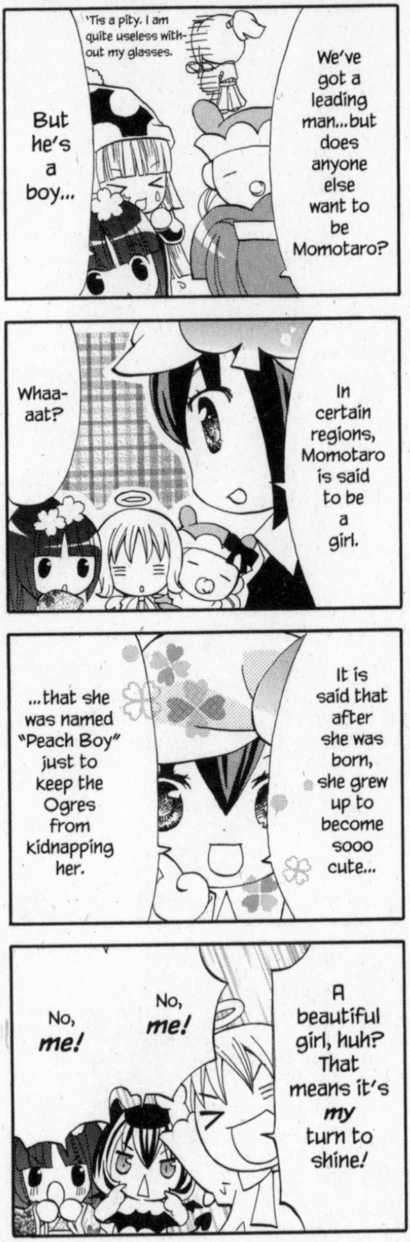
We've got a leading man...but does anyone else want to be Momotaro?
'Tis a pity. I am quite useless without my glasses.
But he's a boy...
In certain regions, Momotaro is said to be a girl.
Whaa-aat?
It is said that after she was born, she grew up to become sooo cute...
...that she was named "Peach Boy" just to keep the Ogres from kidnapping her.
A beautiful girl, huh? That means it's *my* turn to shine!
No, **me!**
No, **me!**

A pink butt

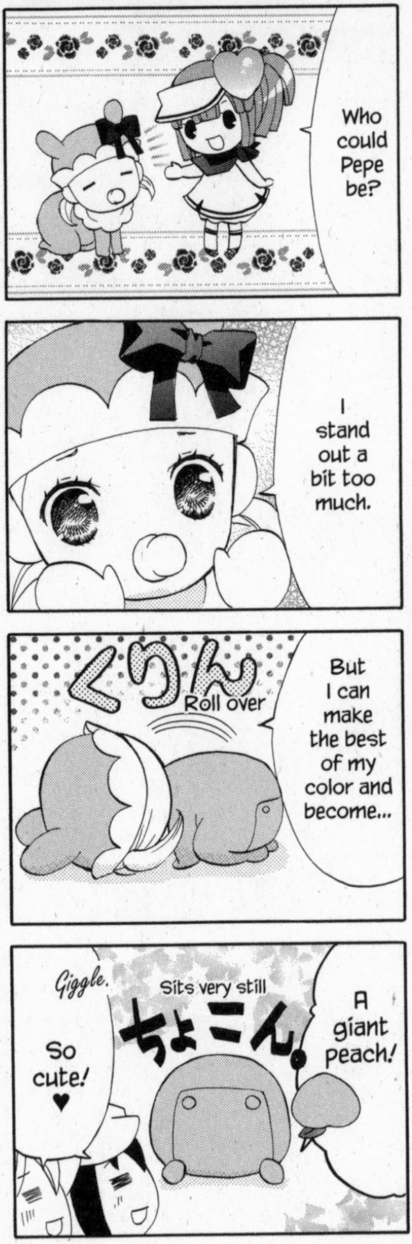
Who could Pepe be?
I stand out a bit too much.
But I can make the best of my color and become...
くりん
Roll over
A giant peach!
ちょこん
Sits very still
Giggle.
So cute! ♥

Different tastes

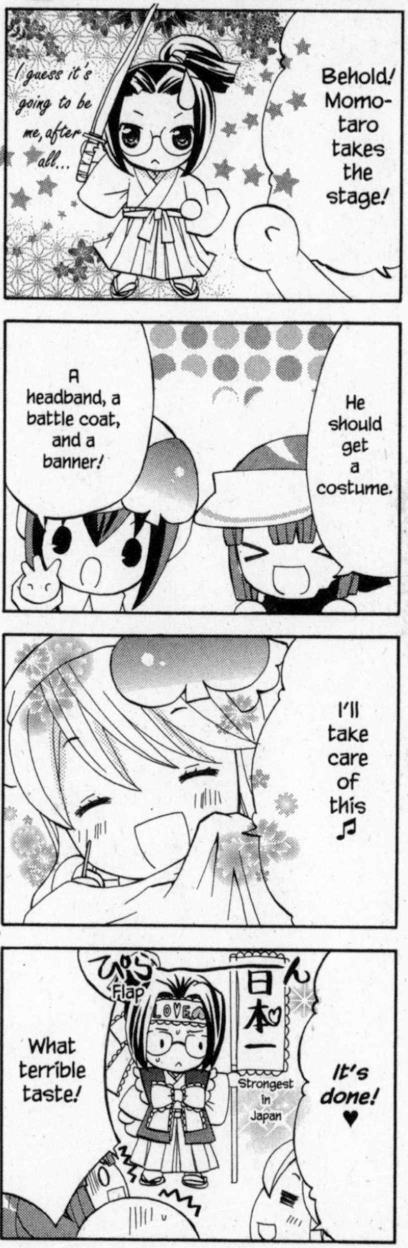
Behold! Momotaro takes the stage!
I guess it's going to be me, after all...
He should get a costume.
A headband, a battle coat, and a banner!
I'll take care of this ♫
It's done! ♥
Strongest in Japan
日本一
LOVE
Flap
What terrible taste!

Looks like fun

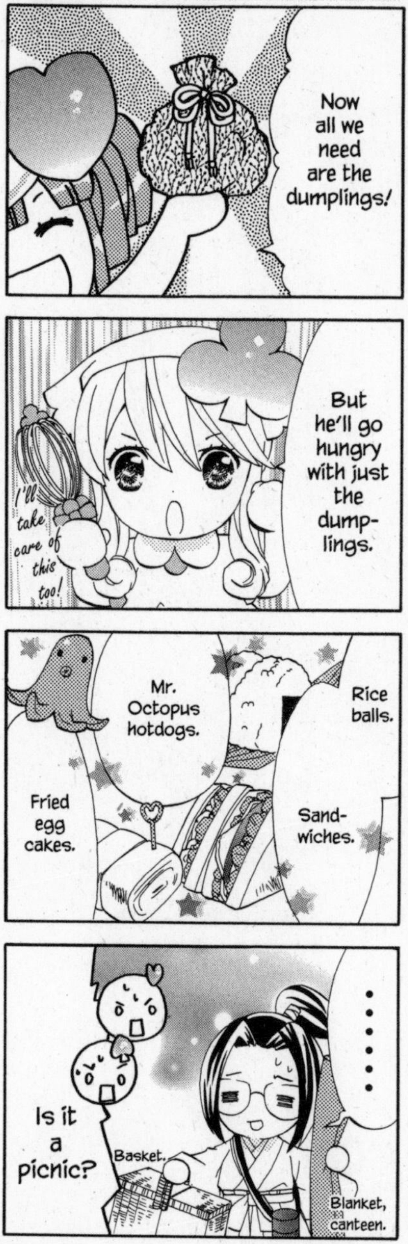
Now all we need are the dumplings!
But he'll go hungry with just the dumplings.
I'll take care of this too!
Rice balls.
Sandwiches.
Mr. Octopus hotdogs.
Fried egg cakes.
......
Blanket, canteen.
Basket.
Is it a picnic?

The price of servitude

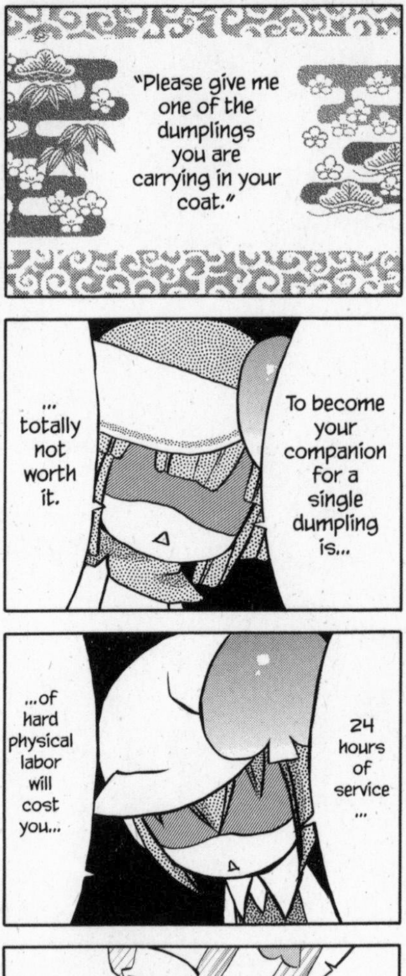
"Please give me one of the dumplings you are carrying in your coat."
To become your companion for a single dumpling is...
...totally not worth it.
24 hours of service...
...of hard physical labor will cost you...
12000 Yen per day!*
Oh please! You're ruining this classic tale!

*$120

Fashion

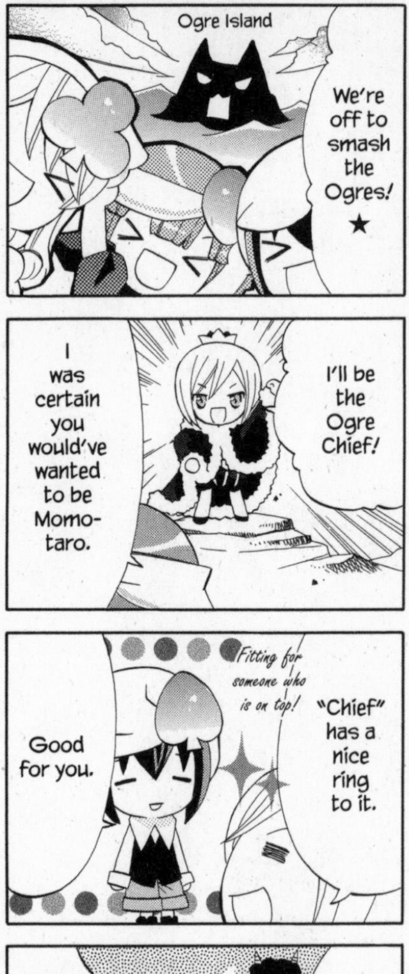
Ogre Island
We're off to smash the Ogres! ★
I'll be the Ogre Chief!
I was certain you would've wanted to be Momotaro.
"Chief" has a nice ring to it.
Fitting for someone who is on top!
Good for you.
Your undies seem fitting for an Ogre as well.
How rude!
Don't compare them to underpants.

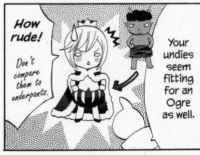

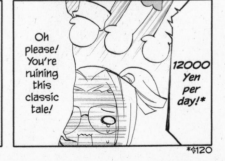

Still not over it

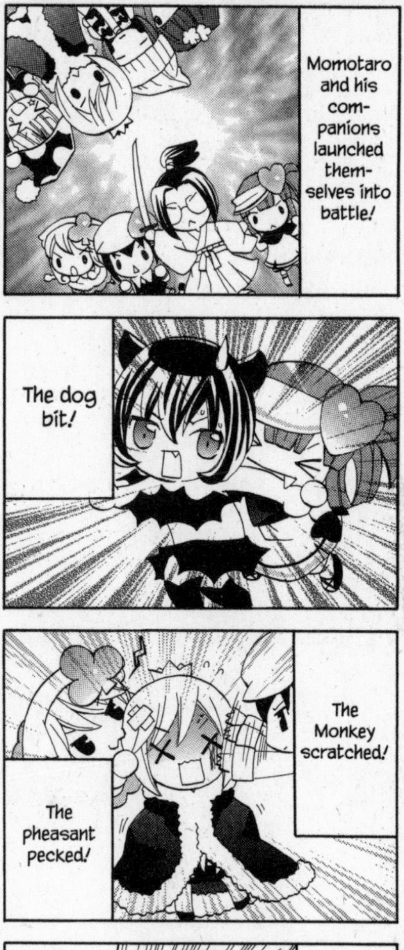
Momotaro and his companions launched themselves into battle!
The dog bit!
The Monkey scratched!
The pheasant pecked!
The cat frolicked!
Wave
MEOW! ♥
That's why we said we don't need a cat!

The secret's out

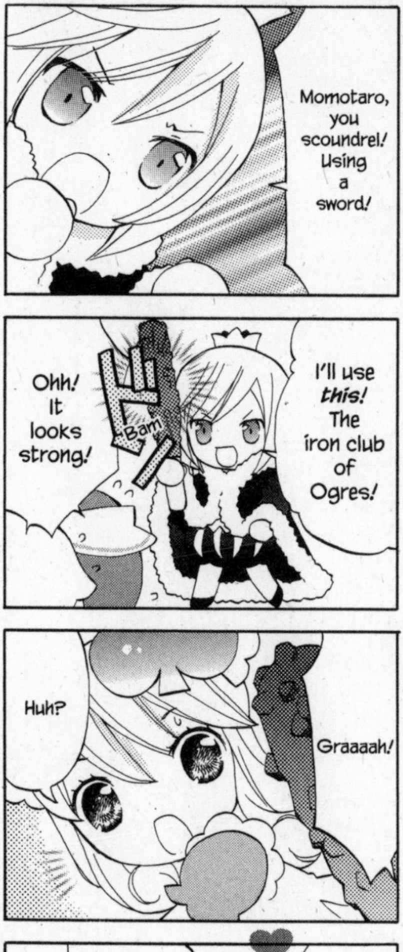
Momotaro, you scoundrel! Using a sword!
I'll use *this!* The iron club of Ogres!
Bam
Ohh! It looks strong!
Graaaah!
Huh?
It's an almond-sprinkled chocolate Pocky ♥
Looks just like an iron club ♪
Don't eat it!

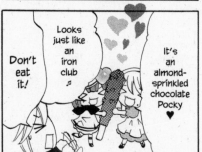

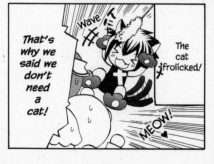

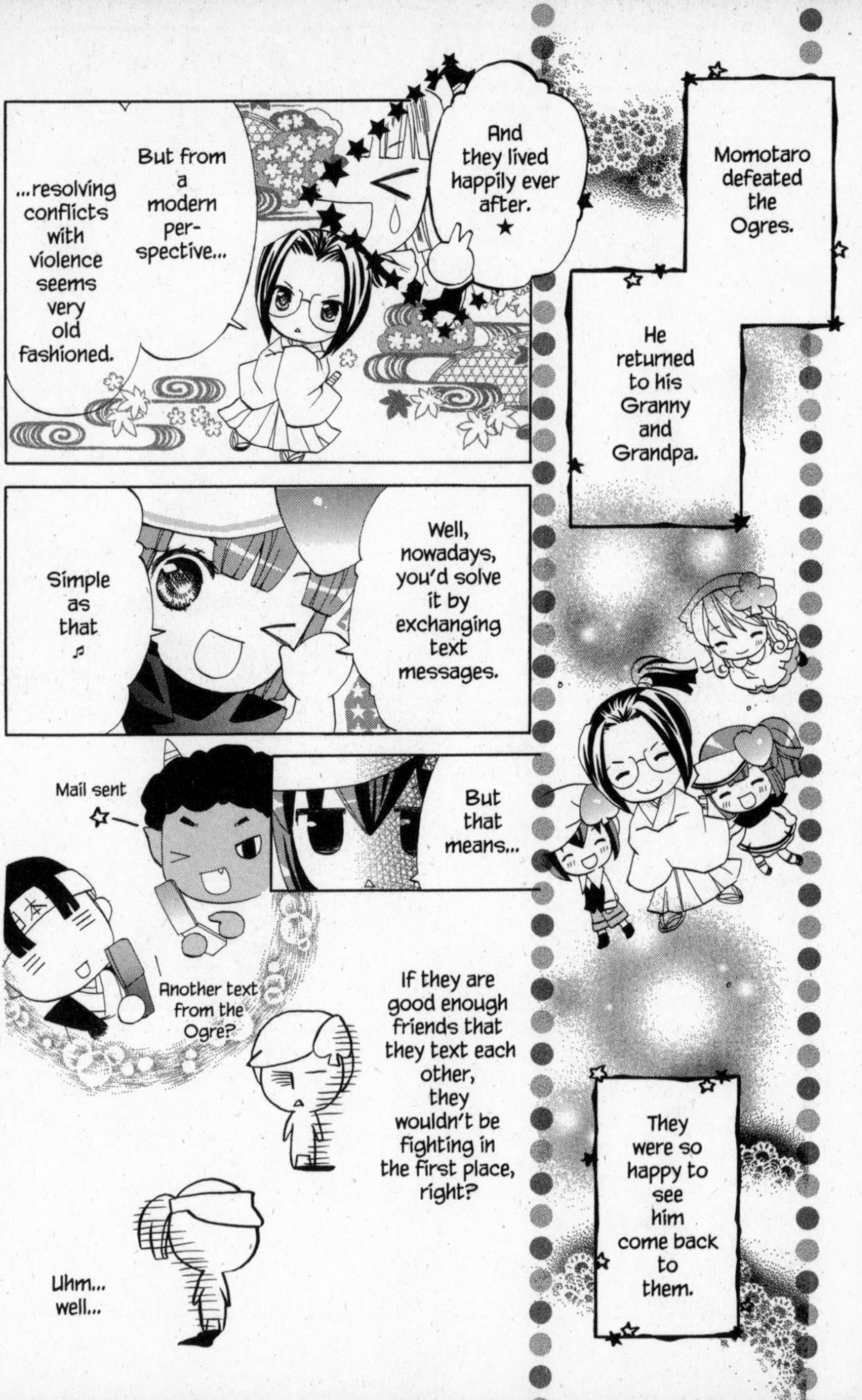
Momotaro defeated the Ogres.
He returned to his Granny and Grandpa.
They were so happy to see him come back to them.
And they lived happily ever after. ★
But from a modern per-spective...
...resolving conflicts with violence seems very old fashioned.
Well, nowadays, you'd solve it by exchanging text messages.
Simple as that ♪
But that means...
Mail sent
Another text from the Ogre?
If they are good enough friends that they text each other, they wouldn't be fighting in the first place, right?
Uhm... well...

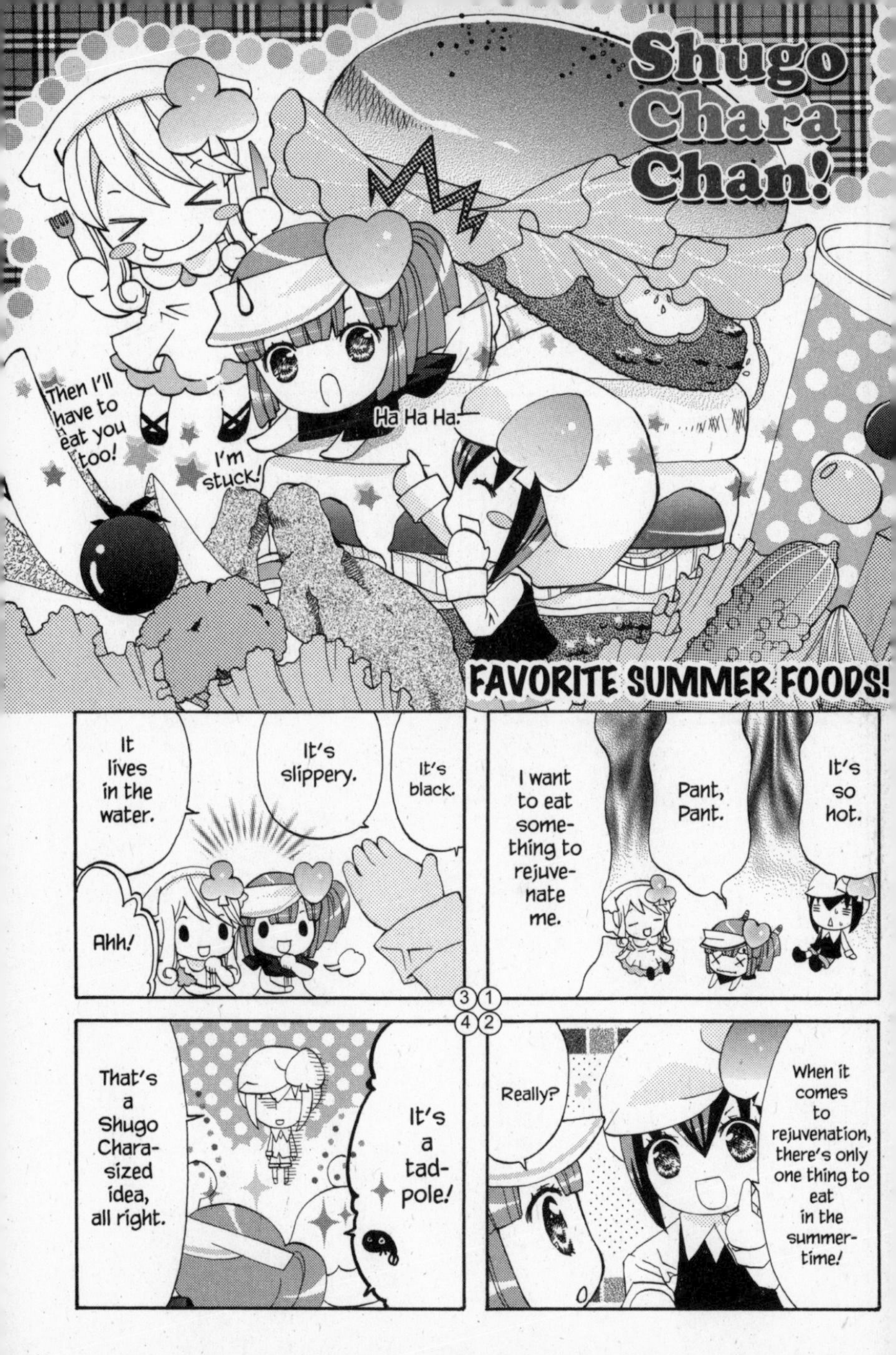
Shugo Chara Chan!
Ha Ha Ha.
I'm stuck!
Then I'll have to eat you too!
FAVORITE SUMMER FOODS!
It's so hot.
Pant, Pant.
I want to eat something to rejuvenate me.
When it comes to rejuvenation, there's only one thing to eat in the summertime!
Really?
It's black.
It's slippery.
It lives in the water.
Ahh!
It's a tadpole!
That's a Shugo Chara-sized idea, all right.

The downside

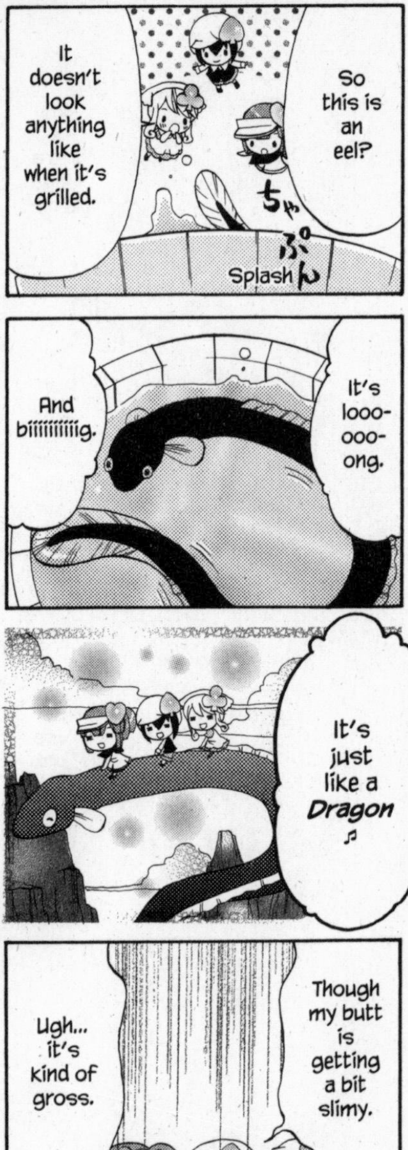
So this is an eel?
It doesn't look anything like when it's grilled.
ちゃぷん
Splash
It's looo-ooo-ong.
And biiiiiiiiiig.
It's just like a Dragon ♪
Though my butt is getting a bit slimy.
Ugh... it's kind of gross.

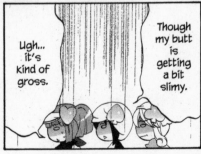

Ugh...it's kind of gross

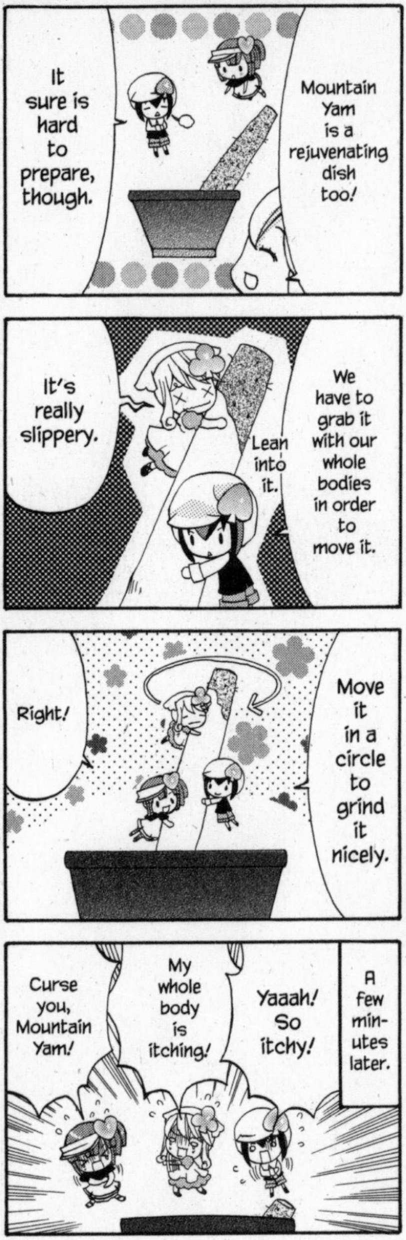
Mountain Yam is a rejuvenating dish too!
It sure is hard to prepare, though.
We have to grab it with our whole bodies in order to move it.
Lean into it.
It's really slippery.
Move it in a circle to grind it nicely.
Right!
A few minutes later.
Yaaah! So itchy!
My whole body is itching!
Curse you, Mountain Yam!

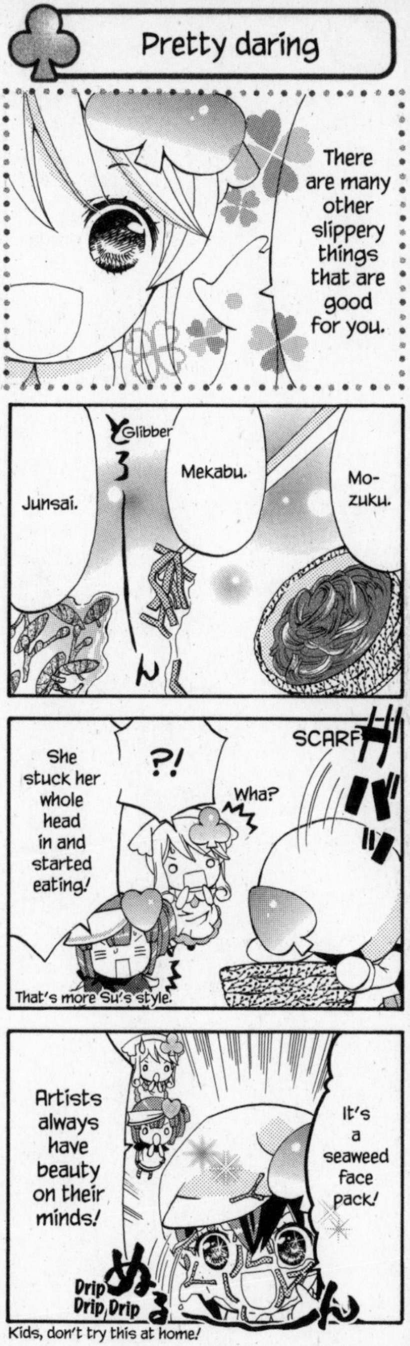
Pretty daring
There are many other slippery things that are good for you.
Mo-zuku.
Mekabu.
Glibber
Junsai.
SCARF
Wha?
?!
She stuck her whole head in and started eating!
That's more Su's style.
It's a seaweed face pack!
Artists always have beauty on their minds!
Drip Drip Drip
Kids, don't try this at home!

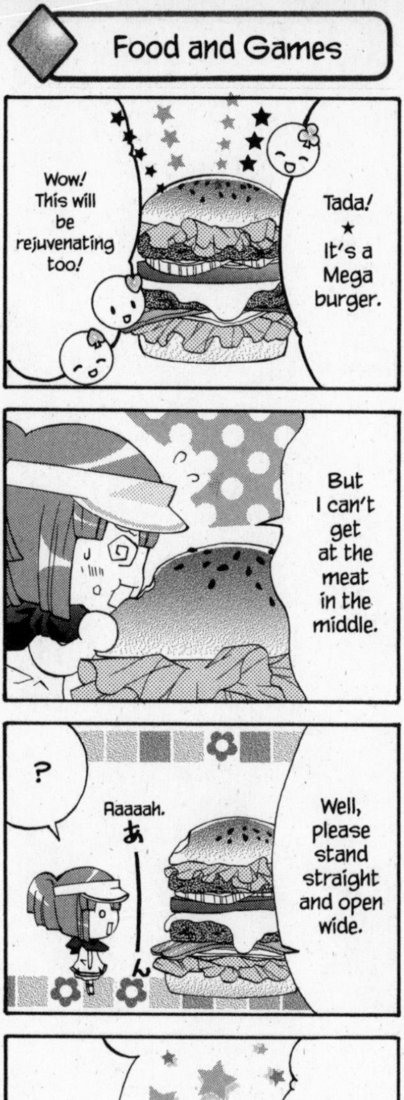
Food and Games
Tada! ★ It's a Mega burger.
Wow! This will be rejuvenating too!
But I can't get at the meat in the middle.
Well, please stand straight and open wide.
Aaaaah.
あ―ん
?
I'm going for the patty!
A Ham-burger daruma otoshi?

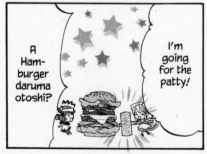

Cheap and easy

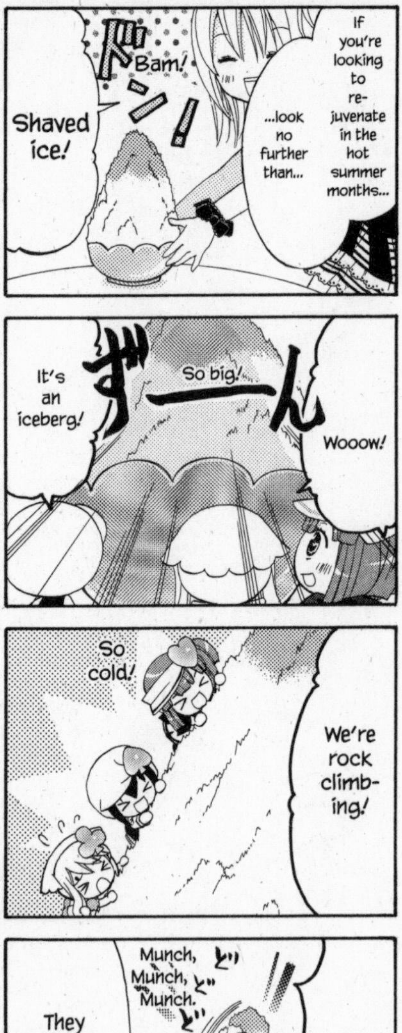
If you're looking to re-juvenate in the hot summer months...
...look no further than...
Bam!
Shaved ice!
Wooow!
So big!
It's an iceberg!
We're rock climb-ing!
So cold!
Ava-lanche!
Munch, Munch, Munch.
They sure are excited about shaved ice...

An honest mistake

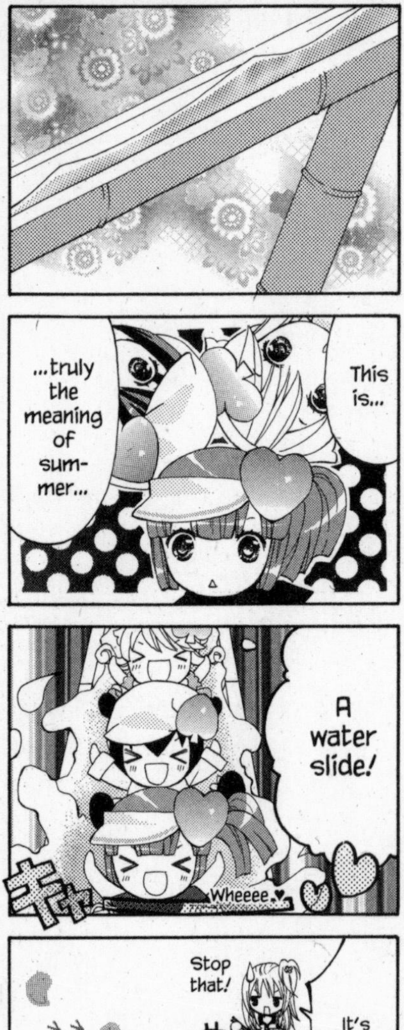
This is...
...truly the meaning of sum-mer...
A water slide!
Wheeee.♥
It's a *nagashi somen* noodle slide!
Stop that!

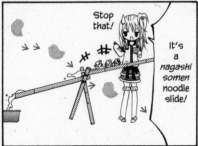

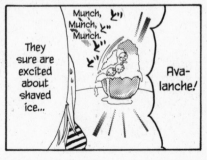

Shugo Chara Chan!

ONE-PANEL MANGA★

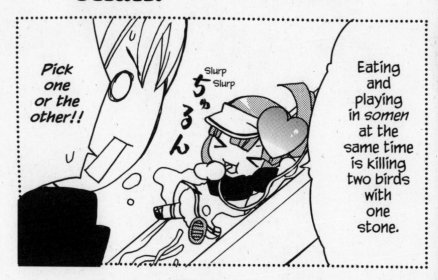

Eating and playing in *somen* at the same time is killing two birds with one stone.
Slurp Slurp
ちゅるん
Pick one or the other!!

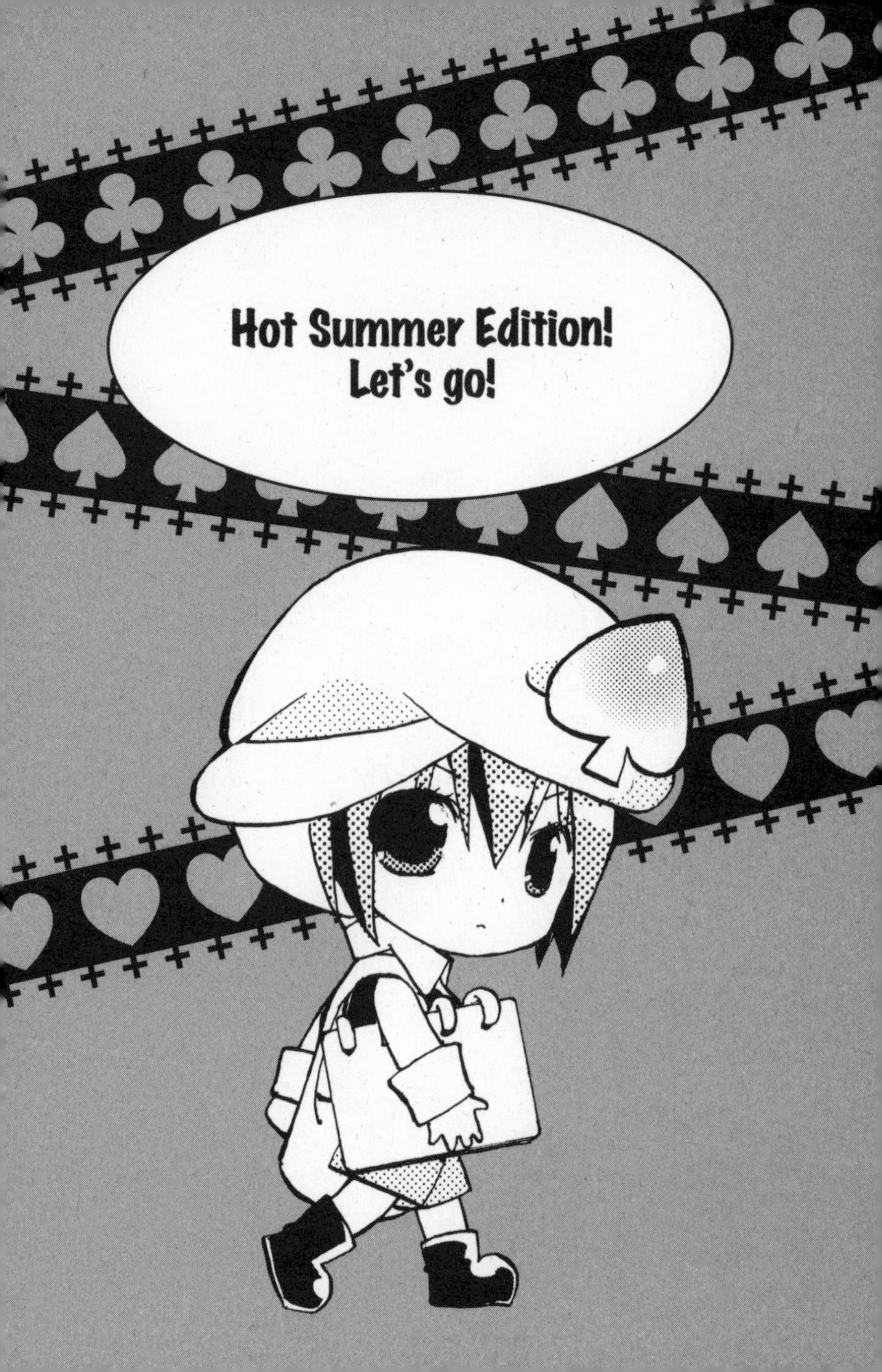
Hot Summer Edition!
Let's go!

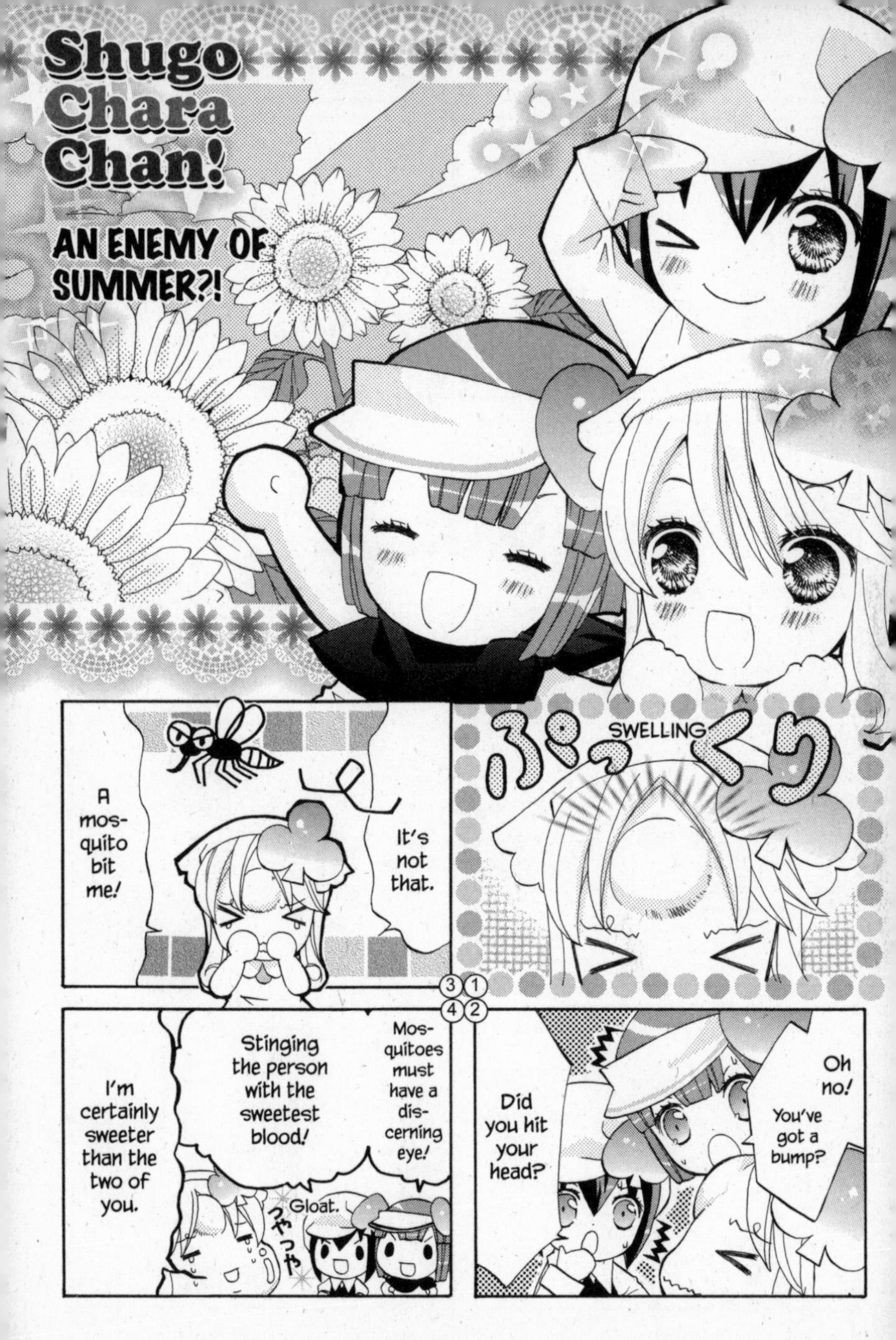
Shugo Chara Chan!
AN ENEMY OF SUMMER?!
ぷっくり
SWELLING
Oh no!
You've got a bump?
Did you hit your head?
It's not that.
A mos-quito bit me!
Mos-quitoes must have a dis-cerning eye!
Stinging the person with the sweetest blood!
I'm certainly sweeter than the two of you.
つやっや
Gloat.

Bodybuilding

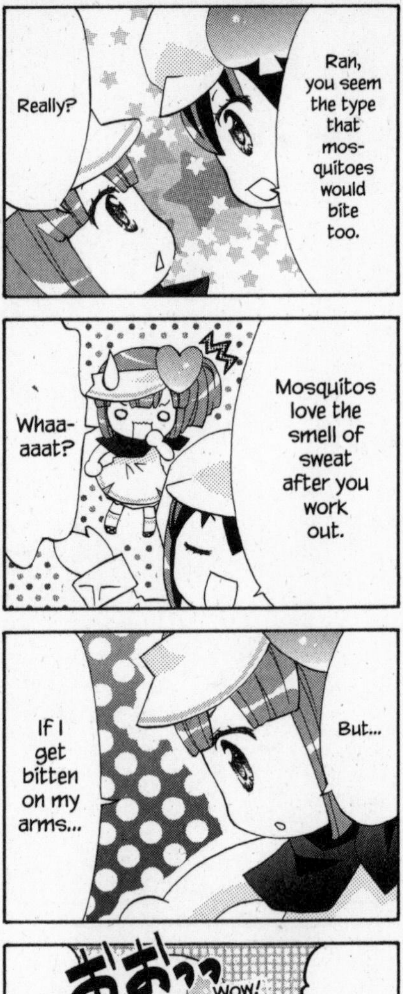
Ran, you seem the type that mosquitoes would bite too.
Really?
Mosquitos love the smell of sweat after you work out.
Whaa-aaat?
But...
If I get bitten on my arms...
The bumps will look like biceps!
おおっっ
WOW!
That's an easy way to get buff!
Flex.
ぷくー

Mr. Pig Shock

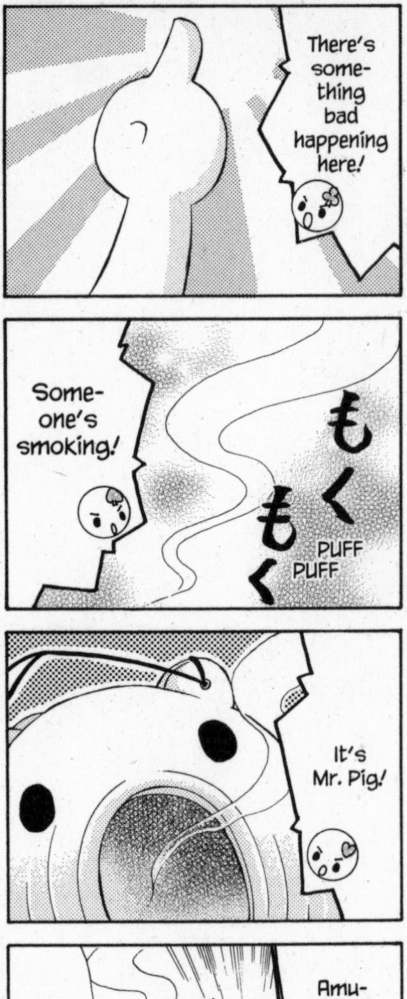
There's something bad happening here!
もくもく
PUFF PUFF
Someone's smoking!
It's Mr. Pig!
Amu-Chan, you're his guardian, right? Teach him the error of his ways!
Uh...
It's a *katori-buta* to keep the mosquitos away.

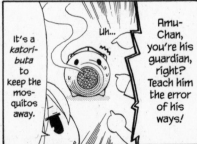

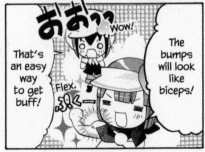

The way to use it is...

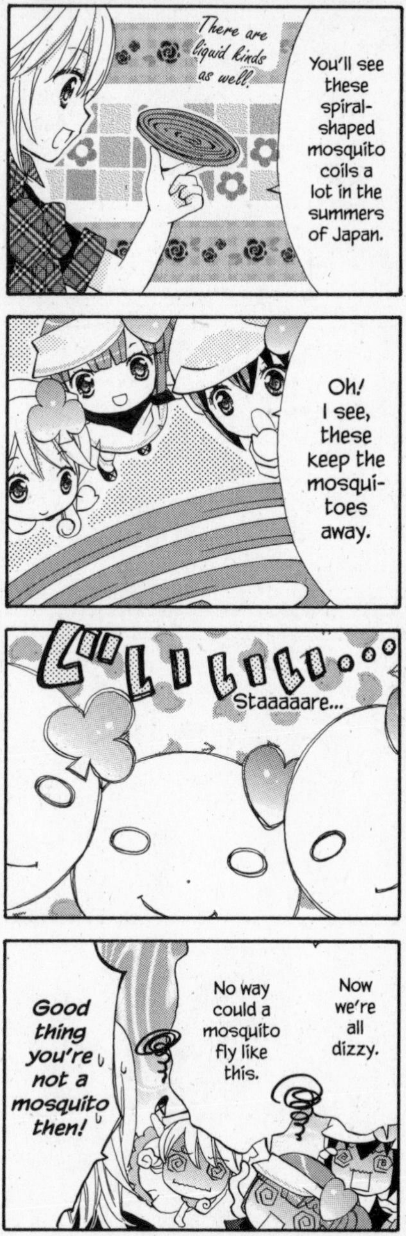
You'll see these spiral-shaped mosquito coils a lot in the summers of Japan.
There are liquid kinds as well.
Oh! I see, these keep the mosquitoes away.
Staaaaare...
Now we're all dizzy.
No way could a mosquito fly like this.
Good thing you're not a mosquito then!

It seemed possible

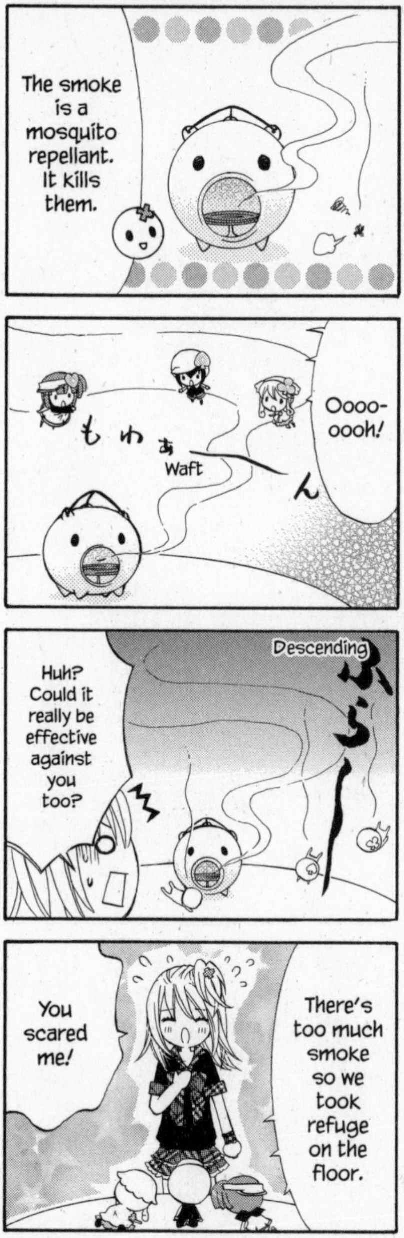
The smoke is a mosquito repellant. It kills them.
Oooo-oooh!
もわぁ
Waft
Descending
Huh? Could it really be effective against you too?
There's too much smoke so we took refuge on the floor.
You scared me!

Uh Oh...

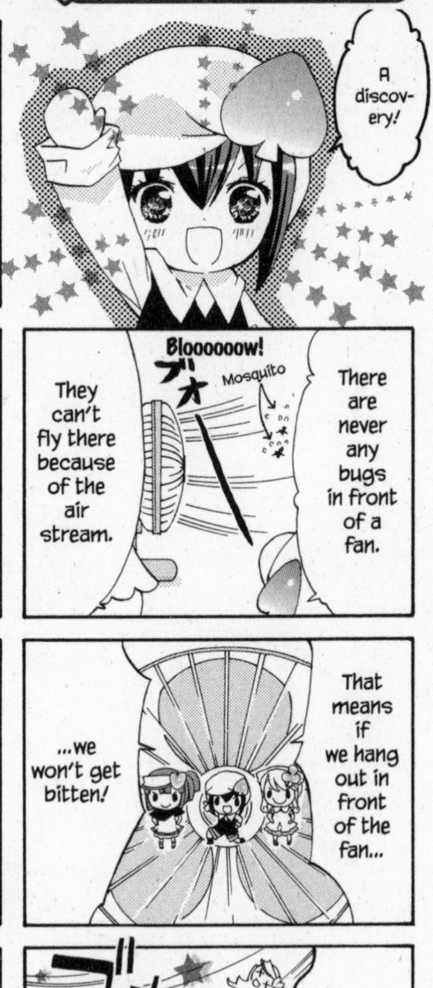
A discovery!
There are never any bugs in front of a fan.
Mosquito
They can't fly there because of the air stream.
Blooooow!
ブオ
That means if we hang out in front of the fan...
...we won't get bitten!
We're getting blown away too!
ゴオオオ
Bloooooow!
キャー
Yaaaah!

Peace of mind

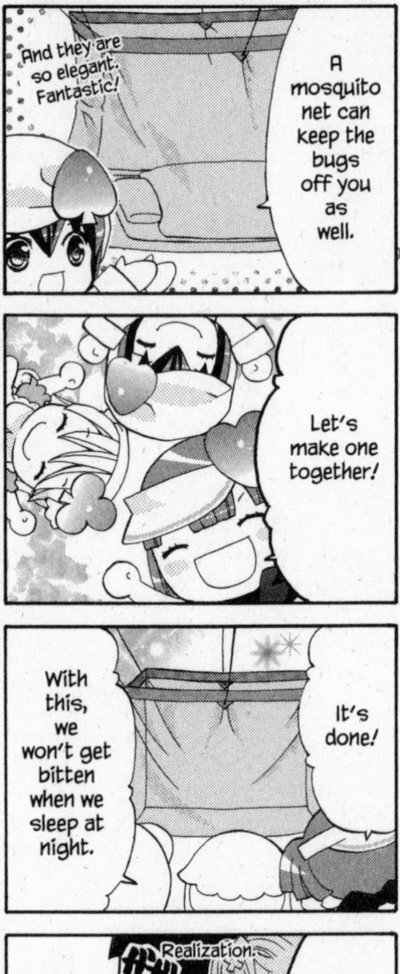
A mosquito net can keep the bugs off you as well.
And they are so elegant. Fantastic!
Let's make one together!
It's done!
With this, we won't get bitten when we sleep at night.
Since you sleep in your eggs, isn't this pointless anyway?
Realization.
There's that cool and biting *retort* again!

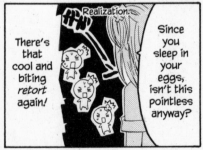

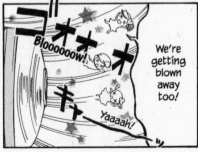

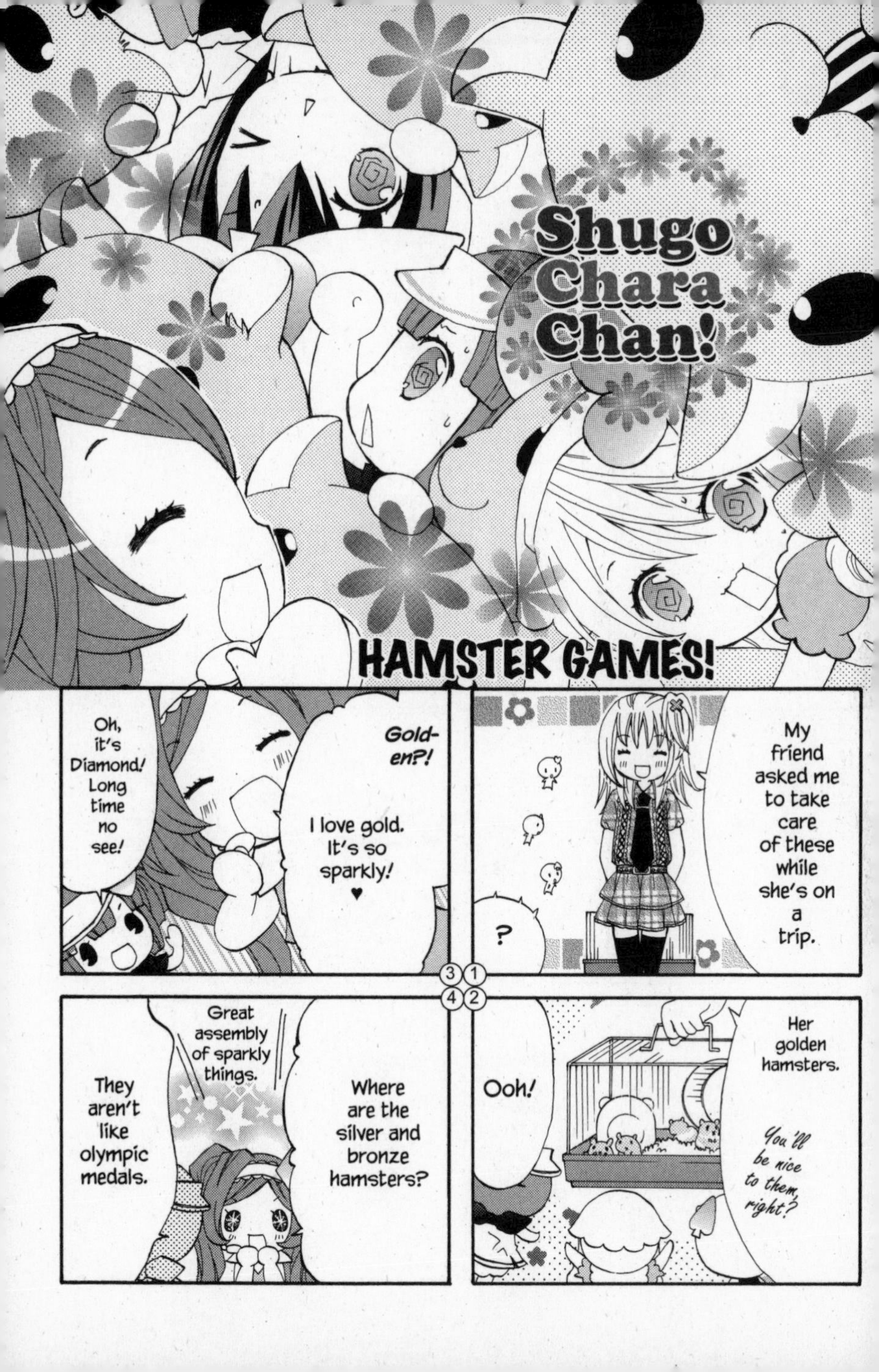
Shugo Chara Chan!
HAMSTER GAMES!
My friend asked me to take care of these while she's on a trip.
?
Her golden hamsters.
You'll be nice to them, right?
Ooh!
Gold-en?!
I love gold. It's so sparkly! ♥
Oh, it's Diamond! Long time no see!
Where are the silver and bronze hamsters?
Great assembly of sparkly things.
They aren't like olympic medals.

It's plain to see

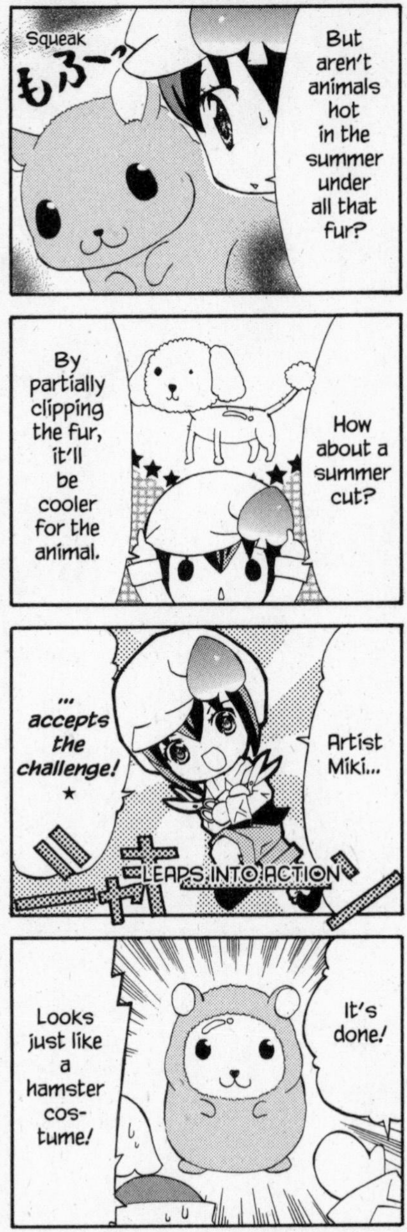
But aren't animals hot in the summer under all that fur?
Squeak
もふーっ
How about a summer cut?
By partially clipping the fur, it'll be cooler for the animal.
Artist Miki...
... *accepts the challenge!* ★
LEAPS INTO ACTION
It's done!
Looks just like a hamster costume!

Don't try to imitate!

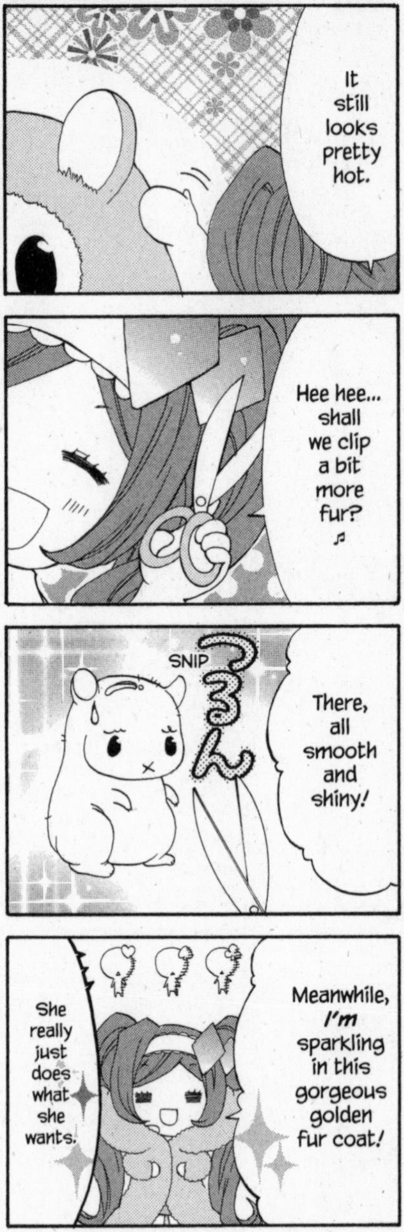
It still looks pretty hot.
Hee hee... shall we clip a bit more fur? ♪
There, all smooth and shiny!
SNIP
つるん
Meanwhile, *I'm* sparkling in this gorgeous golden fur coat!
She really just does what she wants.

Bad instincts

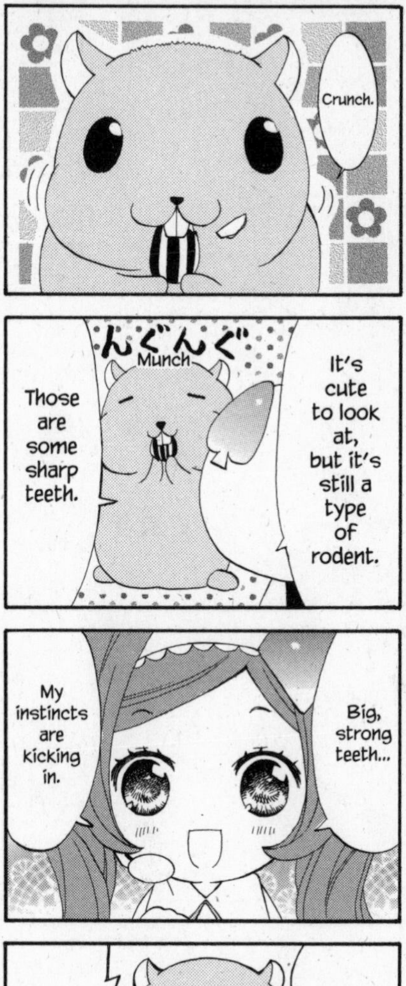
Crunch.
んぐんぐ
Munch
It's cute to look at, but it's still a type of rodent.
Those are some sharp teeth.
Big, strong teeth...
My instincts are kicking in.
I want to give him some shiny, gold teeth! ♥
Stop acting so spoiled!

Life is hard

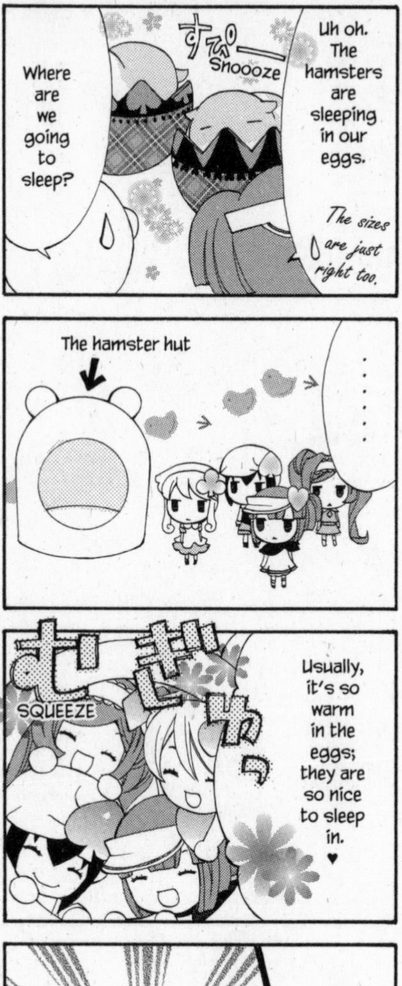
Uh oh. The hamsters are sleeping in our eggs.
すぴー
Snoooze
The sizes are just right too.
Where are we going to sleep?
......
The hamster hut
Usually, it's so warm in the eggs; they are so nice to sleep in. ♥
むぎゅっ
SQUEEZE
But it's summer now, and it's way too hot!

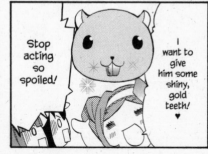

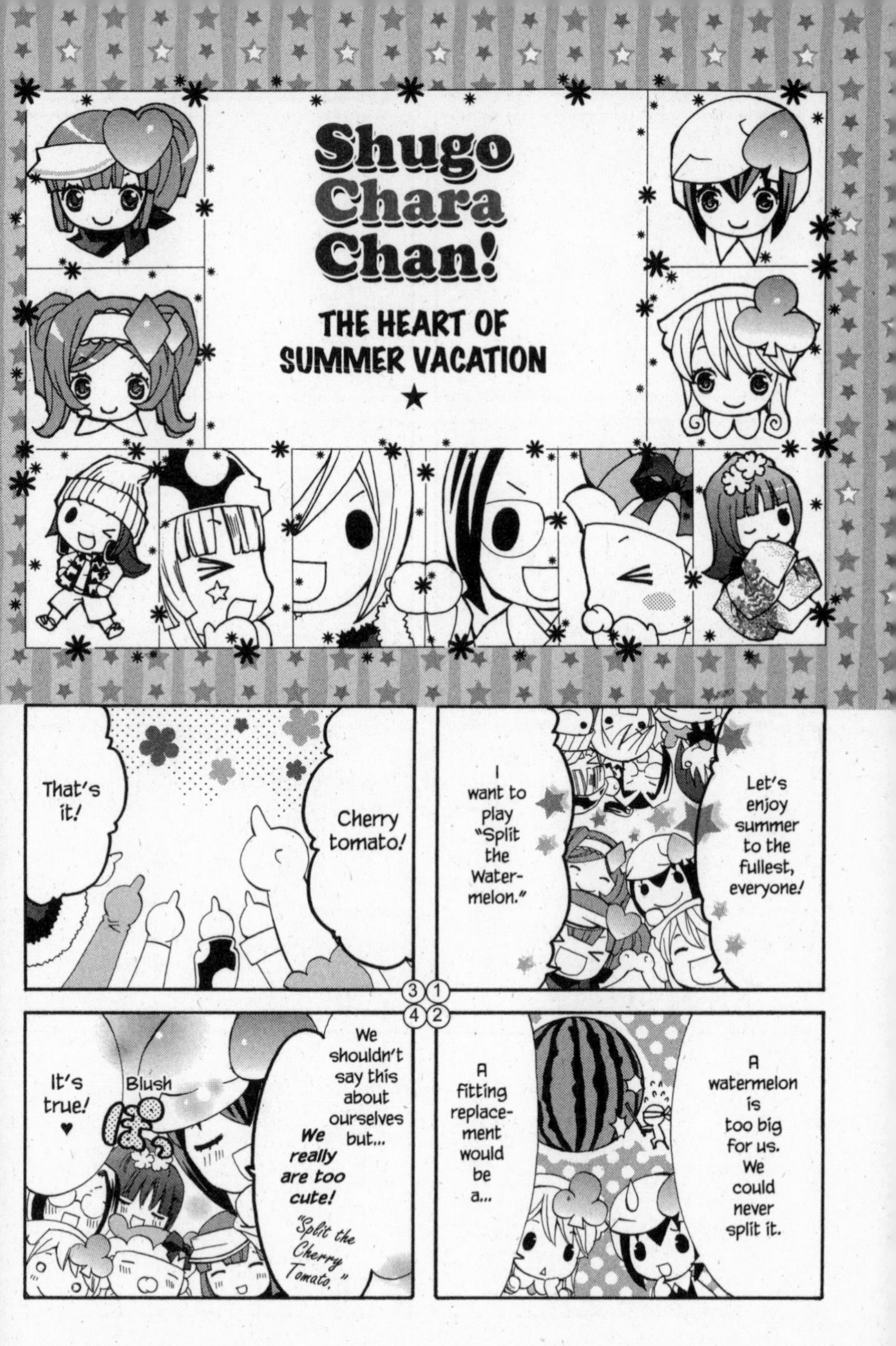
Shugo Chara Chan!
THE HEART OF SUMMER VACATION ★
Let's enjoy summer to the fullest, everyone!
I want to play "Split the Watermelon."
A watermelon is too big for us. We could never split it.
A fitting replacement would be a...
Cherry tomato!
That's it!
We shouldn't say this about ourselves but...
We really are too cute!
"Split the Cherry Tomato."
Blush
It's true! ♥

Fun, no matter what ♪

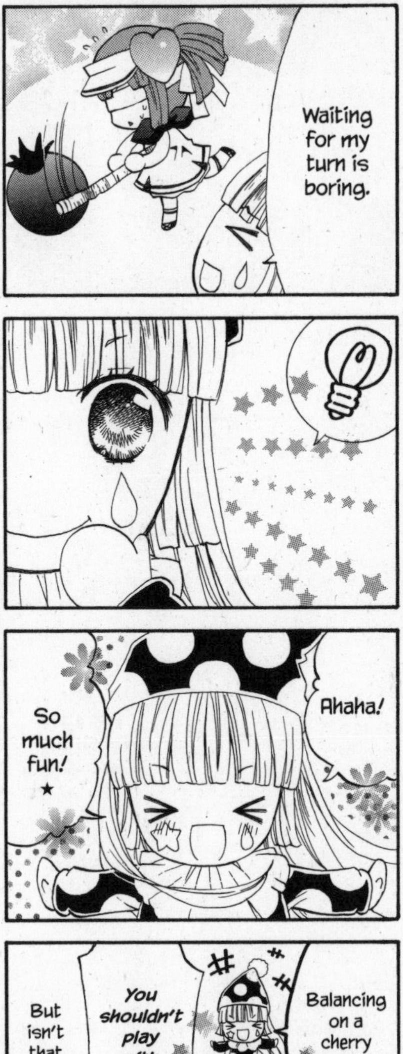
Waiting for my turn is boring.
Ahaha!
So much fun! ★
Balancing on a cherry tomato!
You shouldn't play with your food!
But isn't that what we're doing?

Think green

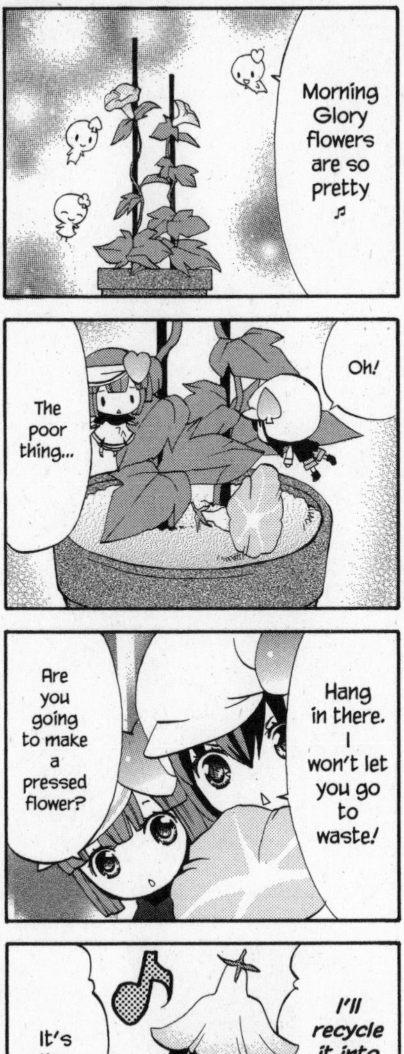
Morning Glory flowers are so pretty ♪
Oh!
The poor thing...
Hang in there. I won't let you go to waste!
Are you going to make a pressed flower?
I'll recycle it into a hat!
It's like a fairy tale!

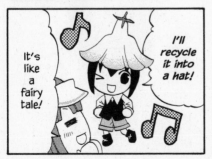

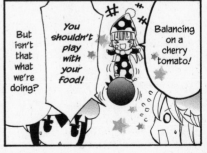

The beautiful flower language

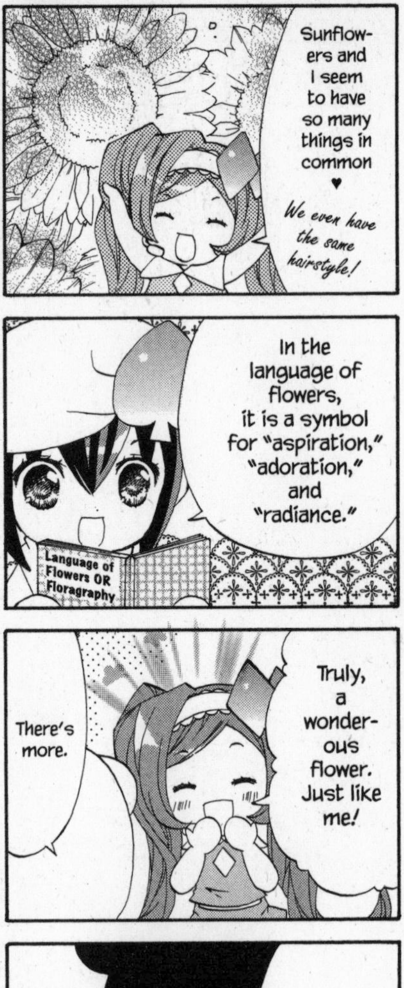
Sunflowers and I seem to have so many things in common ♥
We even have the same hairstyle!
In the language of flowers, it is a symbol for "aspiration," "adoration," and "radiance."
Language of Flowers OR Floragraphy
Truly, a wonderous flower. Just like me!
There's more.
It can also mean "falsehood" and "fake gold."
Say what?

Too gross

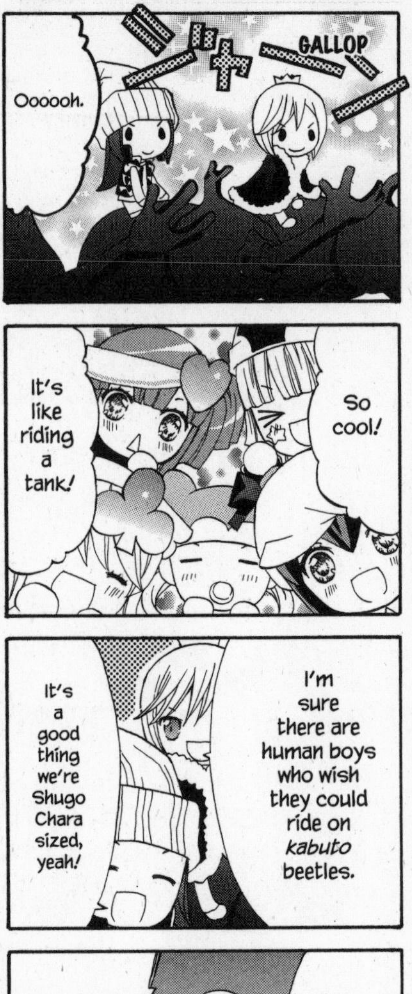
GALLOP
Ooooh.
So cool!
It's like riding a tank!
I'm sure there are human boys who wish they could ride on *kabuto* beetles.
It's a good thing we're Shugo Chara sized, yeah!
At this size, you could even ride the larva!
Crawl!
We respectfully refuse!

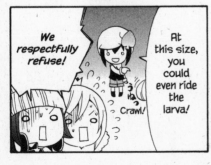

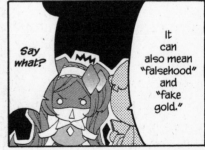

What could be inside?

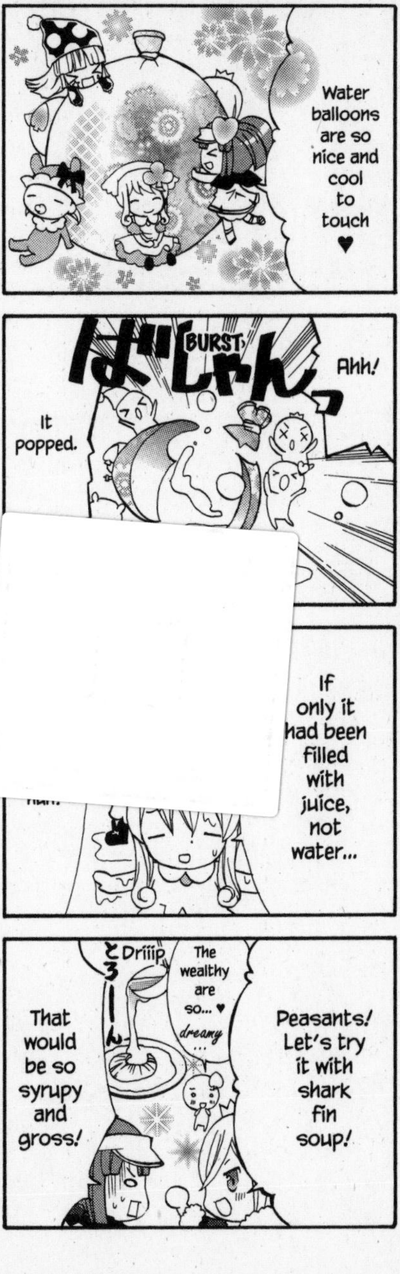
Water balloons are so nice and cool to touch ♥
ばしゃんっ
BURST
Ahh!
It popped.
If only it had been filled with juice, not water...
Peasants! Let's try it with shark fin soup!
The wealthy are so... ♥ dreamy...
とろーん
Driiip
That would be so syrupy and gross!

Personal jiggle

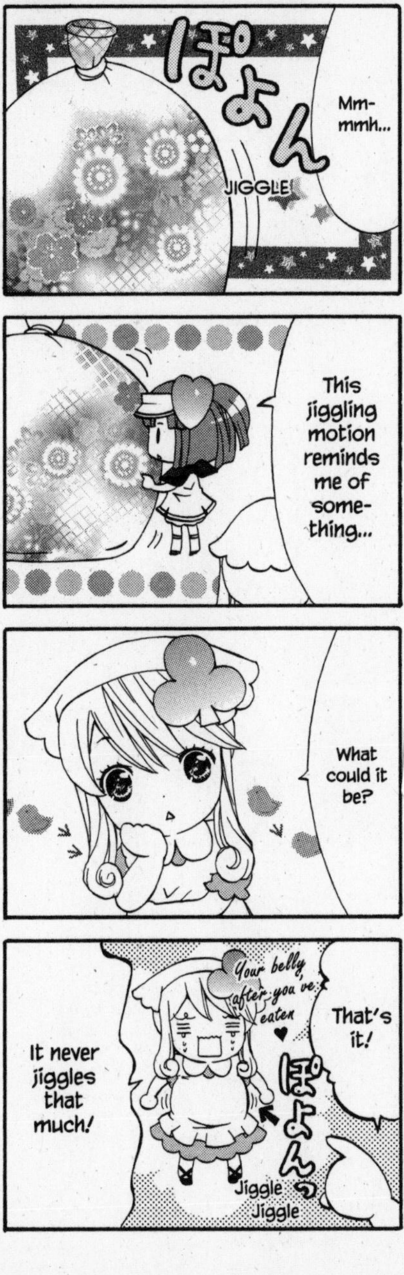
Mm-mmh...
ぽよん
JIGGLE
This jiggling motion reminds me of something...
What could it be?
That's it!
Your belly after you've eaten ♥
ぽよんっ
Jiggle Jiggle
It never jiggles that much!

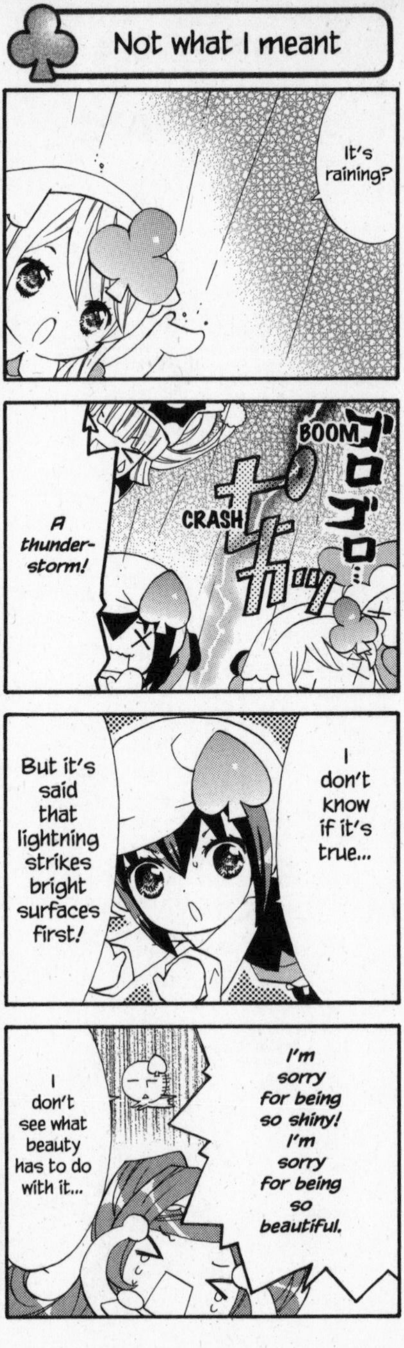
Not what I meant
It's raining?
BOOM
ゴロゴロ…
CRASH
ピカッ
A thunderstorm!
I don't know if it's true...
But it's said that lightning strikes bright surfaces first!
I'm sorry for being so shiny! I'm sorry for being so beautiful.
I don't see what beauty has to do with it...

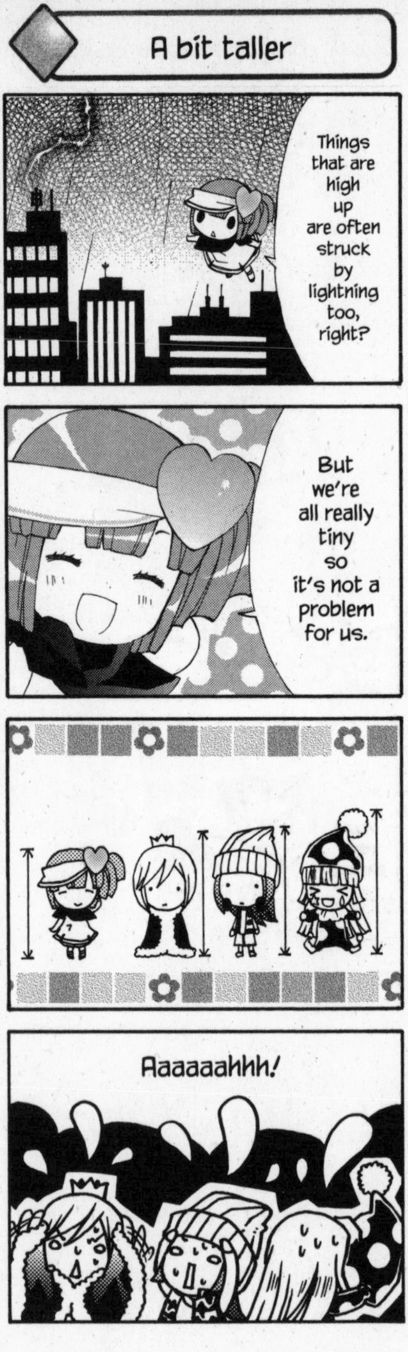
A bit taller
Things that are high up are often struck by lightning too, right?
But we're all really tiny so it's not a problem for us.
Aaaaaahhh!

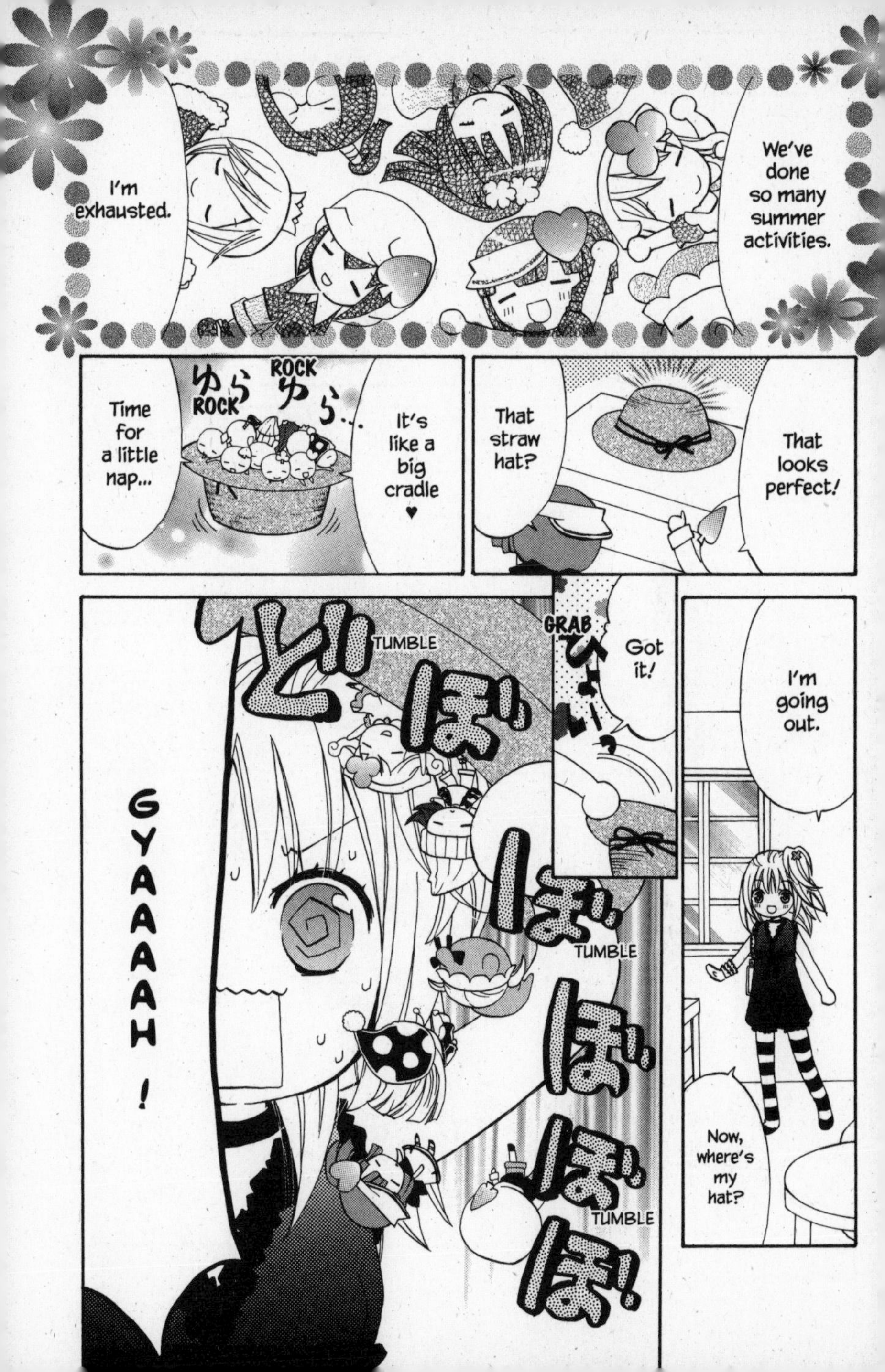

We've done so many summer activities.
I'm exhausted.
That looks perfect!
That straw hat?
It's like a big cradle ♥
ゆらゆら…
ROCK ROCK
Time for a little nap...
I'm going out.
Now, where's my hat?
Got it!
ひょいっ
GRAB
どぼぼぼぼぼ!
TUMBLE
TUMBLE
TUMBLE
GYAAAAAH!

Shugo Chara Chan!

ONE PANEL MANGA

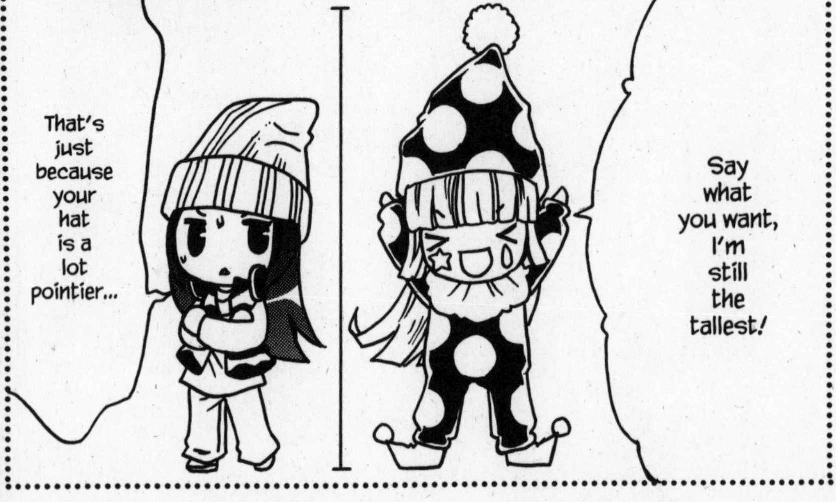
Say what you want, I'm still the tallest!
That's just because your hat is a lot pointier...

Shugo Chara Chan!

HOMEWORK CHALLENGE!

Summer homework sure looks hard.

But the hard work put in now will really pay off later in life.

First, let's make a picture diary.

DIARY

③①
④②

Who's the athlete here?

A workout schedule?

Morning, 1 hour jog	100 crunches	Stretching	Noon, 1-hour jog	20 squats	100 push-ups	Stretching

Let's study hard and improve ourselves!

So we should do it too!

Anticipation

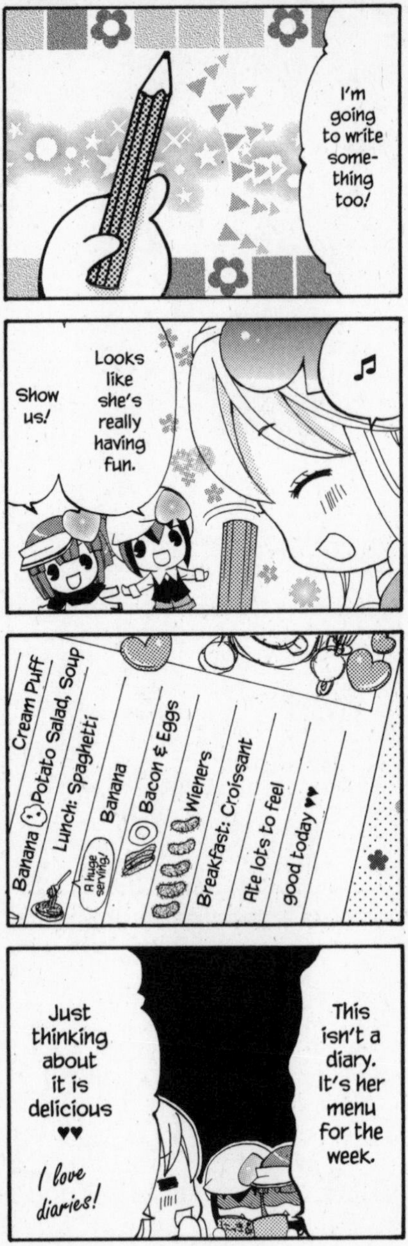
I'm going to write something too!
♪
Looks like she's really having fun.
Show us!
Cream Puff
Banana Potato Salad, Soup
A huge serving!
Lunch: Spaghetti
Banana
Bacon & Eggs
Wieners
Breakfast: Croissant
Ate lots to feel
good today ♥♥
This isn't a diary. It's her menu for the week.
Just thinking about it is delicious ♥♥
I love diaries!

Put your back into it

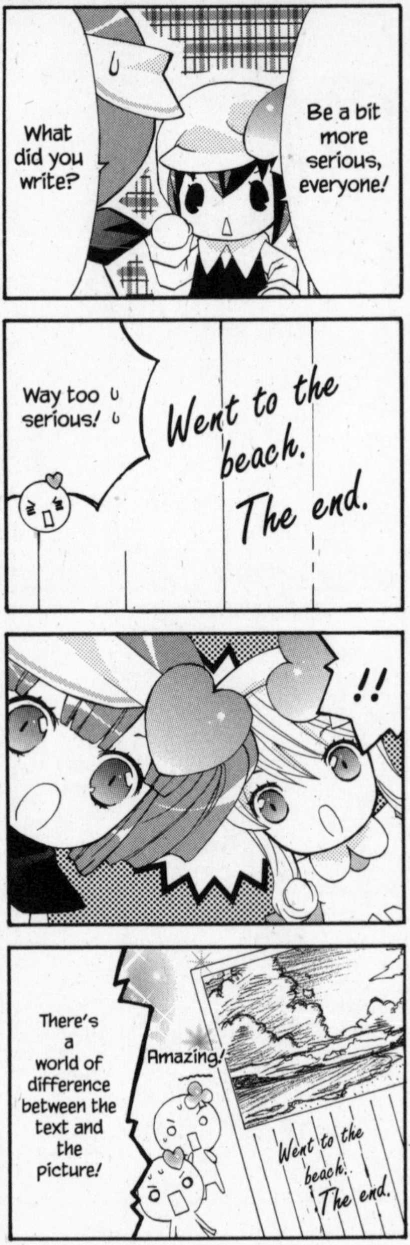
Be a bit more serious, everyone!
What did you write?
Went to the beach. The end.
Way too serious!
!!
Amazing!
Went to the beach. The end.
There's a world of difference between the text and the picture!

Observation Diary

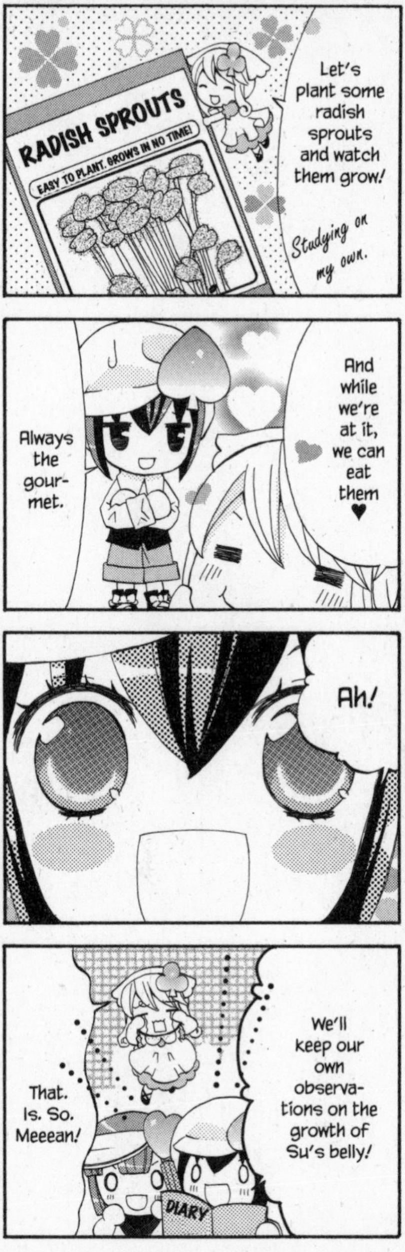
Let's plant some radish sprouts and watch them grow!
RADISH SPROUTS
EASY TO PLANT. GROWS IN NO TIME!
Studying on my own.
And while we're at it, we can eat them ♥
Always the gour-met.
Ah!
We'll keep our own observa-tions on the growth of Su's belly!
That. Is. So. Meeean!
DIARY

Faces

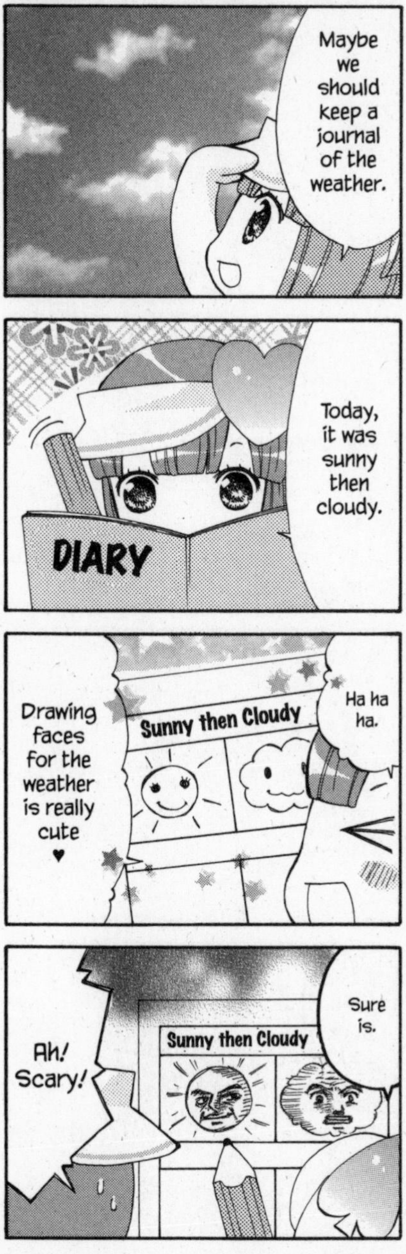
Maybe we should keep a journal of the weather.
Today, it was sunny then cloudy.
DIARY
Ha ha ha.
Sunny then Cloudy
Drawing faces for the weather is really cute ♥
Sure is.
Sunny then Cloudy
Ah! Scary!

That made you cry?

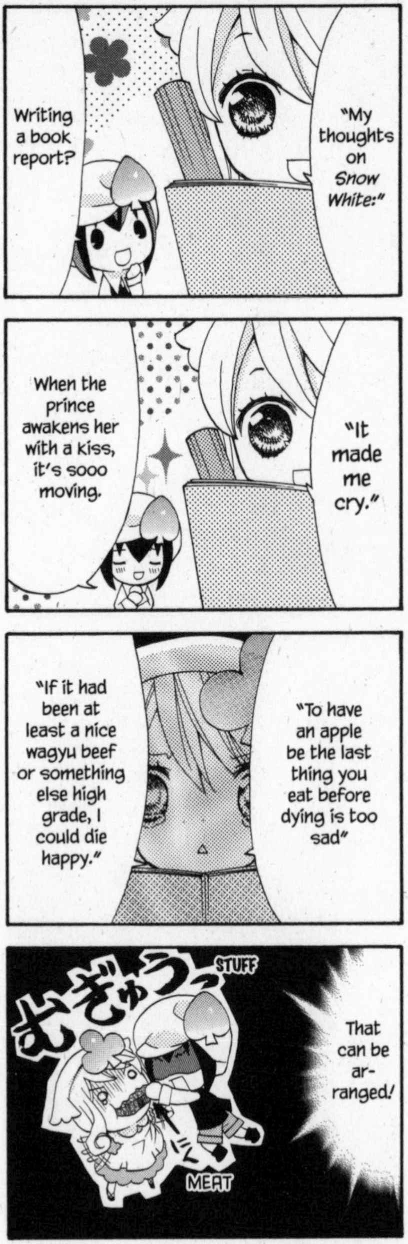
"My thoughts on Snow White:"
Writing a book report?
"It made me cry."
When the prince awakens her with a kiss, it's sooo moving.
"To have an apple be the last thing you eat before dying is too sad"
"If it had been at least a nice wagyu beef or something else high grade, I could die happy."
That can be arranged!
むぎゅうっ STUFF
にく MEAT

Just like that!

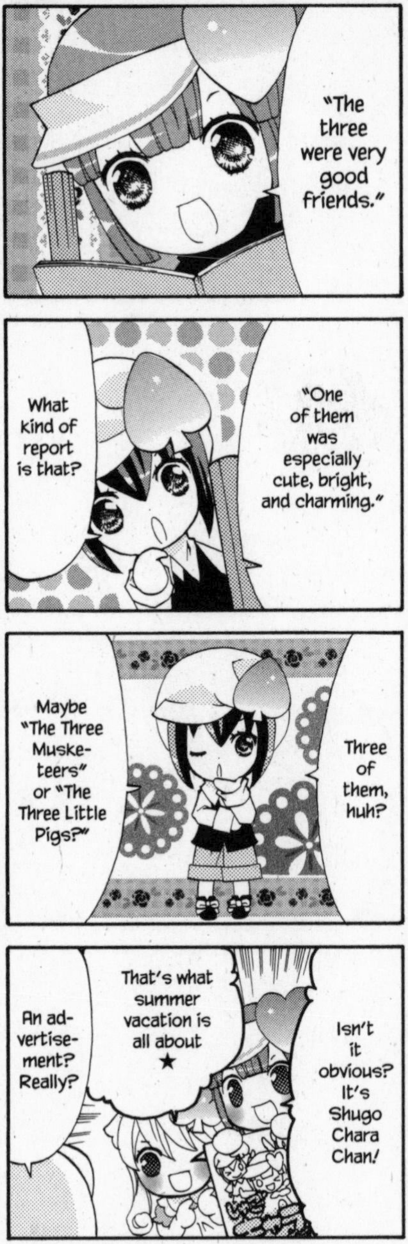
"The three were very good friends."
"One of them was especially cute, bright, and charming."
What kind of report is that?
Three of them, huh?
Maybe "The Three Musketeers" or "The Three Little Pigs?"
Isn't it obvious? It's Shugo Chara Chan!
That's what summer vacation is all about ★
An advertisement? Really?

Shugo Chara Chan!

ONE PANEL MANGA

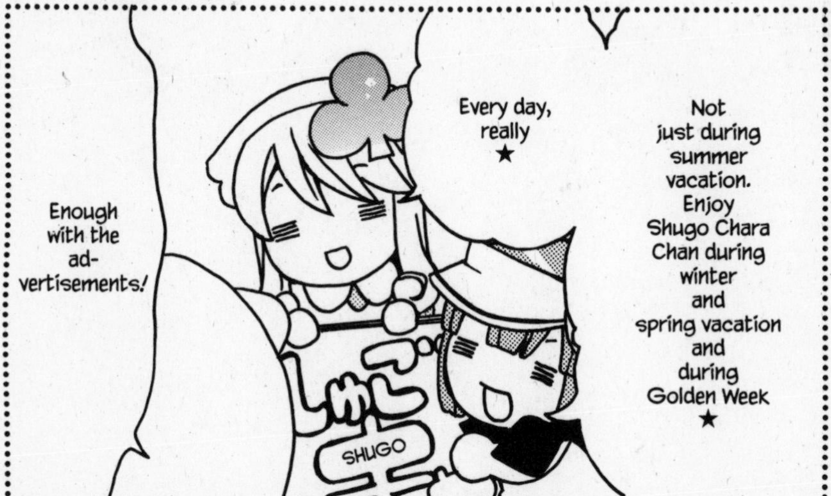
Not just during summer vacation. Enjoy Shugo Chara Chan during winter and spring vacation and during Golden Week ★
Every day, really ★
Enough with the ad-vertisements!
SHUGO

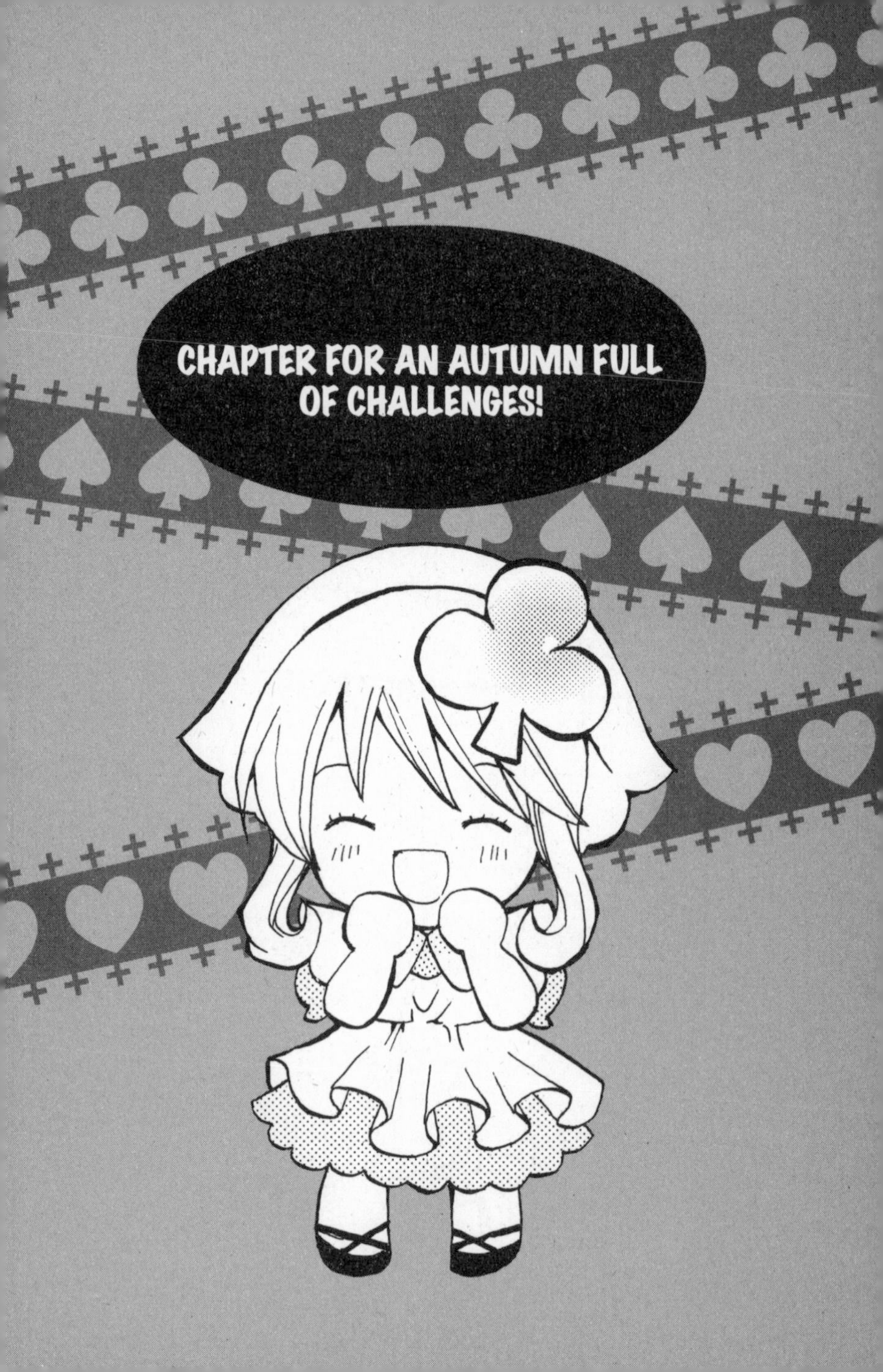
CHAPTER FOR AN AUTUMN FULL OF CHALLENGES!

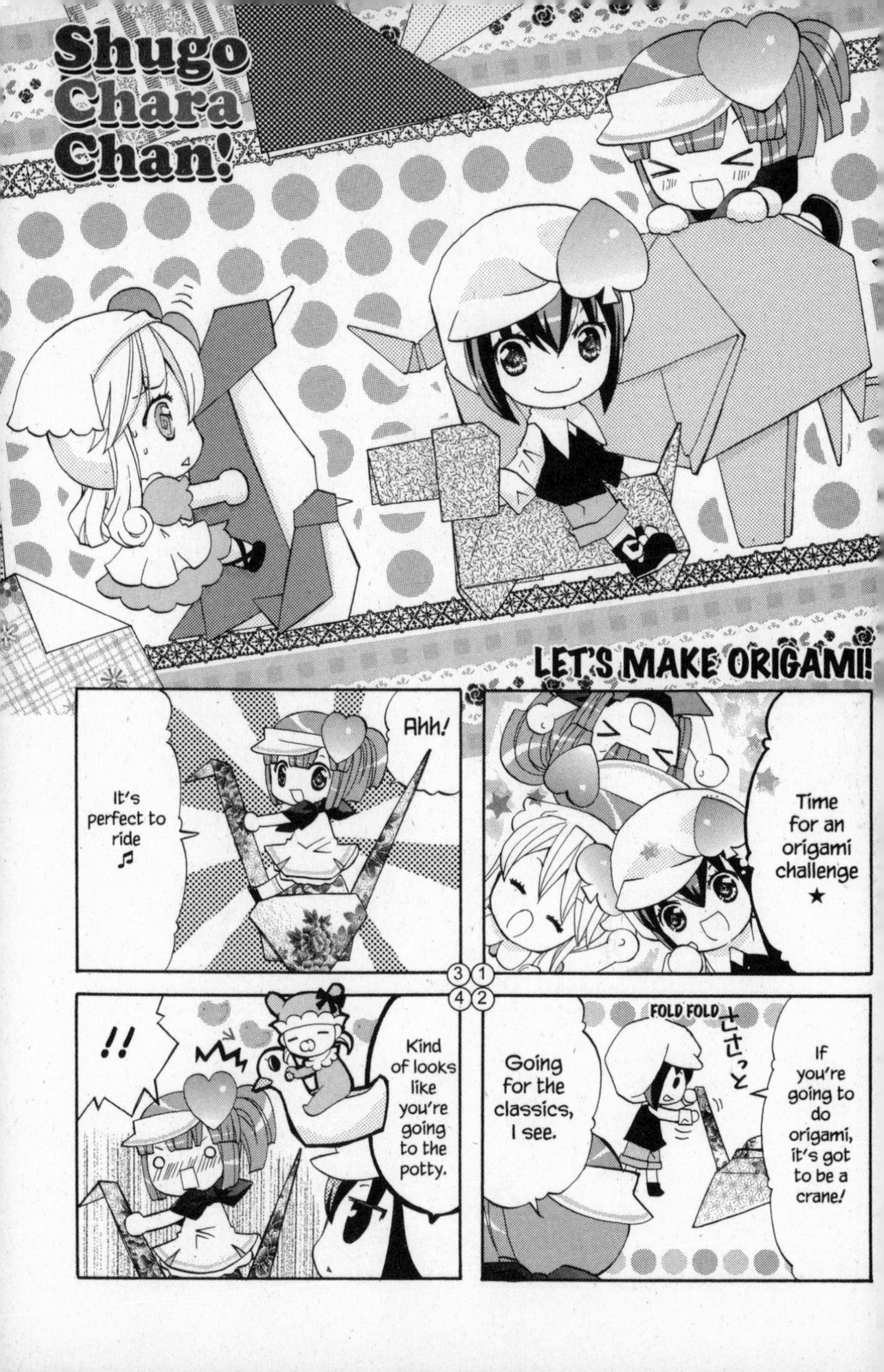
Shugo Chara Chan!
LET'S MAKE ORIGAMI!
Time for an origami challenge ★
If you're going to do origami, it's got to be a crane!
FOLD FOLD
Going for the classics, I see.
Ahh!
It's perfect to ride ♫
Kind of looks like you're going to the potty.
!!

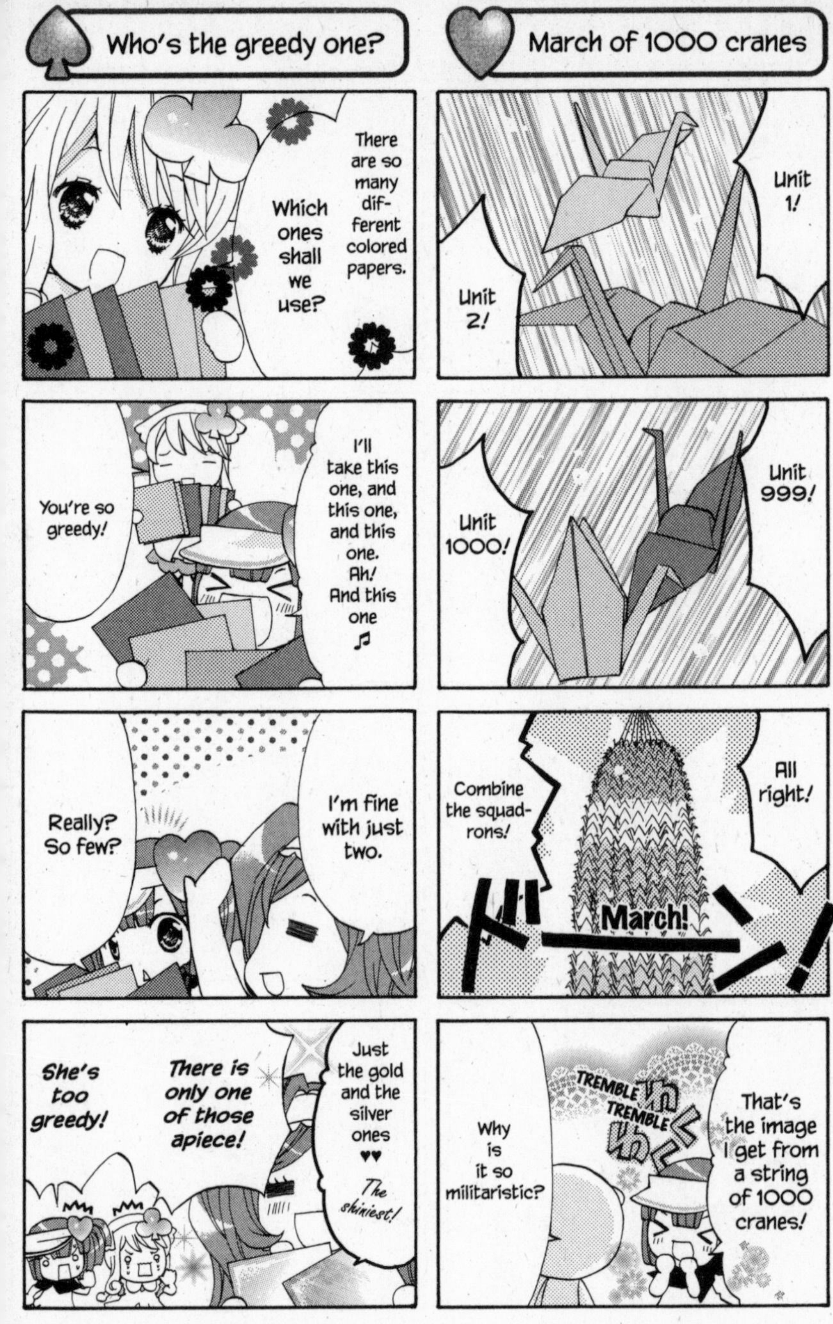
March of 1000 cranes
Unit 1!
Unit 2!
Unit 999!
Unit 1000!
All right!
Combine the squad-rons!
March!
That's the image I get from a string of 1000 cranes!
TREMBLE TREMBLE
Why is it so militaristic?
Who's the greedy one?
There are so many dif-ferent colored papers.
Which ones shall we use?
I'll take this one, and this one, and this one. Ah! And this one ♫
You're so greedy!
I'm fine with just two.
Really? So few?
Just the gold and the silver ones ♥♥
The shiniest!
There is only one of those apiece!
She's too greedy!

Realization

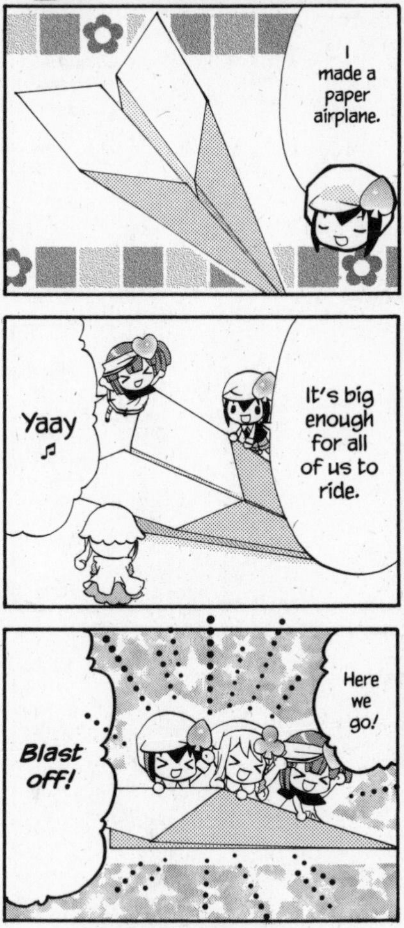
I made a paper airplane.
It's big enough for all of us to ride.
Yaay ♪
Here we go!
Blast off!
Hey! Someone has to throw us!
We all just got on at once...

The real deal?

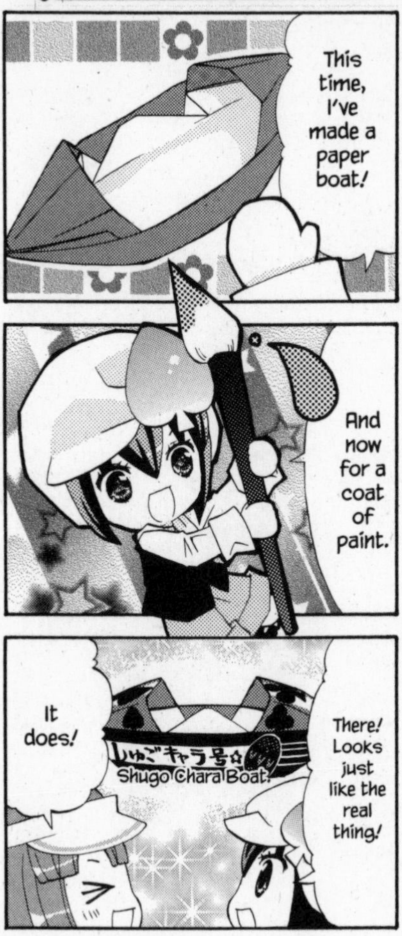
This time, I've made a paper boat!
And now for a coat of paint.
There! Looks just like the real thing!
しゅごキャラ号☆
Shugo Chara Boat!
It does!
Ahh! It's sinkii-iing!
Well, it is made of paper!
BLOOP
BLOOP

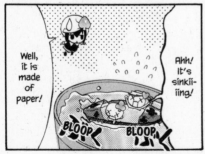

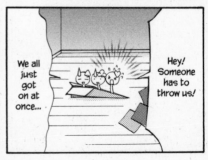

My favorite things are...

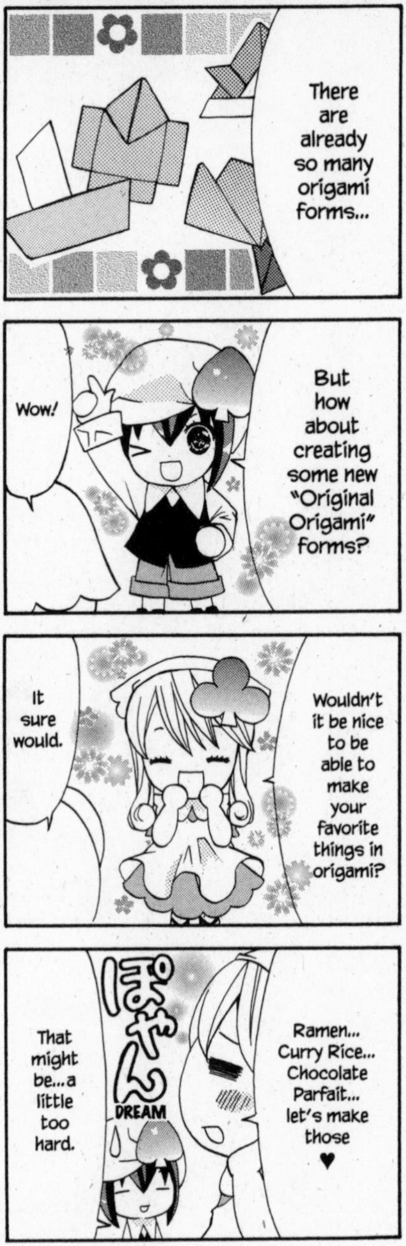
There are already so many origami forms...
But how about creating some new "Original Origami" forms?
Wow!
Wouldn't it be nice to be able to make your favorite things in origami?
It sure would.
Ramen... Curry Rice... Chocolate Parfait... let's make those ♥
ぽやん
DREAM
That might be...a little too hard.

A bit too blunt

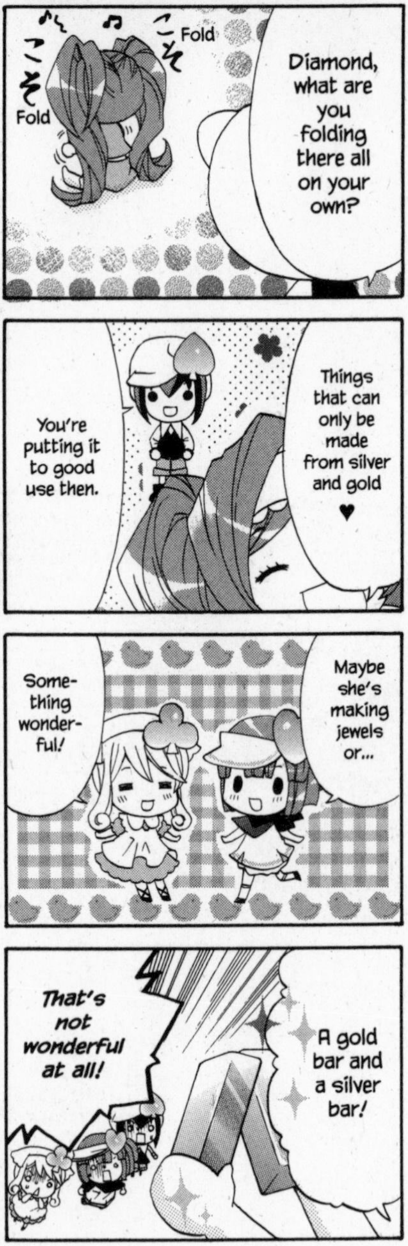
Diamond, what are you folding there all on your own?
こそ Fold
こそ Fold
Things that can only be made from silver and gold ♥
You're putting it to good use then.
Maybe she's making jewels or...
Something wonderful!
A gold bar and a silver bar!
That's not wonderful at all!

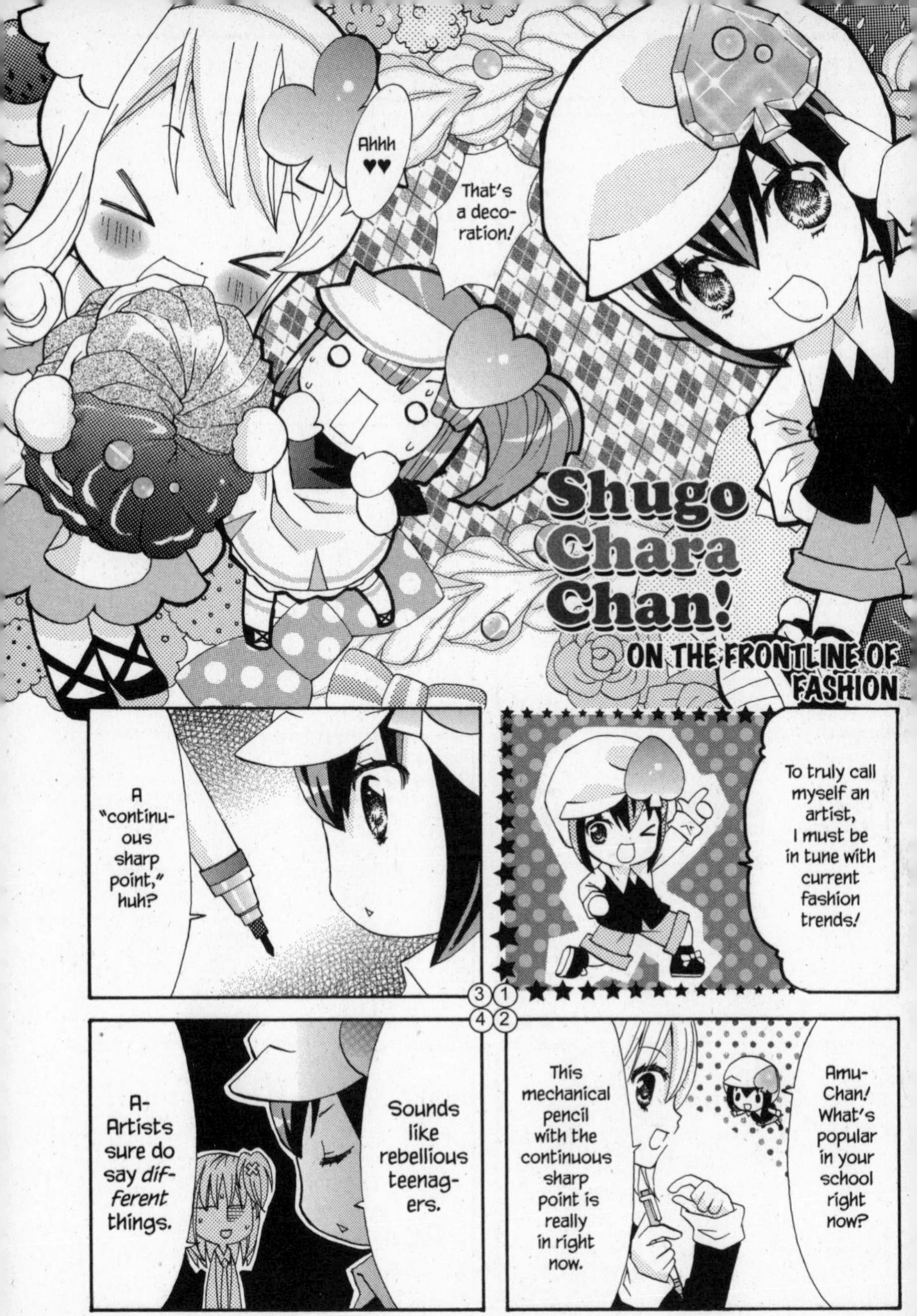
That's a decoration!
Ahhh ♥♥
Shugo Chara Chan!
ON THE FRONTLINE OF FASHION
To truly call myself an artist, I must be in tune with current fashion trends!
Amu-Chan! What's popular in your school right now?
This mechanical pencil with the continuous sharp point is really in right now.
A "continuous sharp point," huh?
Sounds like rebellious teenagers.
A-Artists sure do say *different* things.

The right way to do it

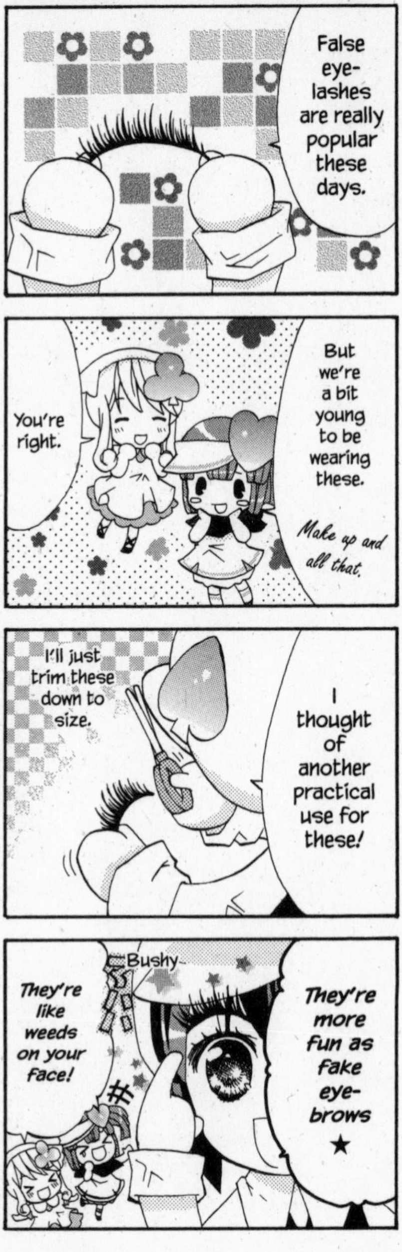
False eye-lashes are really popular these days.
But we're a bit young to be wearing these.
Make up and all that.
You're right.
I thought of another practical use for these!
I'll just trim these down to size.
They're more fun as fake eye-brows ★
Bushy
They're like weeds on your face!

Shaky

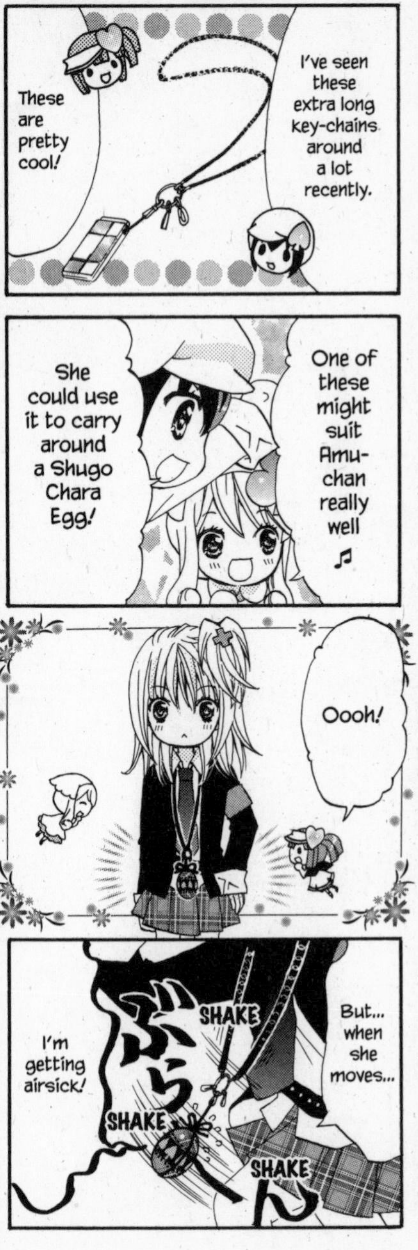
I've seen these extra long key-chains around a lot recently.
These are pretty cool!
One of these might suit Amu-chan really well ♫
She could use it to carry around a Shugo Chara Egg!
Oooh!
But... when she moves...
SHAKE
ぶらん
I'm getting airsick!
SHAKE
SHAKE

It's too hot!

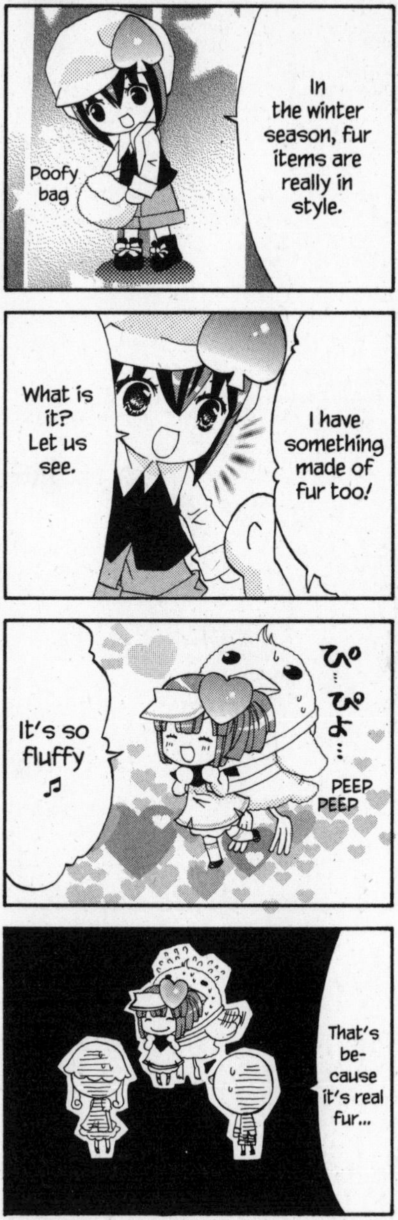
In the winter season, fur items are really in style.
Poofy bag
I have something made of fur too!
What is it? Let us see.
ぴ…ぴよ…
PEEP PEEP
It's so fluffy ♪
That's because it's real fur...

Doughnut breakdown

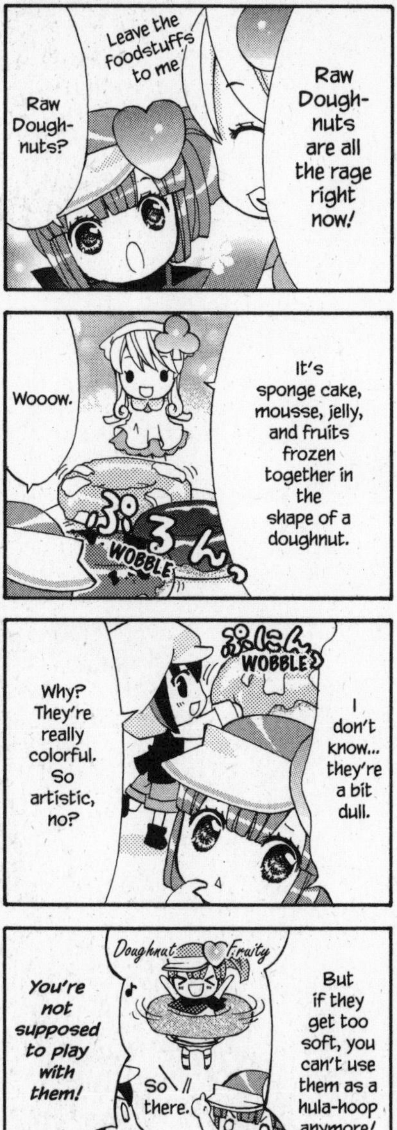
Raw Doughnuts are all the rage right now!
Leave the foodstuffs to me
Raw Doughnuts?
It's sponge cake, mousse, jelly, and fruits frozen together in the shape of a doughnut.
Wooow.
ぷるん
WOBBLE
ぷにん
WOBBLE
I don't know... they're a bit dull.
Why? They're really colorful. So artistic, no?
But if they get too soft, you can't use them as a hula-hoop anymore!
Doughnut Fruity
So there.
You're not supposed to play with them!

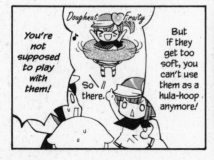

Keep us out of it!

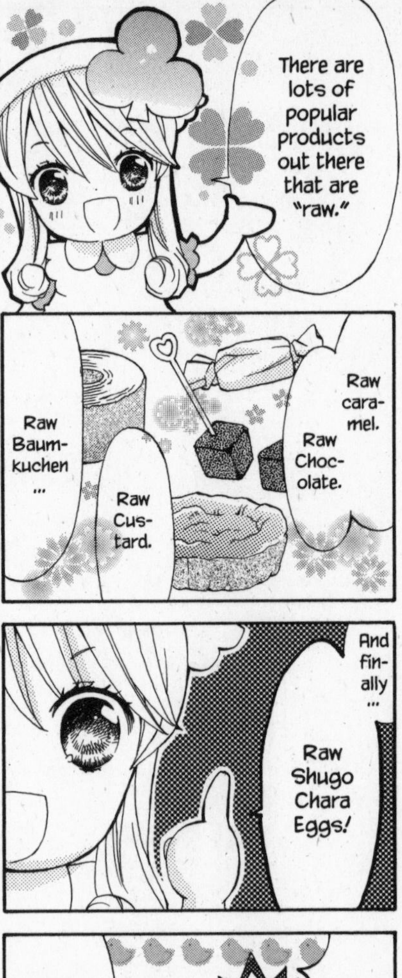

There are lots of popular products out there that are "raw."
Raw caramel.
Raw Chocolate.
Raw Custard.
Raw Baumkuchen ...
And finally ...
Raw Shugo Chara Eggs!
No way!
Aren't they just like normal eggs?

Delicious by degrees

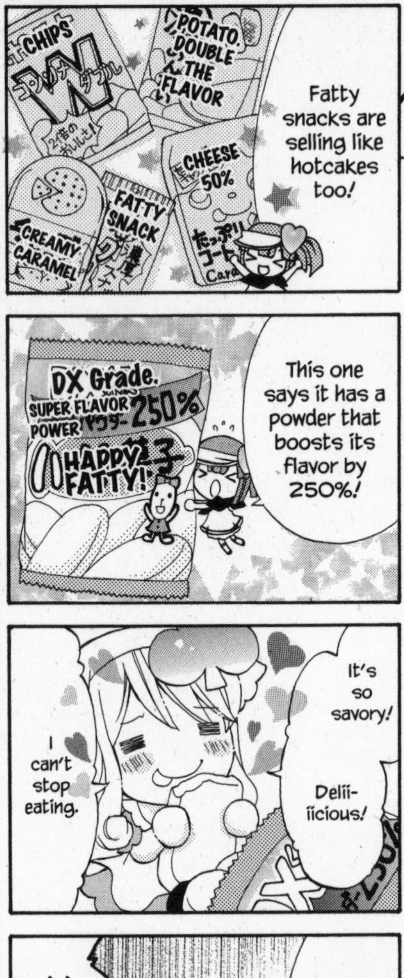

Fatty snacks are selling like hotcakes too!
CHIPS
POTATO DOUBLE THE FLAVOR
CHEESE 50%
FATTY SNACK
CREAMY CARAMEL
This one says it has a powder that boosts its flavor by 250%!
DX Grade.
SUPER FLAVOR POWER 250%
HAPPY FATTY!
It's so savory!
Deliiiicious!
I can't stop eating.
So it'll boost Su's weight by 250% too!
Heh heh...
!!

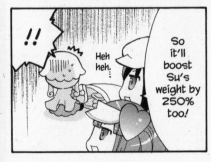

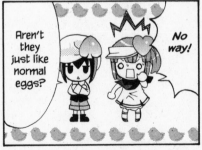

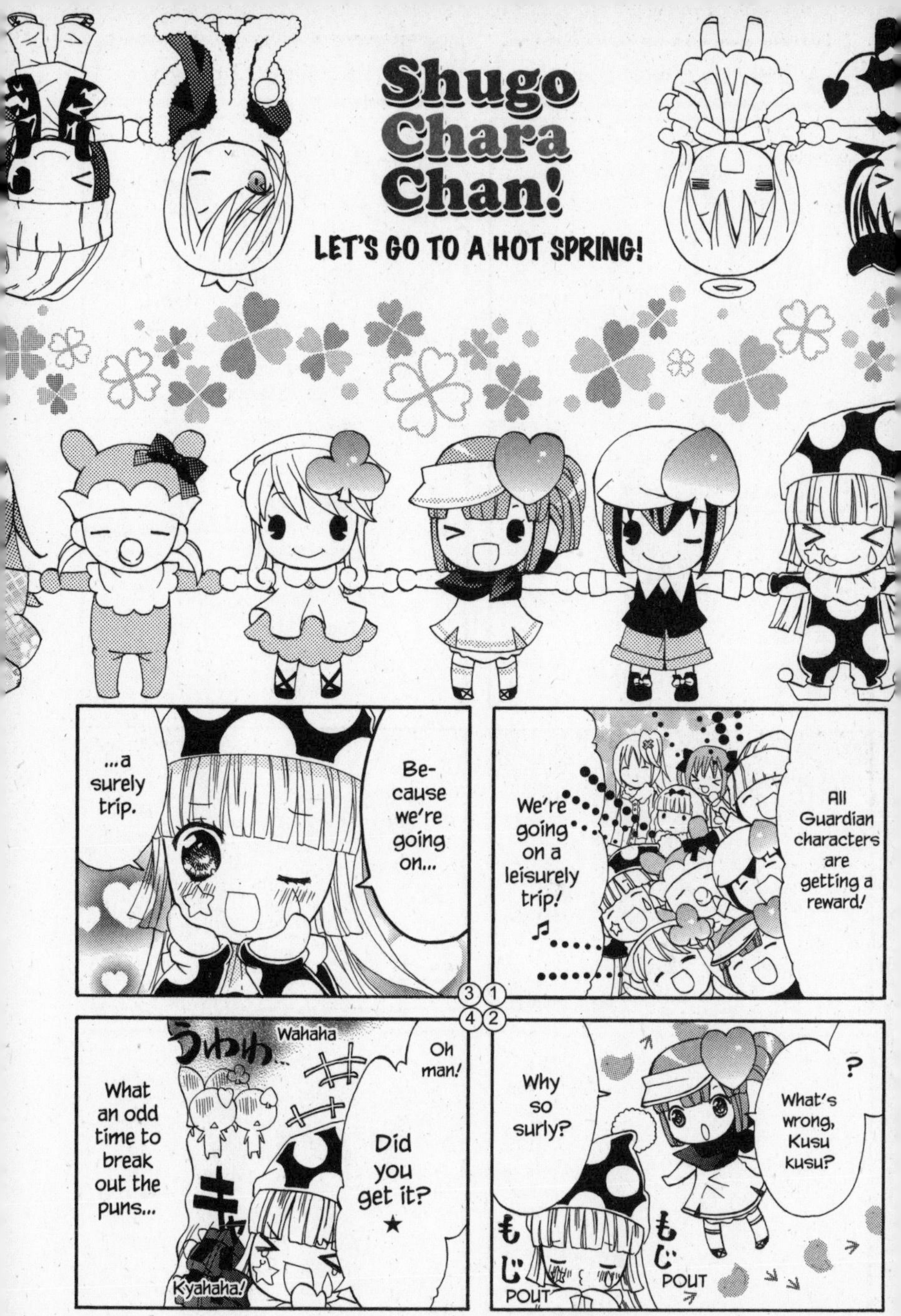
Shugo Chara Chan!
LET'S GO TO A HOT SPRING!
All Guardian characters are getting a reward!
We're going on a leisurely trip! ♪
What's wrong, Kusu kusu?
?
Why so surly?
もじ
POUT
もじ
POUT
Be-cause we're going on...
...a surely trip.
Oh man!
Did you get it? ★
Wahaha
Kyahaha!
What an odd time to break out the puns...

The ravenous *onsen*

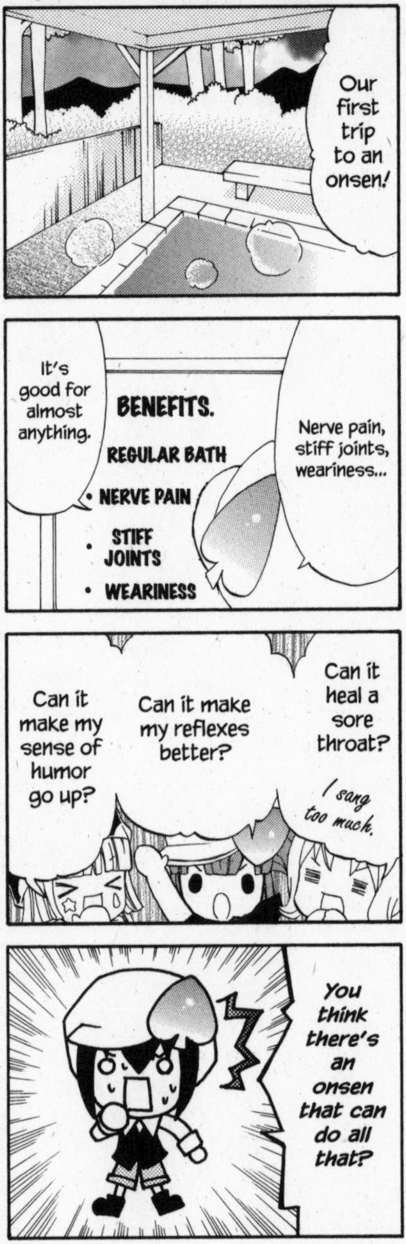

Our first trip to an onsen!
Nerve pain, stiff joints, weariness...
BENEFITS.
REGULAR BATH
• NERVE PAIN
• STIFF JOINTS
• WEARINESS
It's good for almost anything.
Can it heal a sore throat?
I sang too much.
Can it make my reflexes better?
Can it make my sense of humor go up?
You think there's an onsen that can do all that?

Under the circumstances...

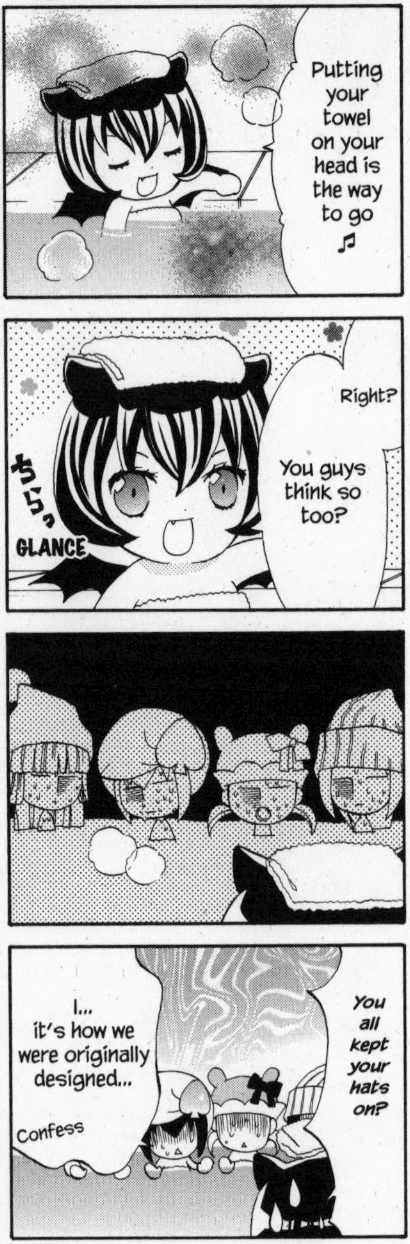

Putting your towel on your head is the way to go ♪
Right?
You guys think so too?
ちらっ
GLANCE
You all kept your hats on?
I... it's how we were originally designed...
Confess

Fall and Summer

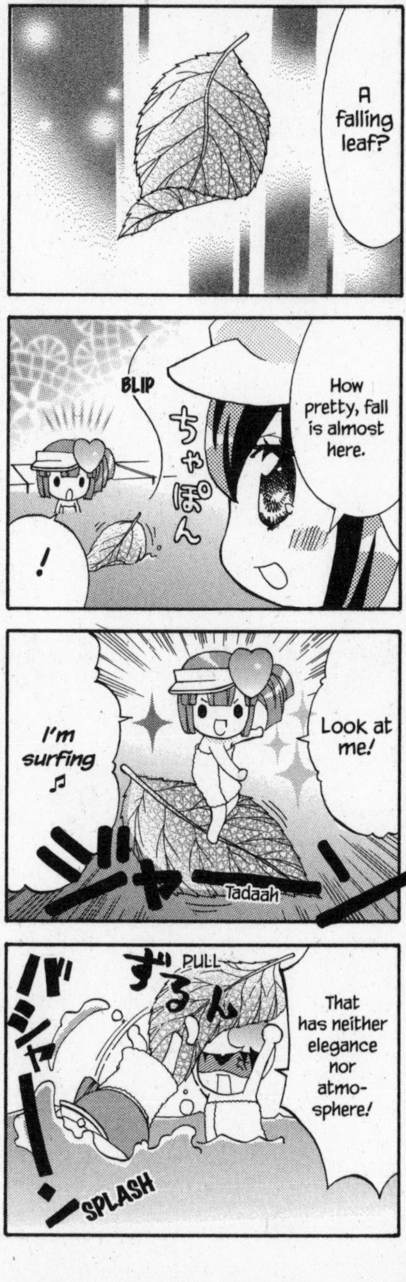
A falling leaf?
How pretty, fall is almost here.
ちゃぽん
BLIP
!
Look at me!
I'm surfing ♪
Tadaah
That has neither elegance nor atmosphere!
ずるん
PULL
バシャー
SPLASH

Smells...tasty

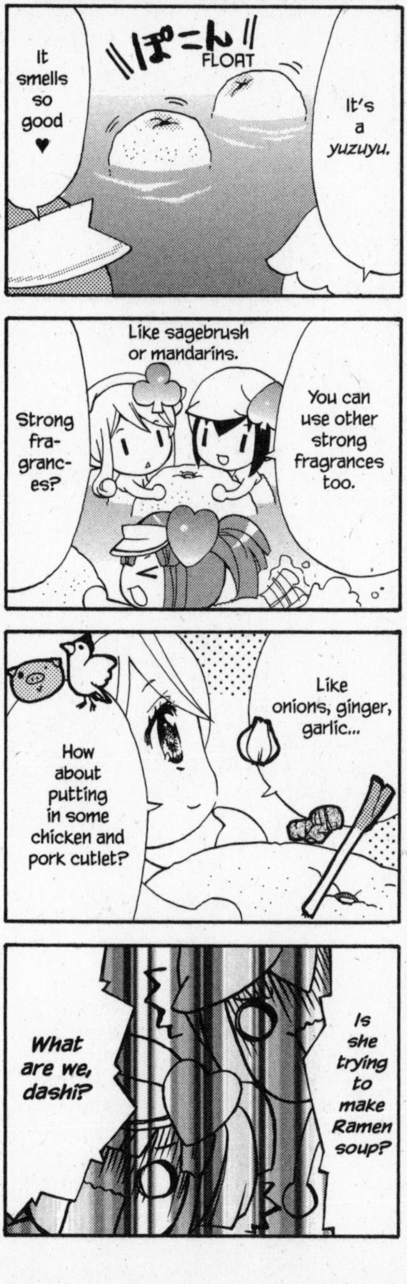
It's a yuzuyu.
ぽこん
FLOAT
It smells so good ♥
You can use other strong fragrances too.
Like sagebrush or mandarins.
Strong fragrances?
Like onions, ginger, garlic...
How about putting in some chicken and pork cutlet?
Is she trying to make Ramen soup?
What are we, dashi?

The heights of luxury

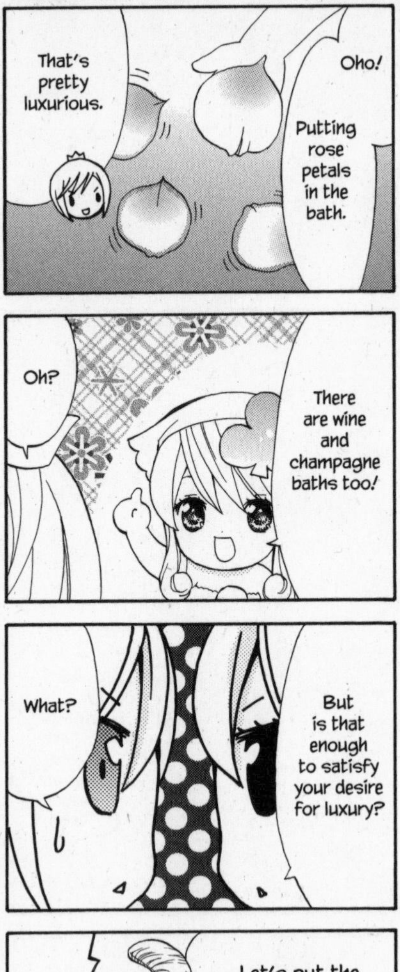
Oho!
Putting rose petals in the bath.
That's pretty luxurious.
There are wine and champagne baths too!
Oh?
But is that enough to satisfy your desire for luxury?
What?
Let's put the three finest delicacies in our bath: shark fin soup, caviar and foie gras!
That's way too fishy!

A nice idea?

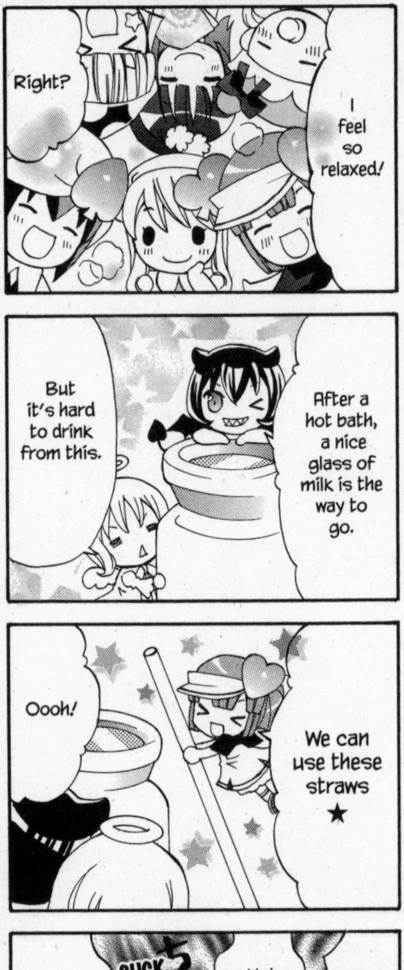
I feel so relaxed!
Right?
After a hot bath, a nice glass of milk is the way to go.
But it's hard to drink from this.
We can use these straws ★
Oooh!
Human sized straws. Too fat!
Not enough lung capacity!
SUCK SUCK
I'm sweating more now than I was before...

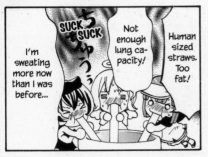

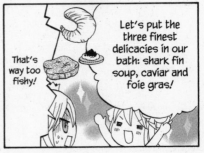

Feel good ice

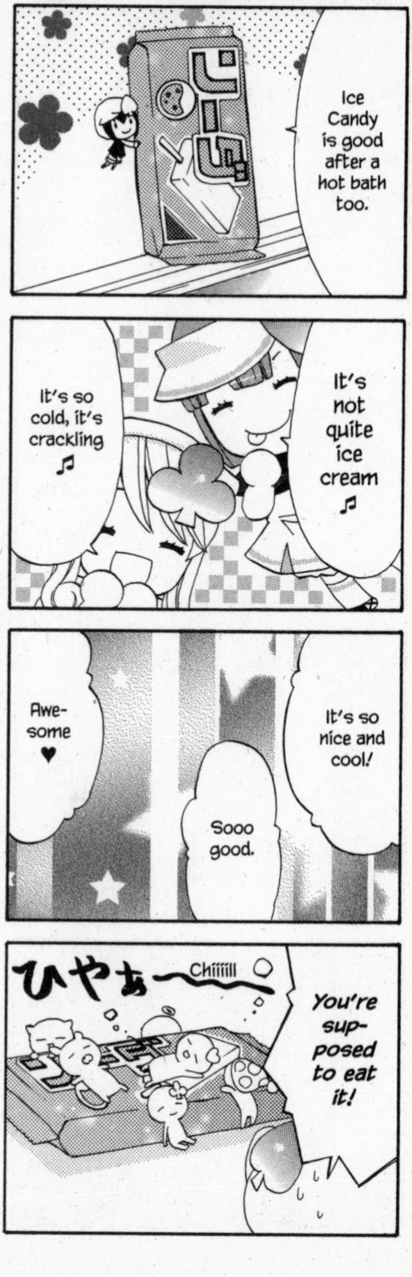
Ice Candy is good after a hot bath too.
It's not quite ice cream ♫
It's so cold, it's crackling ♫
It's so nice and cool!
Sooo good.
Awe-some ♥
You're sup-posed to eat it!
ひやぁ〜
Chiiiill

Playing with your food

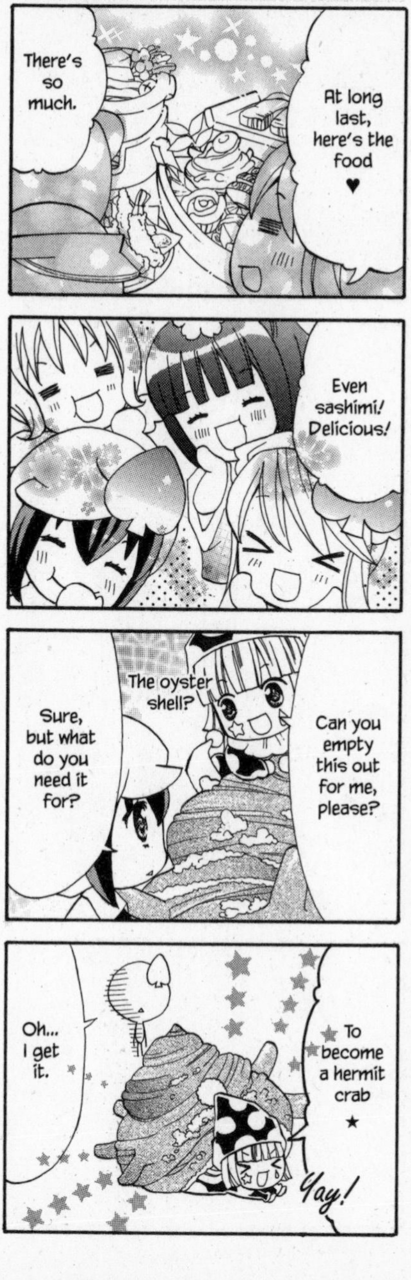
At long last, here's the food ♥
There's so much.
Even sashimi! Delicious!
Can you empty this out for me, please?
The oyster shell?
Sure, but what do you need it for?
To become a hermit crab ★
Oh... I get it.
Yay!

The Pileup

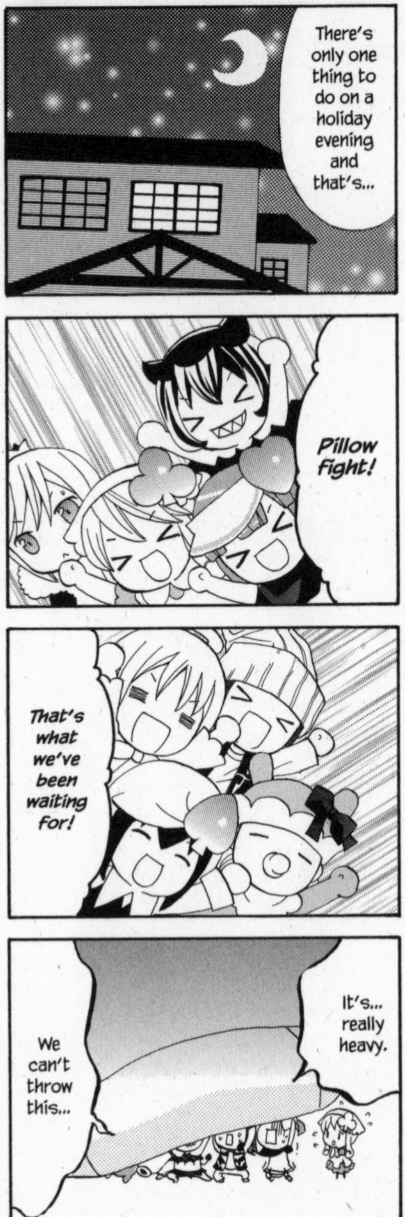
There's only one thing to do on a holiday evening and that's...
Pillow fight!
That's what we've been waiting for!
It's... really heavy.
We can't throw this...

The lives of others

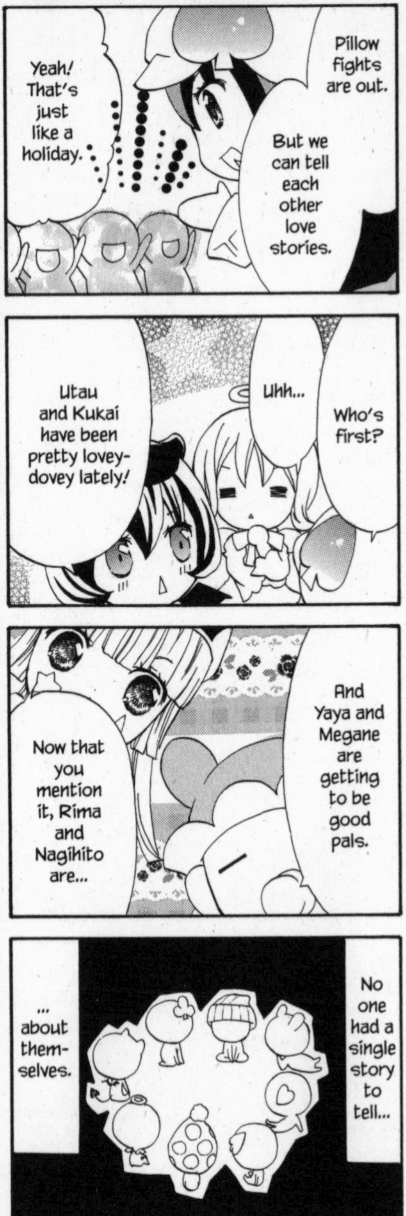
Pillow fights are out.
But we can tell each other love stories.
Yeah! That's just like a holiday.
Who's first?
Uhh...
Utau and Kukai have been pretty lovey-dovey lately!
And Yaya and Megane are getting to be good pals.
Now that you mention it, Rima and Nagihito are...
No one had a single story to tell...
... about them-selves.

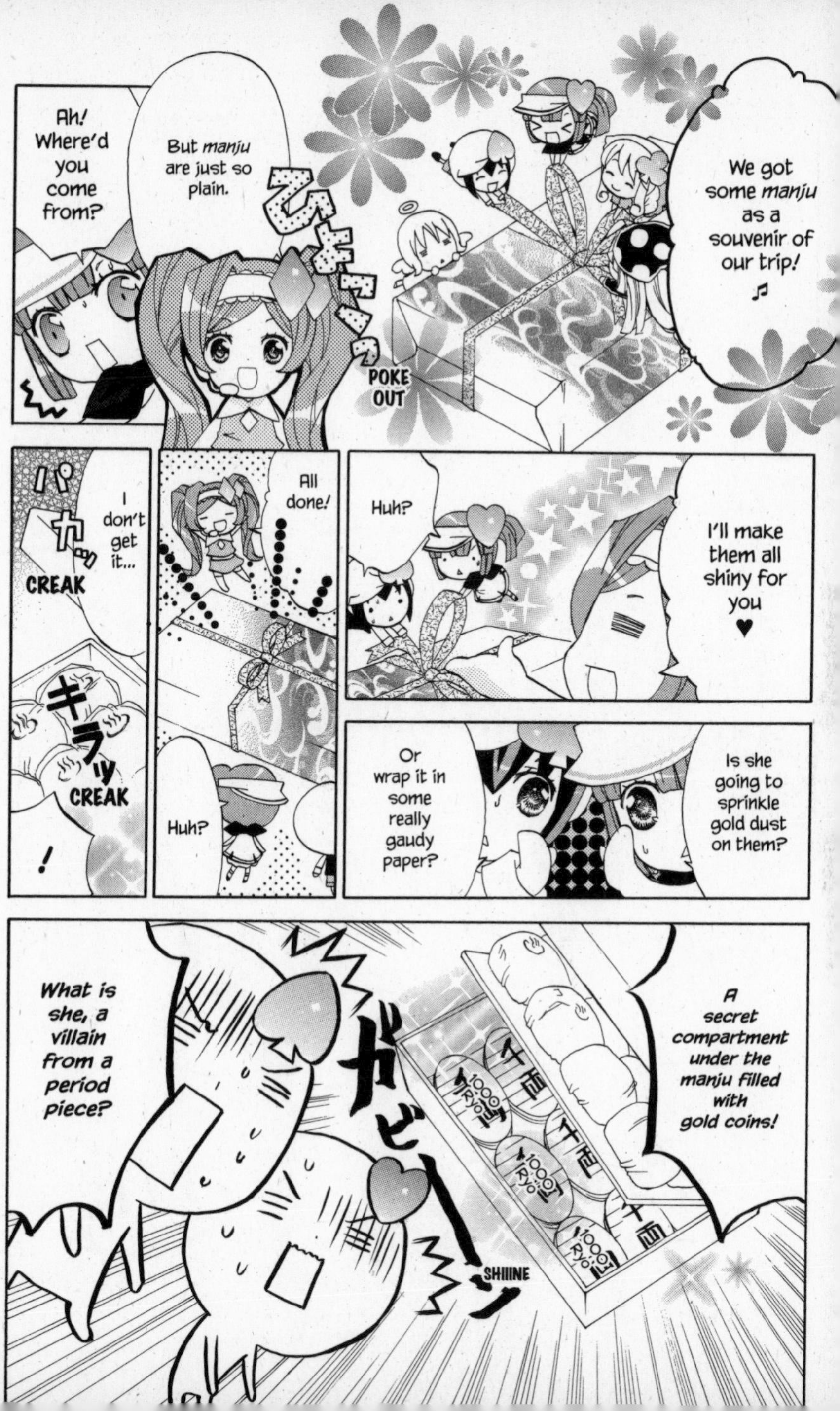

We got some *manju* as a souvenir of our trip! ♪
But *manju* are just so plain.
POKE OUT
Ah! Where'd you come from?
I'll make them all shiny for you ♥
Huh?
Is she going to sprinkle gold dust on them?
Or wrap it in some really gaudy paper?
All done!
Huh?
I don't get it...
CREAK
CREAK
!
A secret compartment under the manju filled with gold coins!
1000 Ryo
1000 Ryo
1000 Ryo
SHIIINE
What is she, a villain from a period piece?

Shugo Chara Chan!

ONE PANEL MANGA.

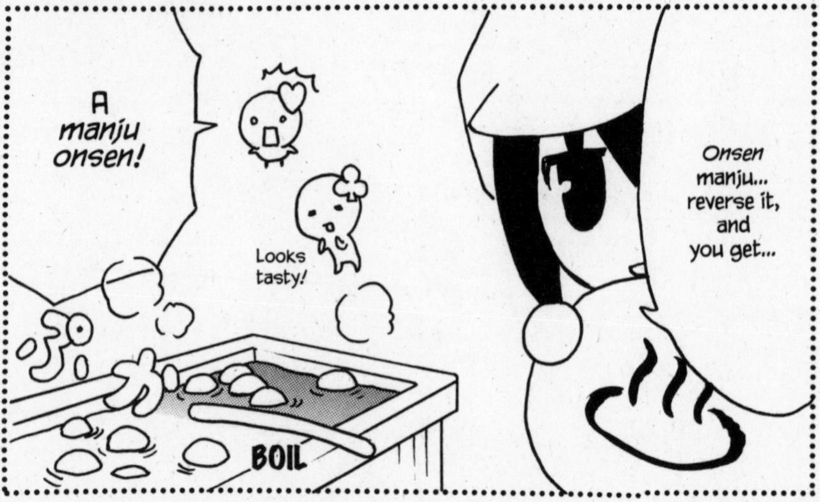
Onsen manju... reverse it, and you get...
A manju onsen!
Looks tasty!
BOIL

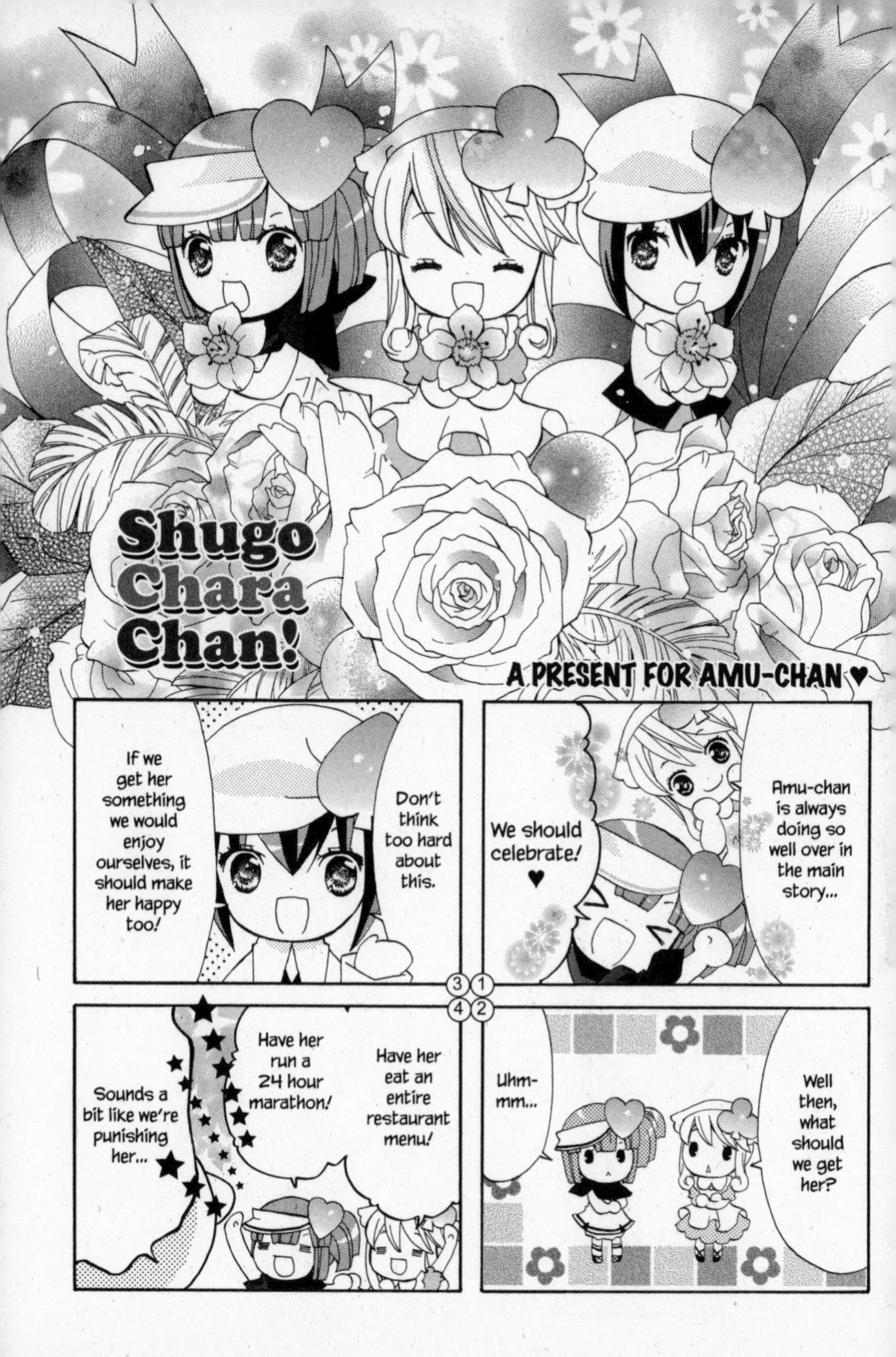
Shugo Chara Chan!
A PRESENT FOR AMU-CHAN ♥
Amu-chan is always doing so well over in the main story...
We should celebrate! ♥
Well then, what should we get her?
Uhmm-mm...
Don't think too hard about this.
If we get her something we would enjoy ourselves, it should make her happy too!
Have her eat an entire restaurant menu!
Have her run a 24 hour marathon!
Sounds a bit like we're punishing her...

What are you saying?

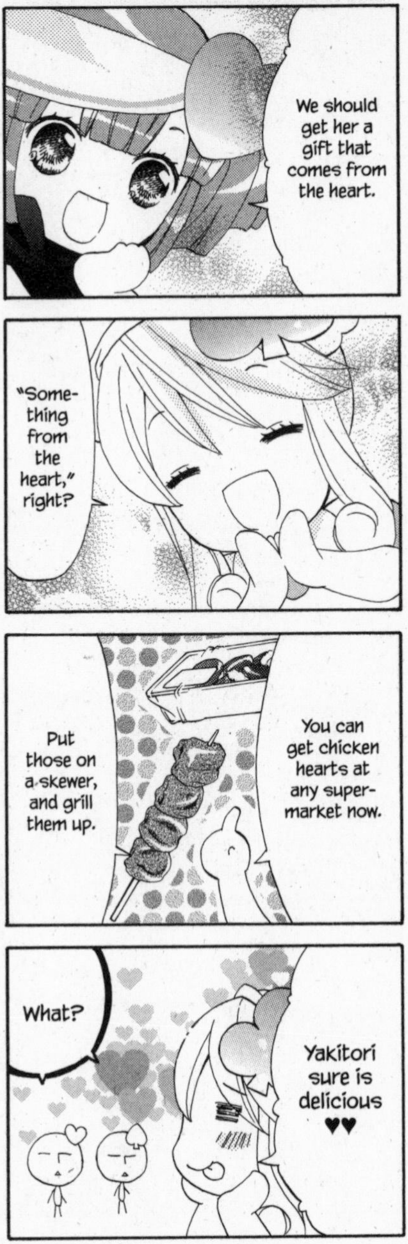
We should get her a gift that comes from the heart.
"Something from the heart," right?
You can get chicken hearts at any supermarket now.
Put those on a skewer, and grill them up.
Yakitori sure is delicious ♥♥
What?

The ego of an artist

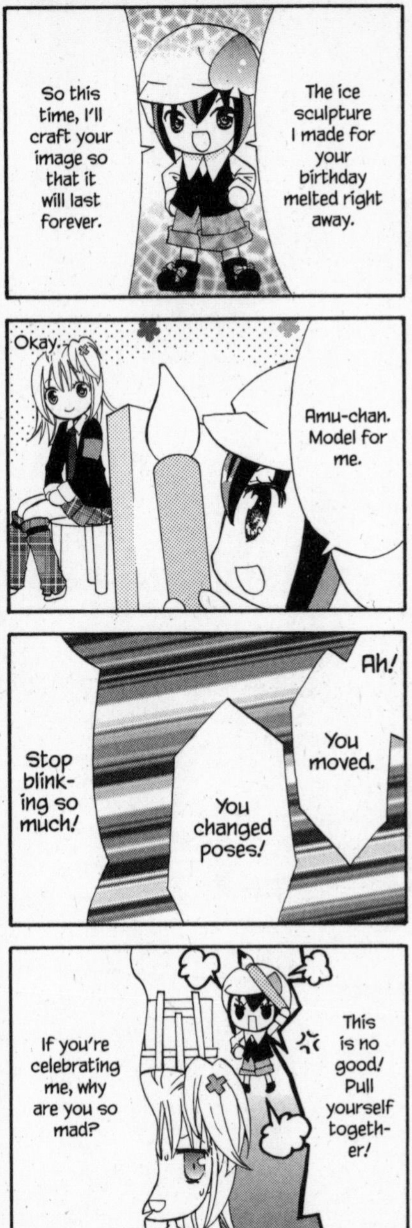
The ice sculpture I made for your birthday melted right away.
So this time, I'll craft your image so that it will last forever.
Amu-chan. Model for me.
Okay.
Ah!
You moved.
You changed poses!
Stop blinking so much!
This is no good! Pull yourself together!
If you're celebrating me, why are you so mad?

Misinterpretation

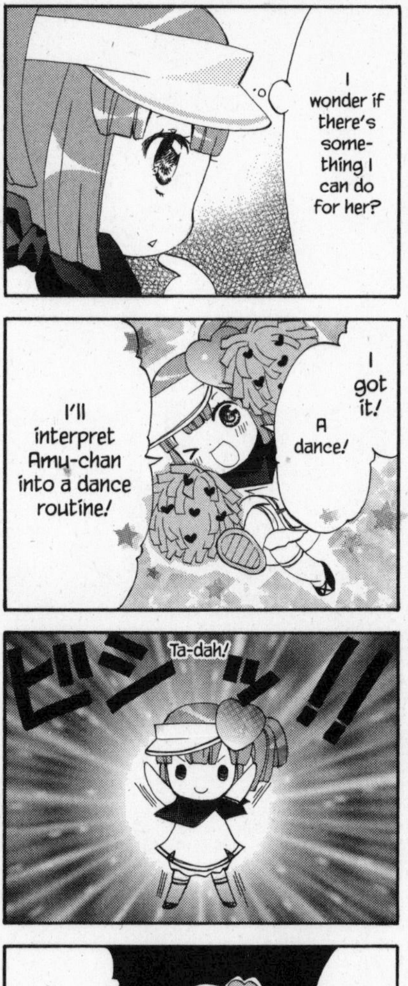
I wonder if there's some-thing I can do for her?
I got it!
A dance!
I'll interpret Amu-chan into a dance routine!
Ta-dah!
What is that?
It's Amu-chan's demerit X-mark!

I want be an adult

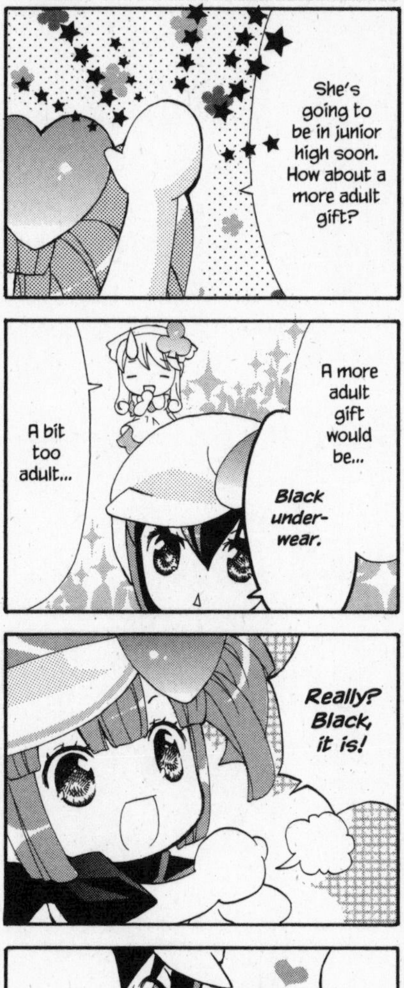
She's going to be in junior high soon. How about a more adult gift?
A more adult gift would be...
Black under-wear.
A bit too adult...
Really? Black, it is!
Well?
That doesn't seem adult at all...
Heh heh ♥

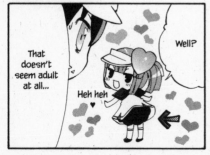

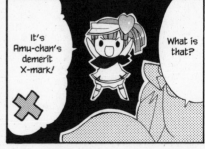

Ouch

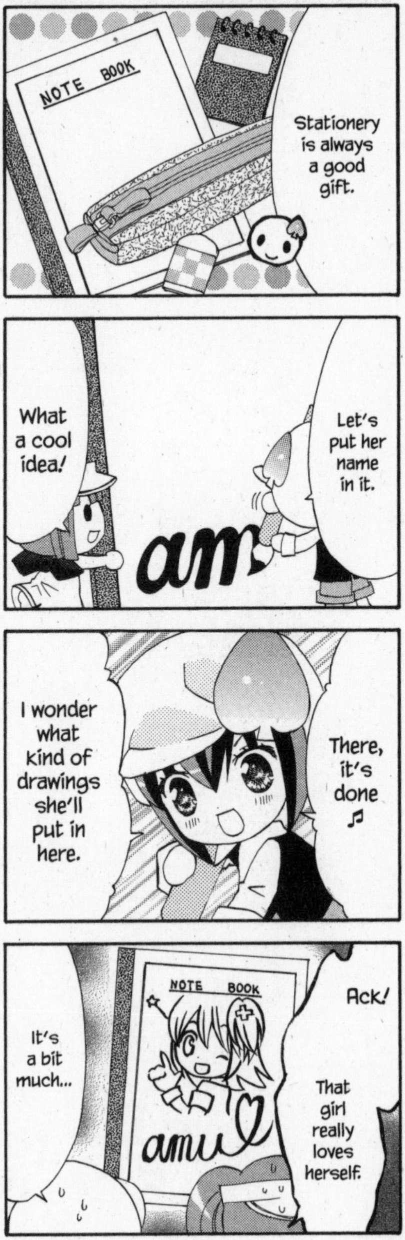
NOTE BOOK
Stationery is always a good gift.
Let's put her name in it.
What a cool idea!
am
There, it's done ♫
I wonder what kind of drawings she'll put in here.
Ack!
That girl really loves herself.
NOTE BOOK
amu
It's a bit much...

Diamond presents

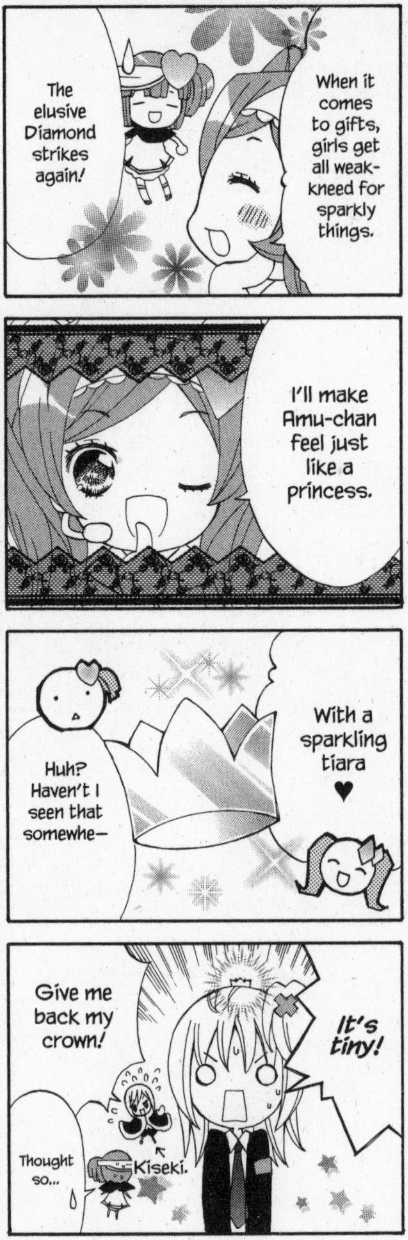
When it comes to gifts, girls get all weak-kneed for sparkly things.
The elusive Diamond strikes again!
I'll make Amu-chan feel just like a princess.
With a sparkling tiara ♥
Huh? Haven't I seen that somewhe–
It's tiny!
Give me back my crown!
Kiseki.
Thought so...

Shugo Chara Chan!

ONE PANEL MANGA.

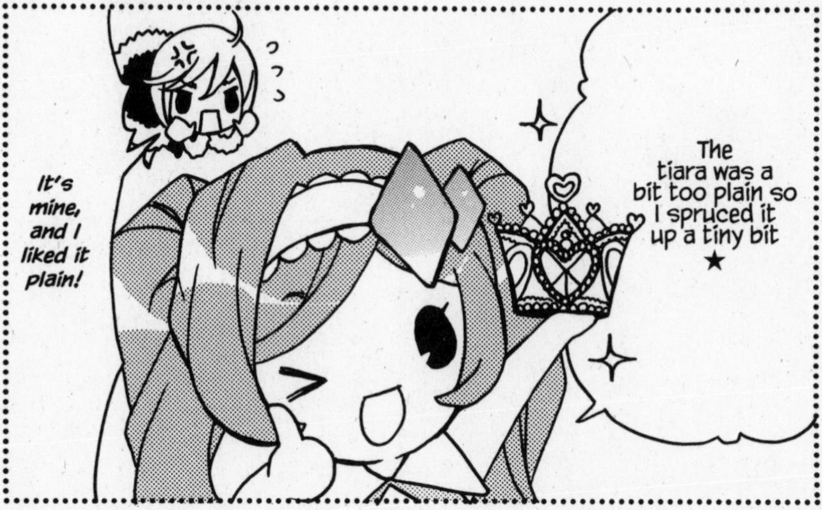
The tiara was a bit too plain so I spruced it up a tiny bit ★
It's mine, and I liked it plain!

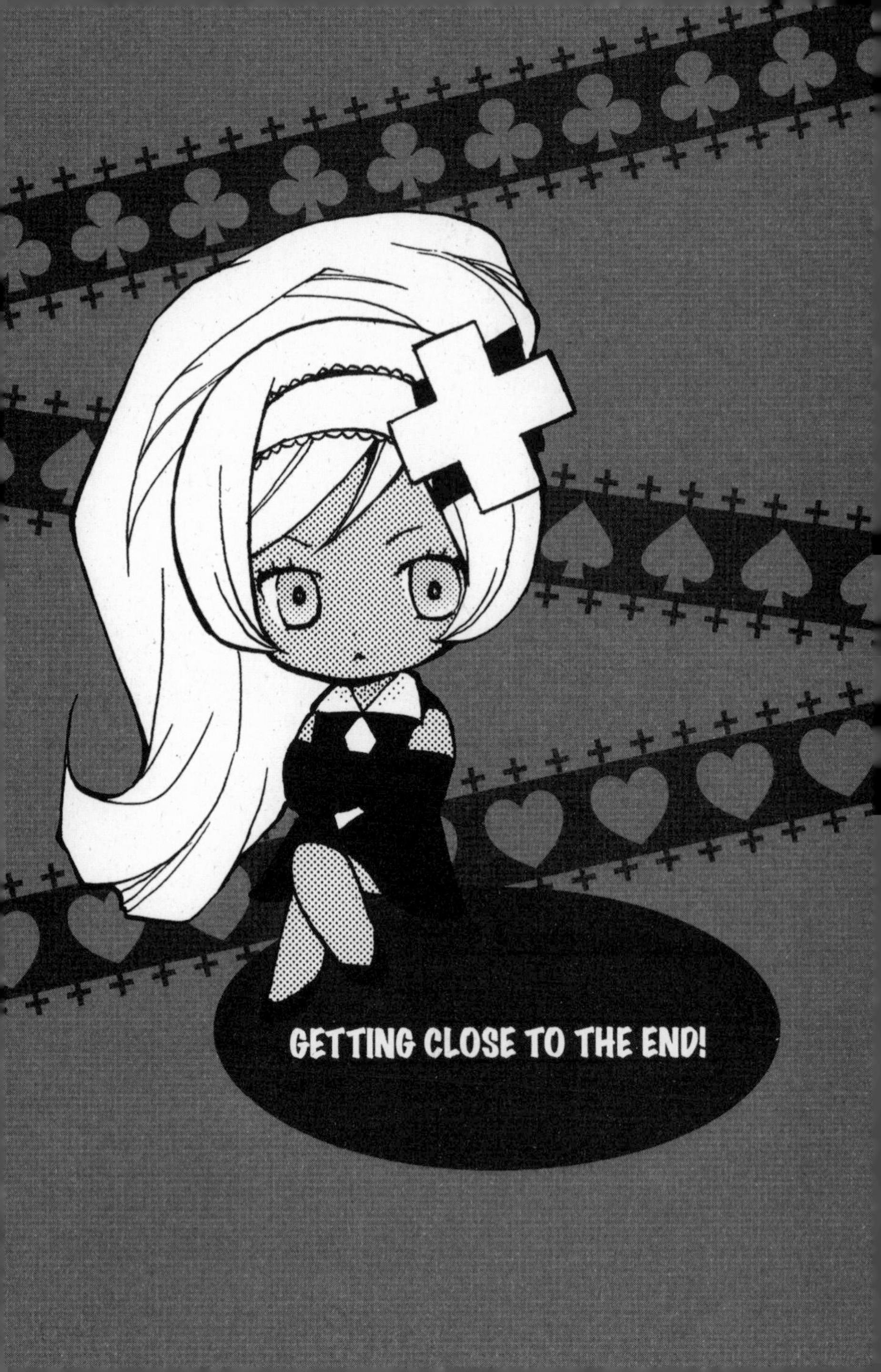
GETTING CLOSE TO THE END!

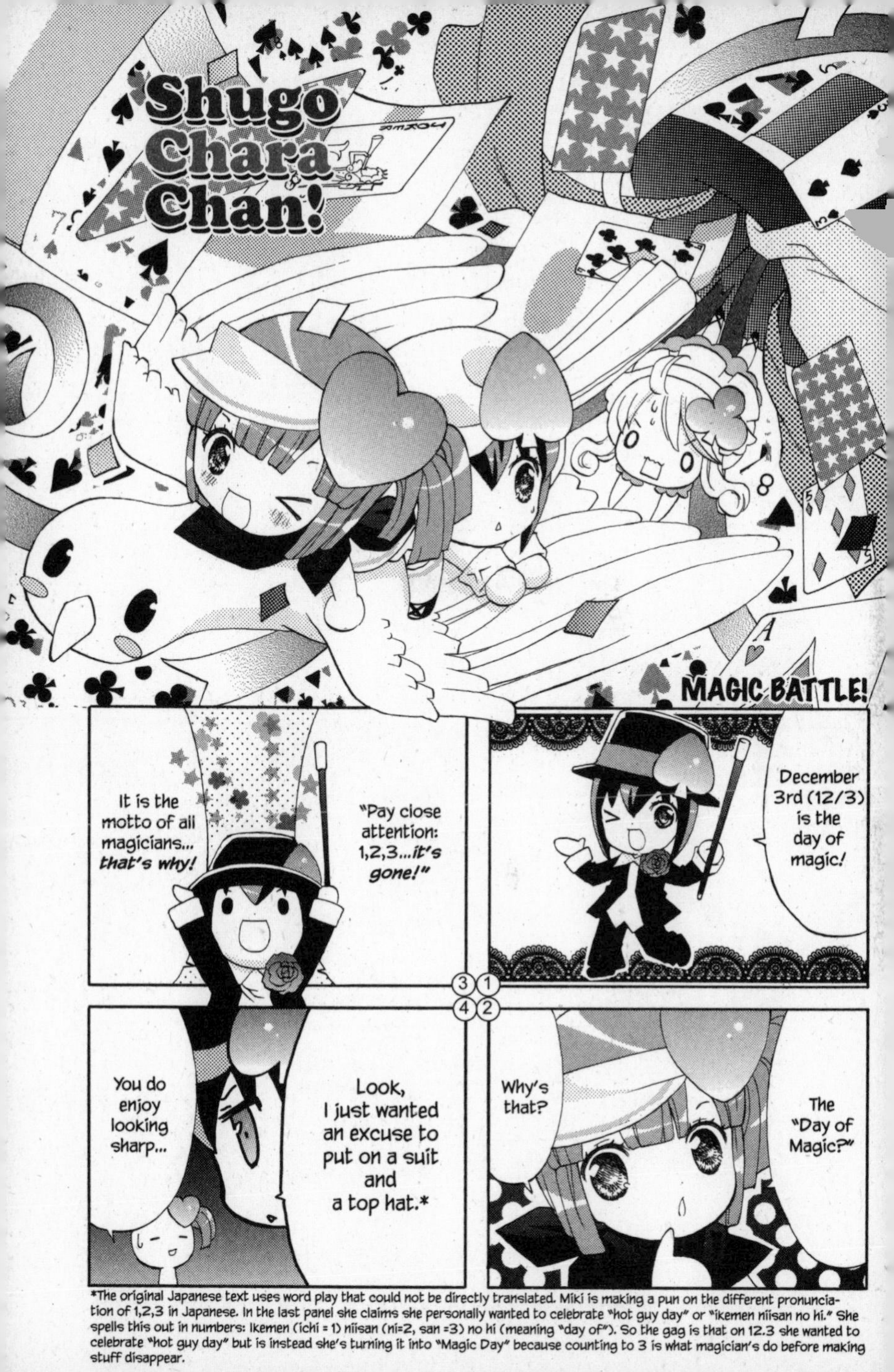
Shugo Chara Chan!
MAGIC BATTLE!
December 3rd (12/3) is the day of magic!
The "Day of Magic?"
Why's that?
"Pay close attention: 1,2,3...*it's gone!*"
It is the motto of all magicians... ***that's why!***
Look, I just wanted an excuse to put on a suit and a top hat.*
You do enjoy looking sharp...

*The original Japanese text uses word play that could not be directly translated. Miki is making a pun on the different pronunciation of 1,2,3 in Japanese. In the last panel she claims she personally wanted to celebrate "hot guy day" or "ikemen niisan no hi." She spells this out in numbers: Ikemen (ichi = 1) niisan (ni=2, san =3) no hi (meaning "day of"). So the gag is that on 12.3 she wanted to celebrate "hot guy day" but is instead she's turning it into "Magic Day" because counting to 3 is what magician's do before making stuff disappear.

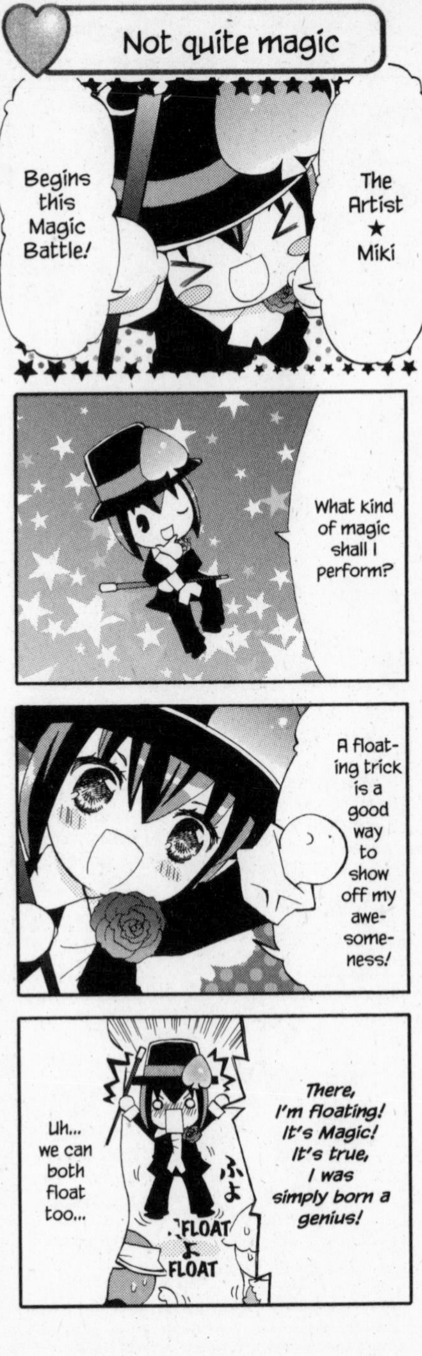
Not quite magic
The Artist ★ Miki
Begins this Magic Battle!
What kind of magic shall I perform?
A floating trick is a good way to show off my awesomeness!
There, I'm floating! It's Magic! It's true, I was simply born a genius!
ふよ FLOAT
ふよ FLOAT
Uh... we can both float too...

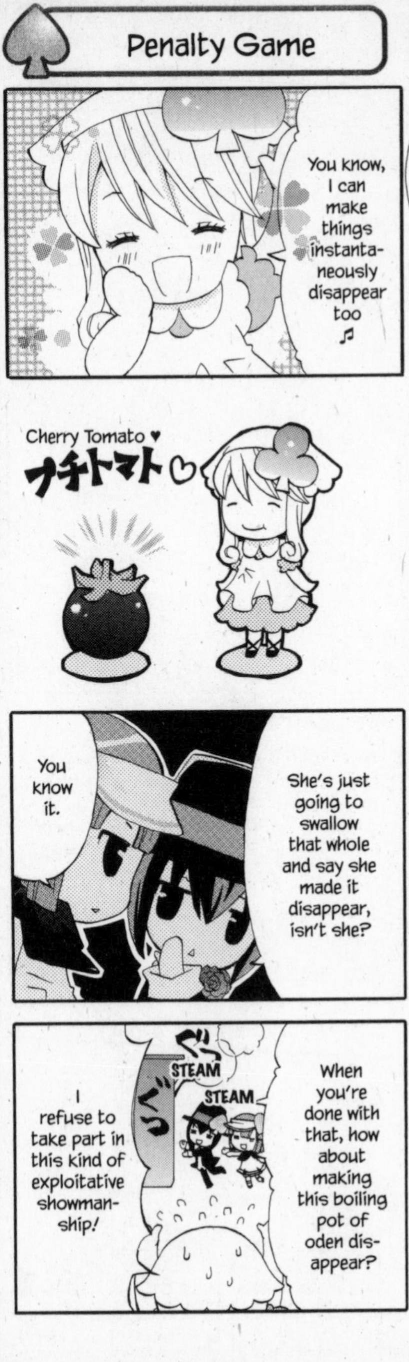
Penalty Game
You know, I can make things instantaneously disappear too ♪
Cherry Tomato ♥
プチトマト♡
She's just going to swallow that whole and say she made it disappear, isn't she?
You know it.
When you're done with that, how about making this boiling pot of oden disappear?
ぐつ STEAM
ぐつ STEAM
I refuse to take part in this kind of exploitative showmanship!

Su, the adult

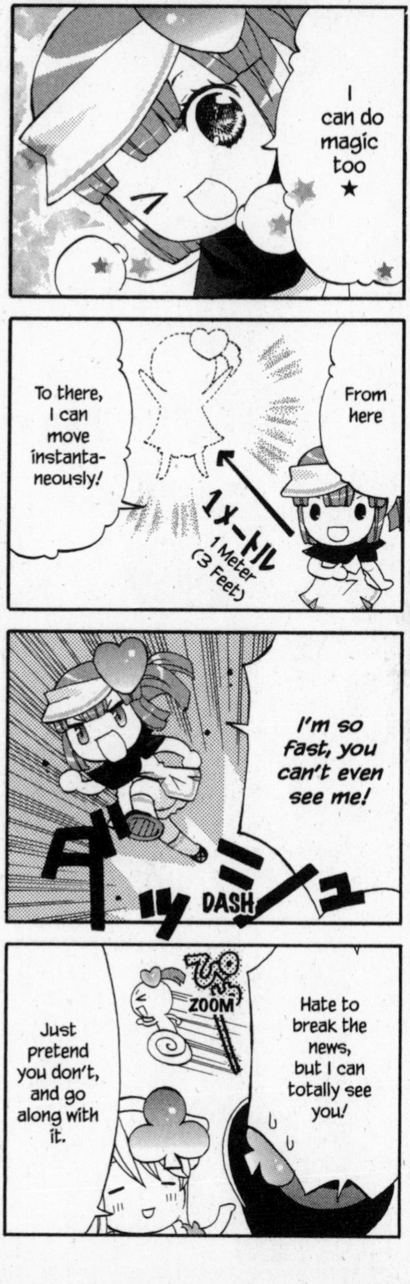
I can do magic too ★
From here
To there, I can move instantaneously!
1メートル
1 Meter (3 Feet)
I'm so fast, you can't even see me!
ダッシュ
DASH
Hate to break the news, but I can totally see you!
ZOOM
Just pretend you don't, and go along with it.

Incredible Powers

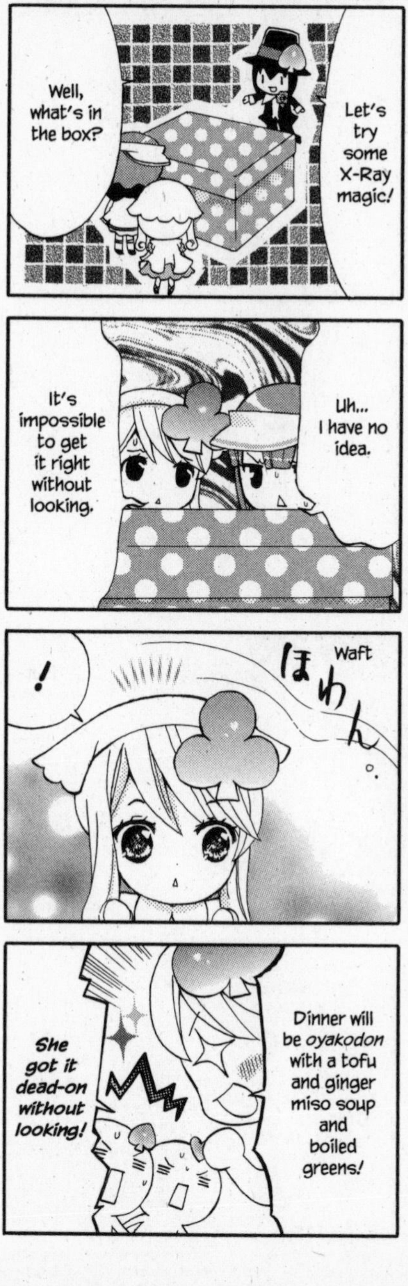
Let's try some X-Ray magic!
Well, what's in the box?
Uh... I have no idea.
It's impossible to get it right without looking.
ほわん
Waft
!
Dinner will be *oyakodon* with a tofu and ginger miso soup and boiled greens!
She got it dead-on without looking!

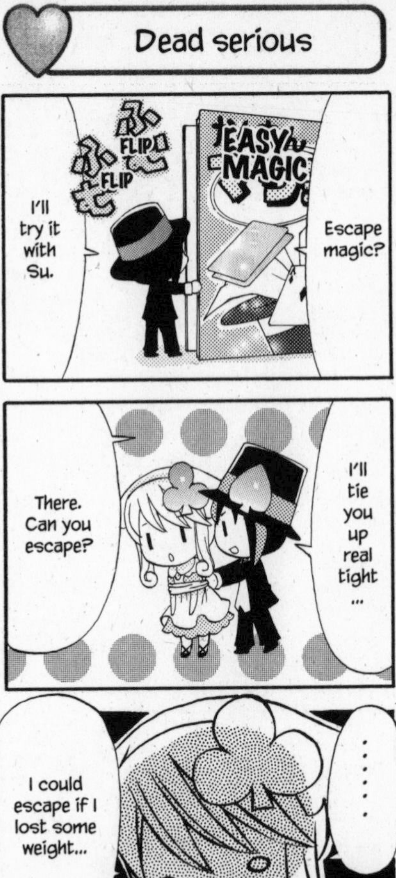
Dead serious
Escape magic?
EASY MAGIC
FLIP
FLIP
I'll try it with Su.
I'll tie you up real tight...
There. Can you escape?
......
I could escape if I lost some weight...
Uh... I guess that's true...
So it's a forced diet...
That's harassment!

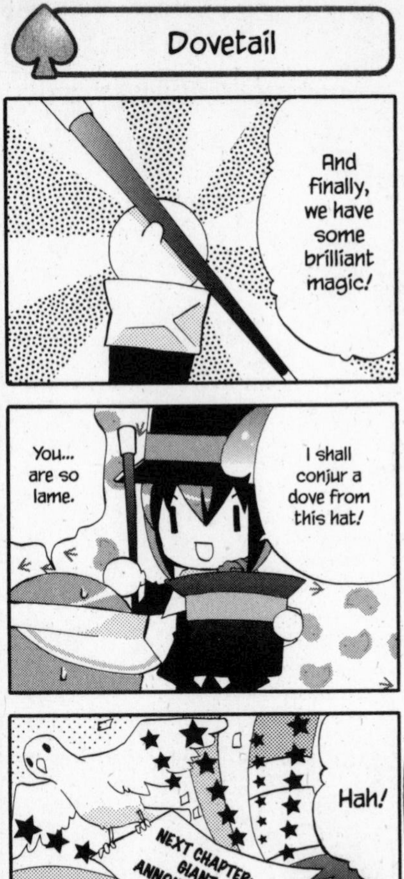
Dovetail
And finally, we have some brilliant magic!
I shall conjur a dove from this hat!
You... are so lame.
Hah!
NEXT CHAPTER: GIANT ANNOUNCEMENT!
Gasp!
The dove's got an announcement!
You're gasping because of the dove, aren't you!*
I said you're lame...

*The original Japanese text involved a joke around the words "Hat", "Dove" and "to be taken aback," as all sound very similar: Hatto (Hat), Hatto (Dove) and hatto shita (to be taken aback). In panel 4 Ran goes "Huh" which is also spelled "Ha" in Japanese. She says that the dove was carrying a note. Miki replies literally: "If it had just been the dove you would've been taken aback, no?" (If it had just been a hato (Dove) you would've been hatto (taken aback).

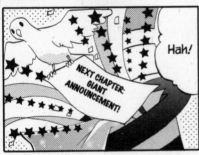

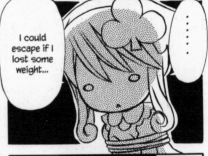

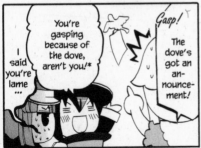

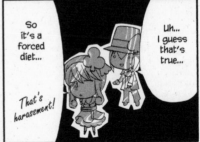

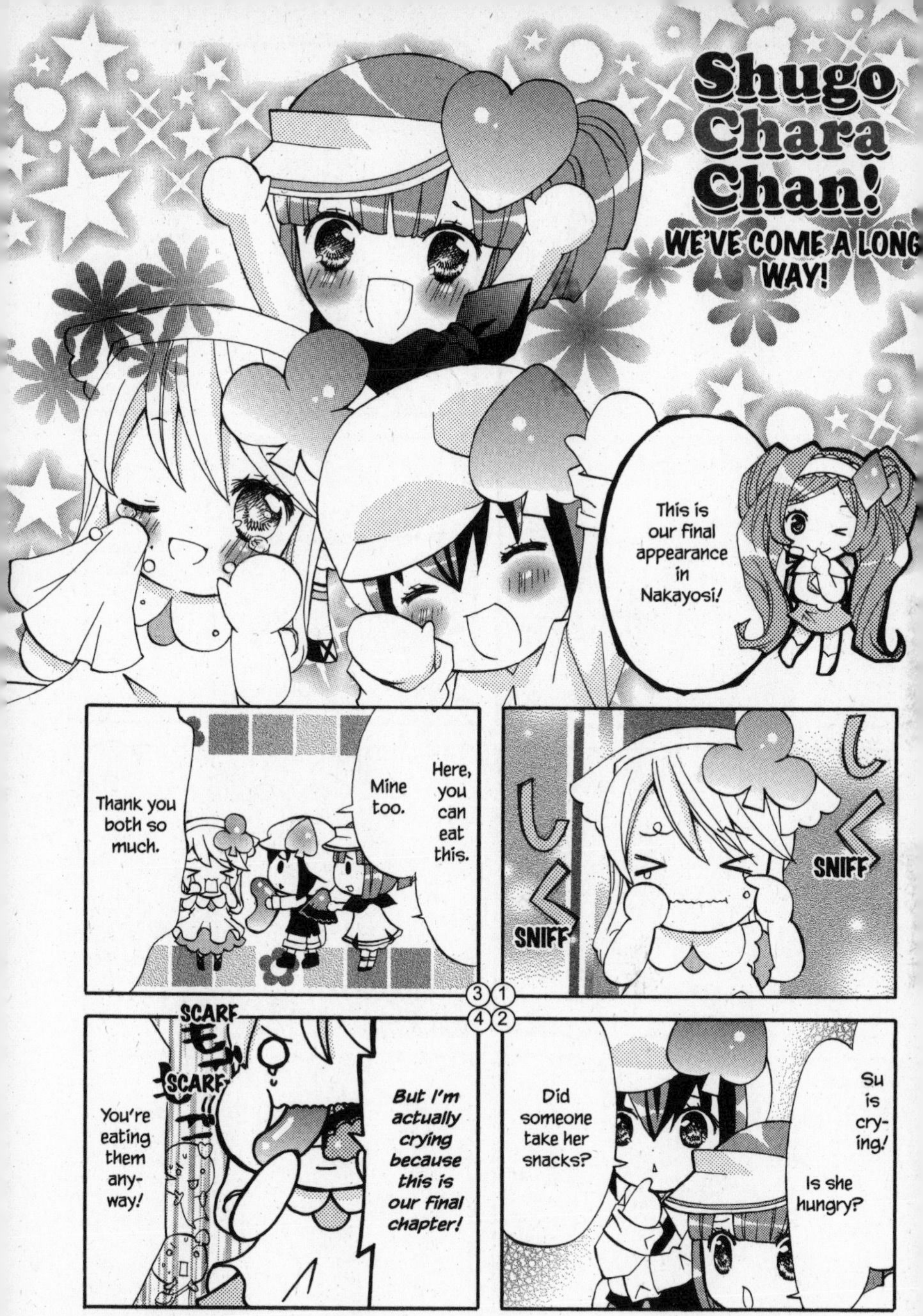
Shugo Chara Chan!
WE'VE COME A LONG WAY!
This is our final appearance in Nakayosi!
SNIFF
SNIFF
Su is crying!
Is she hungry?
Did someone take her snacks?
Here, you can eat this.
Mine too.
Thank you both so much.
But I'm actually crying because this is our final chapter!
SCARF
SCARF
You're eating them anyway!

Real progress

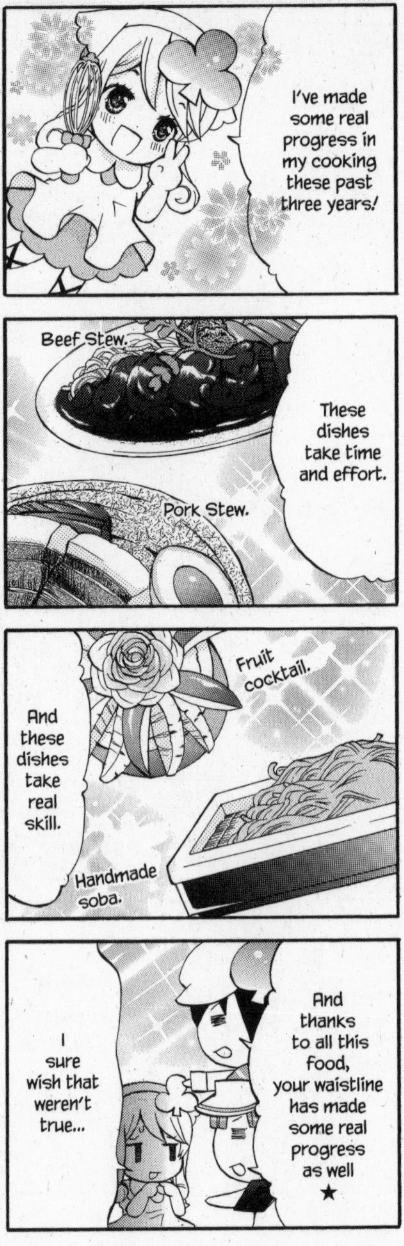
I've made some real progress in my cooking these past three years!
These dishes take time and effort.
Beef Stew.
Pork Stew.
Fruit cocktail.
And these dishes take real skill.
Handmade soba.
And thanks to all this food, your waistline has made some real progress as well ★
I sure wish that weren't true...

Too far!

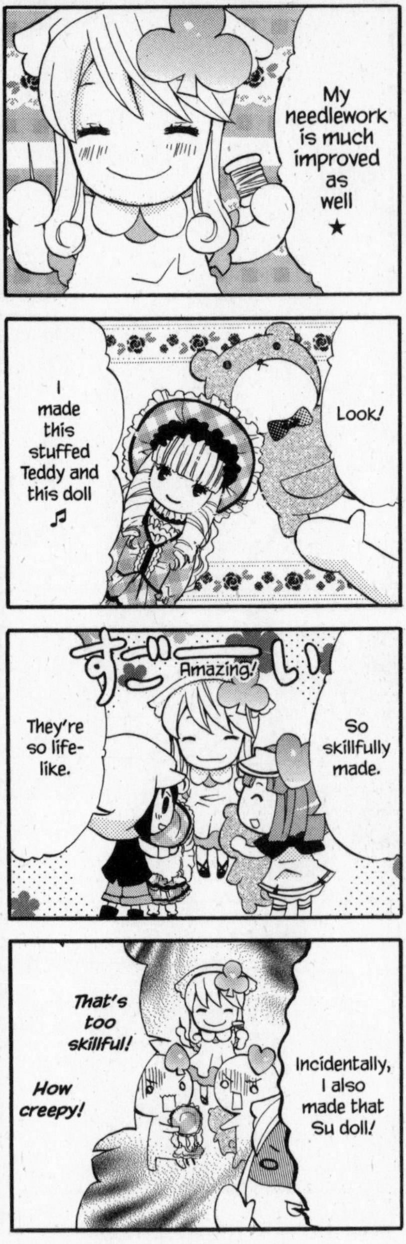
My needlework is much improved as well ★
Look!
I made this stuffed Teddy and this doll ♪
すごーーい
Amazing!
So skillfully made.
They're so life-like.
Incidentally, I also made that Su doll!
That's too skillful!
How creepy!

Take me higher

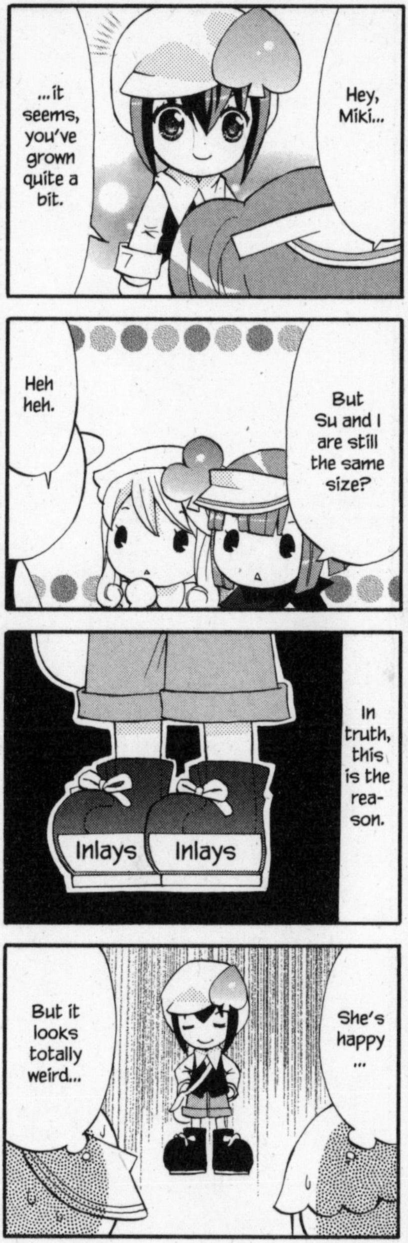
Hey, Miki...
...it seems, you've grown quite a bit.
But Su and I are still the same size?
Heh heh.
In truth, this is the reason.
Inlays
Inlays
She's happy ...
But it looks totally weird...

Even higher!

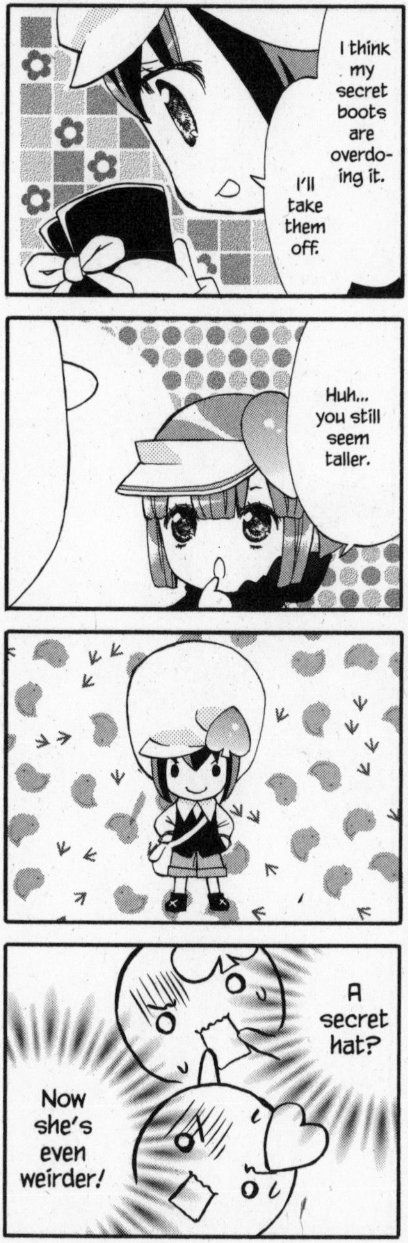
I think my secret boots are overdoing it.
I'll take them off.
Huh... you still seem taller.
A secret hat?
Now she's even weirder!

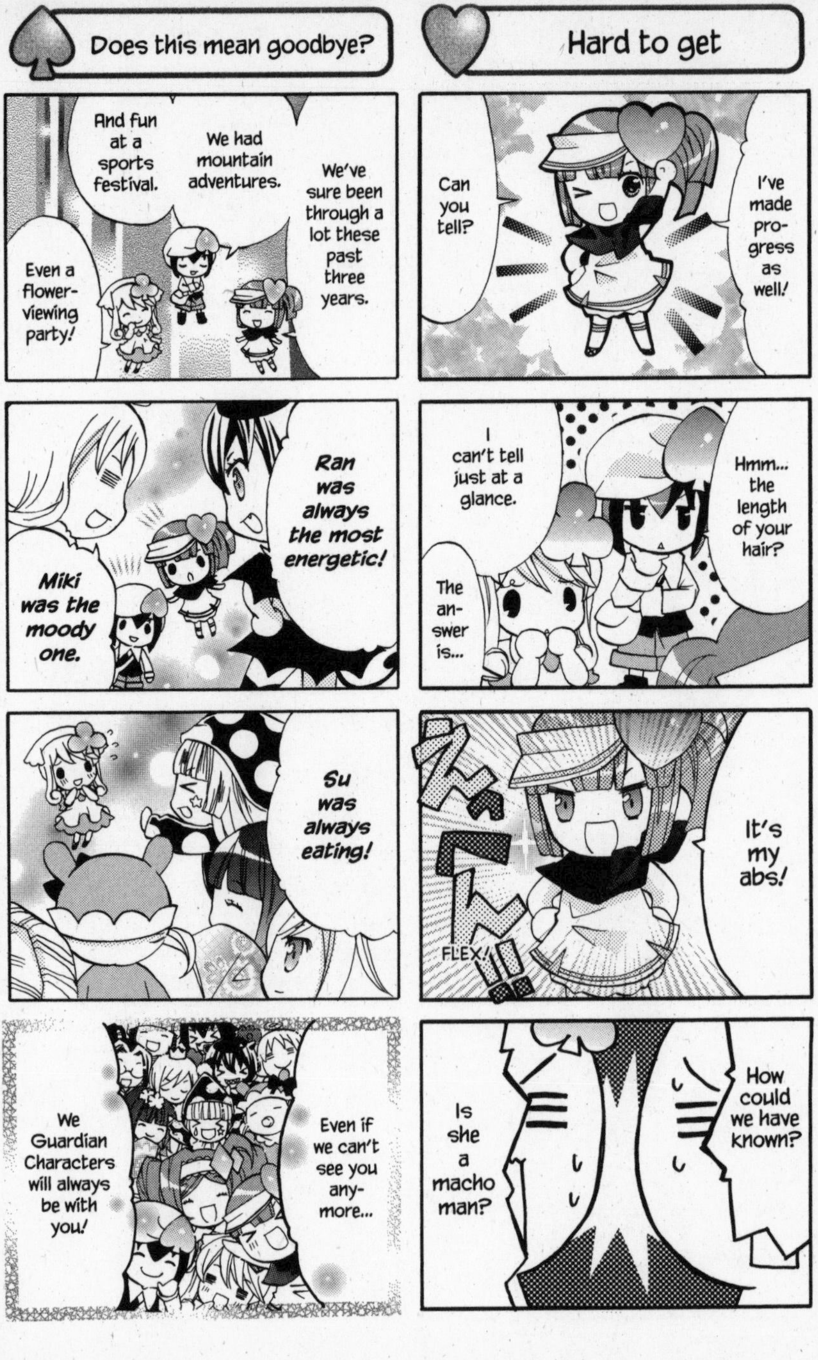
Hard to get
I've made progress as well!
Can you tell?
Hmm... the length of your hair?
I can't tell just at a glance.
The answer is...
It's my abs!
FLEX!
How could we have known?
Is she a macho man?
Does this mean goodbye?
We've sure been through a lot these past three years.
We had mountain adventures.
And fun at a sports festival.
Even a flower-viewing party!
Ran was always the most energetic!
Miki was the moody one.
Su was always eating!
Even if we can't see you anymore...
We Guardian Characters will always be with you!

Shugo Chara Chan!

ONE PANEL MANGA.

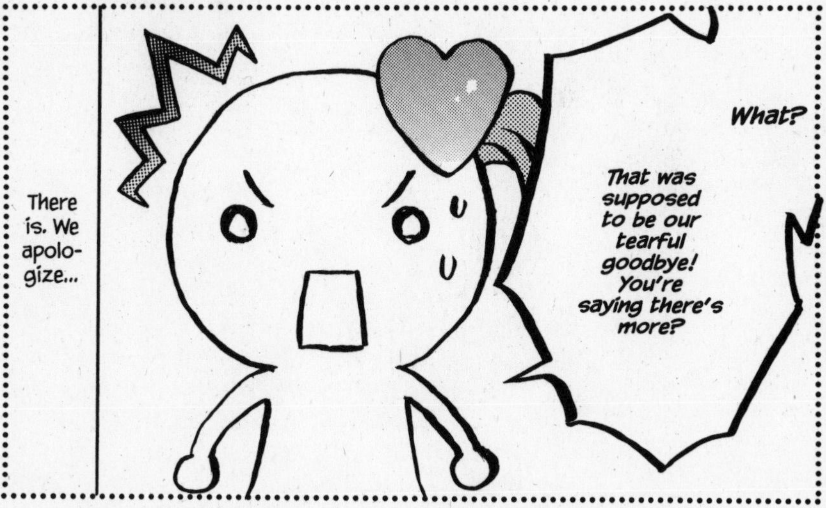
What?
That was supposed to be our tearful goodbye! You're saying there's more?
There is. We apolo-gize...

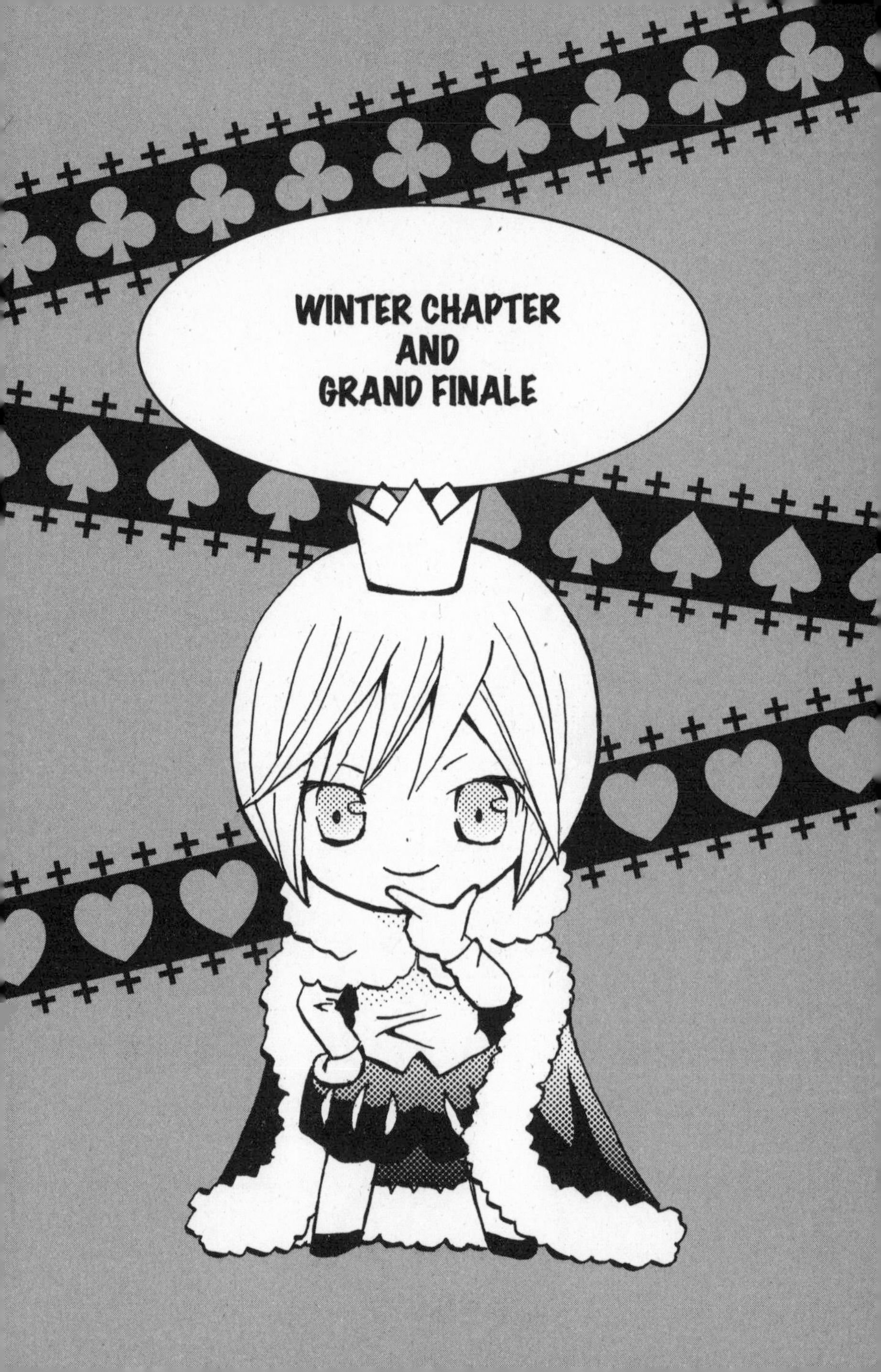
WINTER CHAPTER
AND
GRAND FINALE

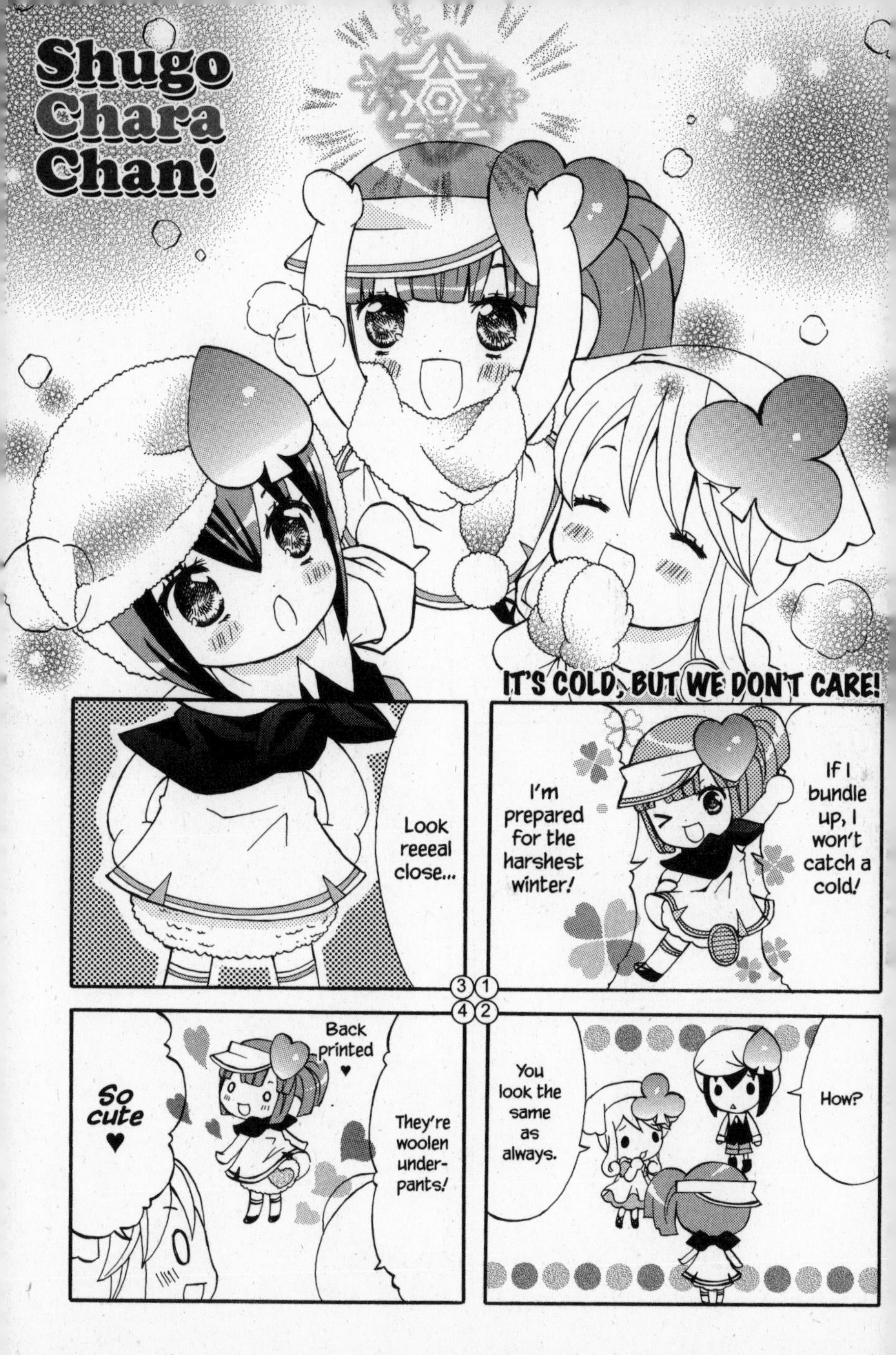
Shugo Chara Chan!
IT'S COLD, BUT WE DON'T CARE!
If I bundle up, I won't catch a cold!
I'm prepared for the harshest winter!
How?
You look the same as always.
Look reeeal close...
They're woolen under-pants!
Back printed ♥
So cute ♥

A cool response

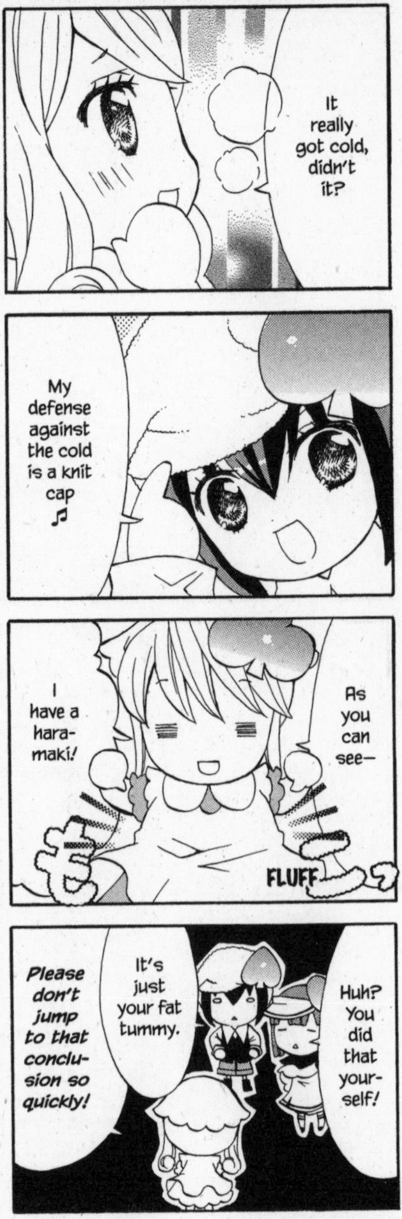
It really got cold, didn't it?
My defense against the cold is a knit cap ♪
As you can see—
I have a hara-maki!
FLUFF
Huh? You did that yourself!
It's just your fat tummy.
Please don't jump to that conclusion so quickly!

Not quite right...

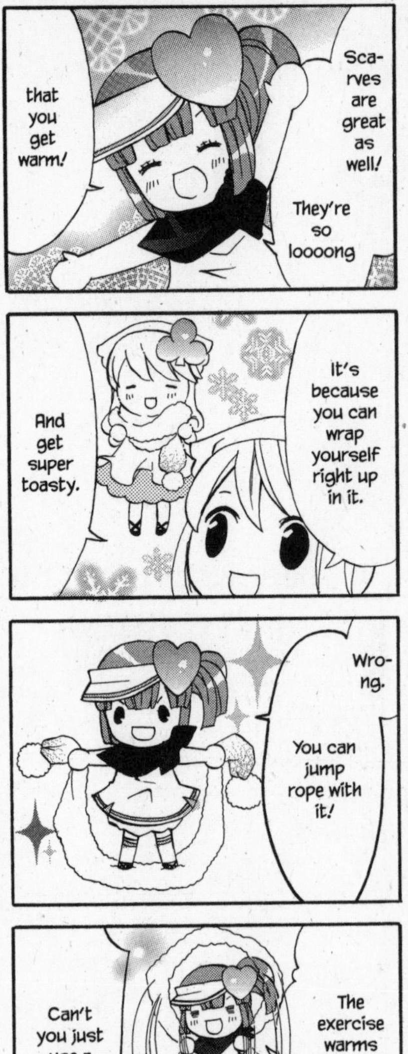
Scarves are great as well!
They're so loooong
that you get warm!
It's because you can wrap yourself right up in it.
And get super toasty.
Wrong.
You can jump rope with it!
The exercise warms you right up.
Can't you just use a normal jump rope?
SKIP
SKIP

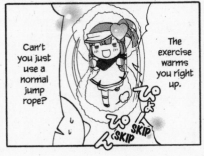

Practical!

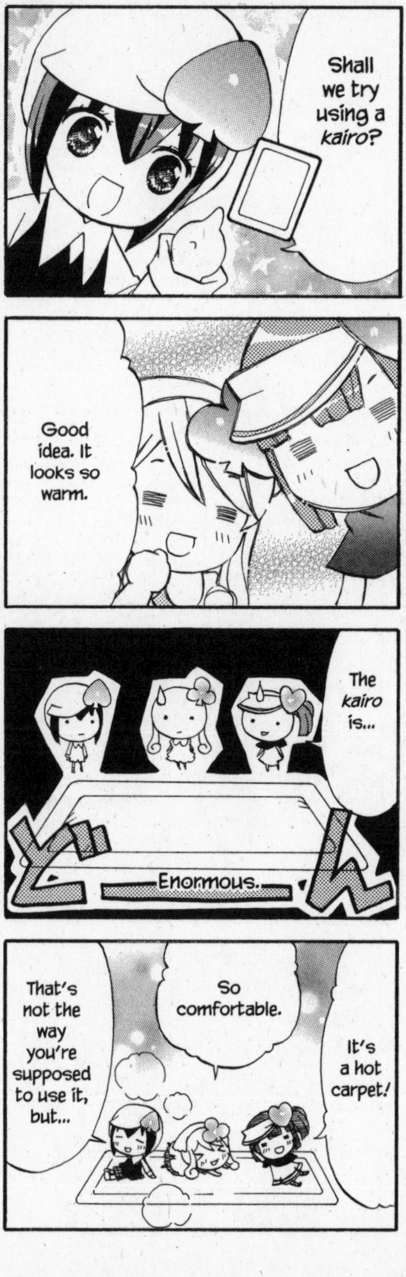
Shall we try using a *kairo*?
Good idea. It looks so warm.
The *kairo* is...
Enormous.
It's a hot carpet!
So comfortable.
That's not the way you're supposed to use it, but...

Wrong answer

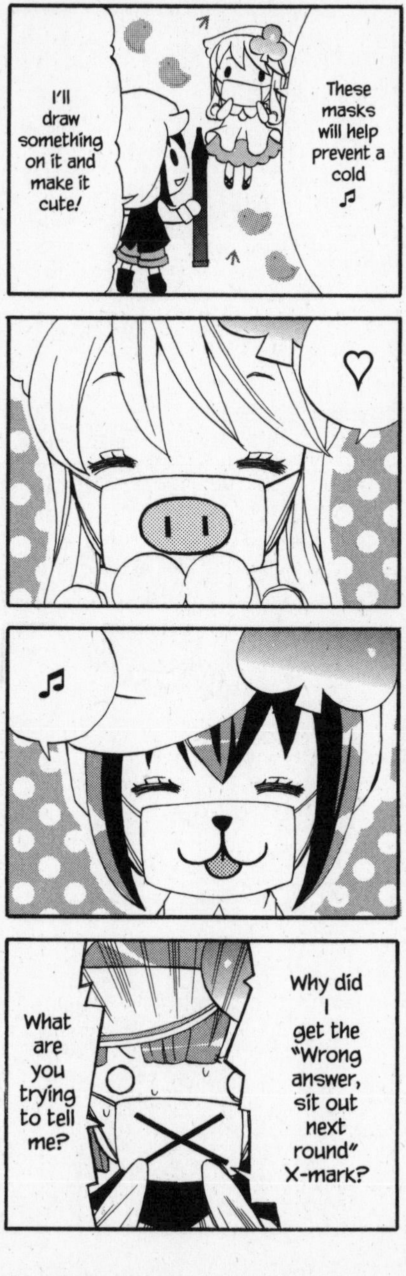
These masks will help prevent a cold ♪
I'll draw something on it and make it cute!
♥
♪
Why did I get the "Wrong answer, sit out next round" X-mark?
What are you trying to tell me?

Pleasant surroundings

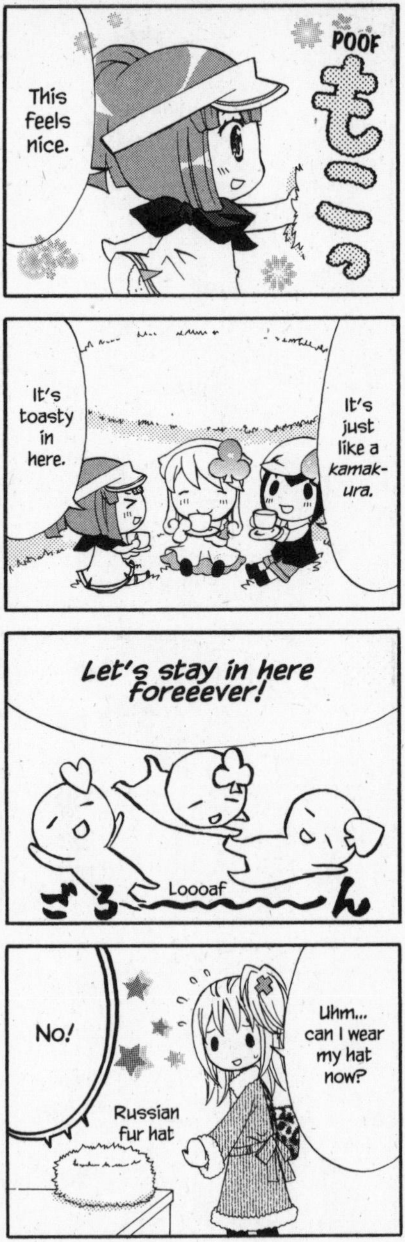
POOF
もこっ
This feels nice.
It's just like a *kamakura.*
It's toasty in here.
Let's stay in here foreeever!
Loooaf
ごろ〜ん
Uhm... can I wear my hat now?
No!
Russian fur hat

More than a little exercise

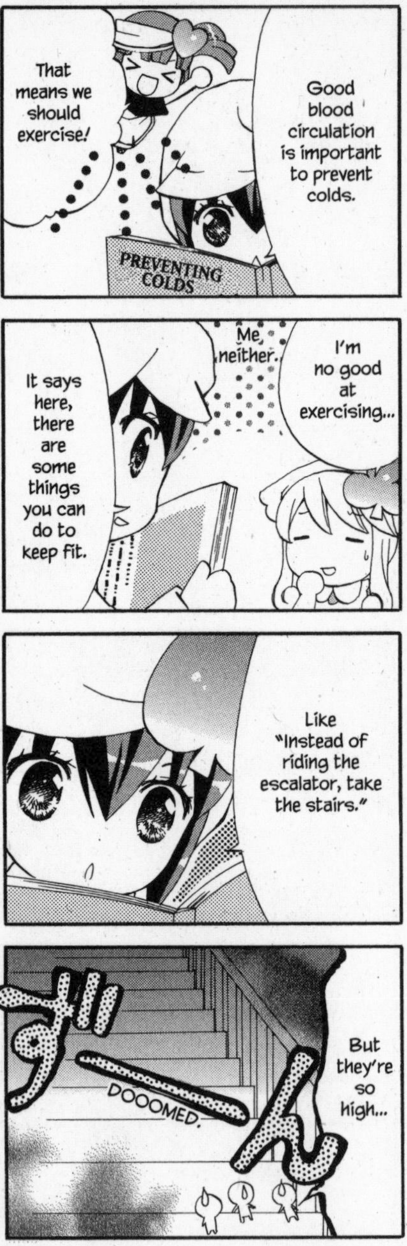
Good blood circulation is important to prevent colds.
That means we should exercise!
PREVENTING COLDS
I'm no good at exercising...
Me, neither.
It says here, there are some things you can do to keep fit.
Like "Instead of riding the escalator, take the stairs."
But they're so high...
ず〜ん
DOOOMED.

Too much moisture

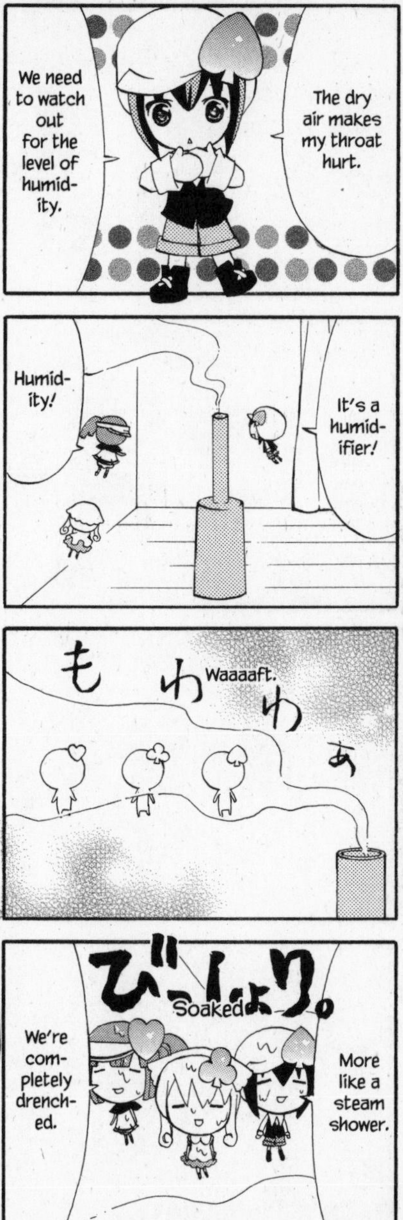
The dry air makes my throat hurt.
We need to watch out for the level of humidity.
It's a humidifier!
Humidity!
Waaaaft.
Soaked
More like a steam shower.
We're completely drenched.

Too good to gargle

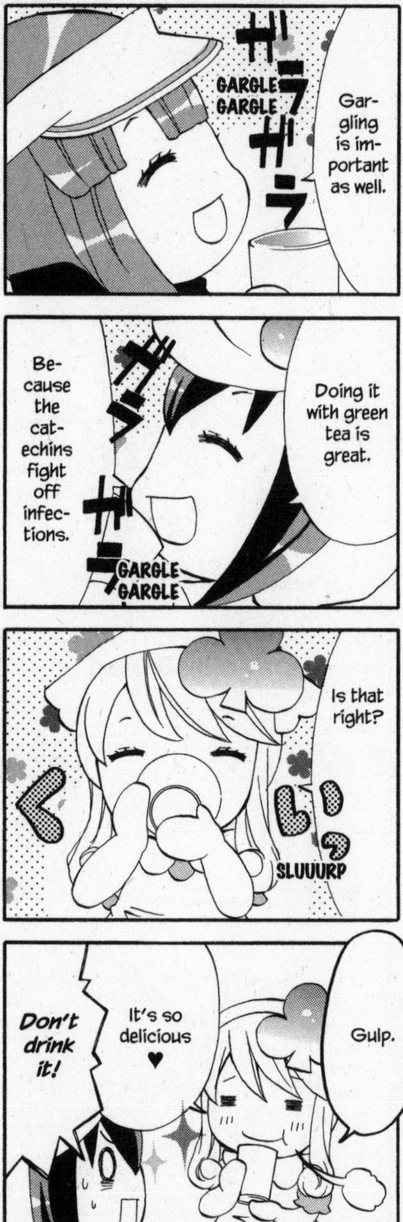
Gargling is important as well.
GARGLE GARGLE
Doing it with green tea is great.
Because the catechins fight off infections.
GARGLE GARGLE
Is that right?
SLUUURP
Gulp.
It's so delicious ♥
Don't drink it!

One more round

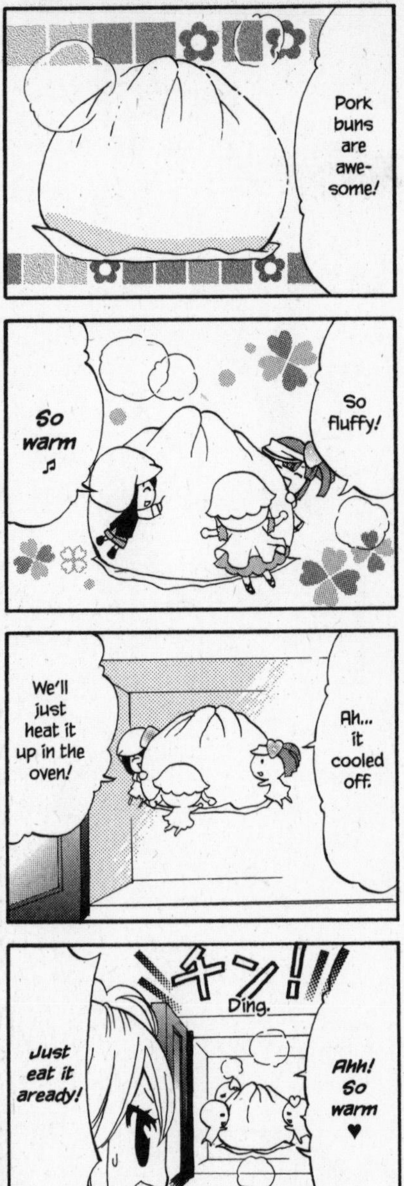
Pork buns are awe-some!
So fluffy!
So warm ♫
Ah... it cooled off.
We'll just heat it up in the oven!
チーン!!
Ding.
Ahh! So warm ♥
Just eat it aready!

Too hot to handle

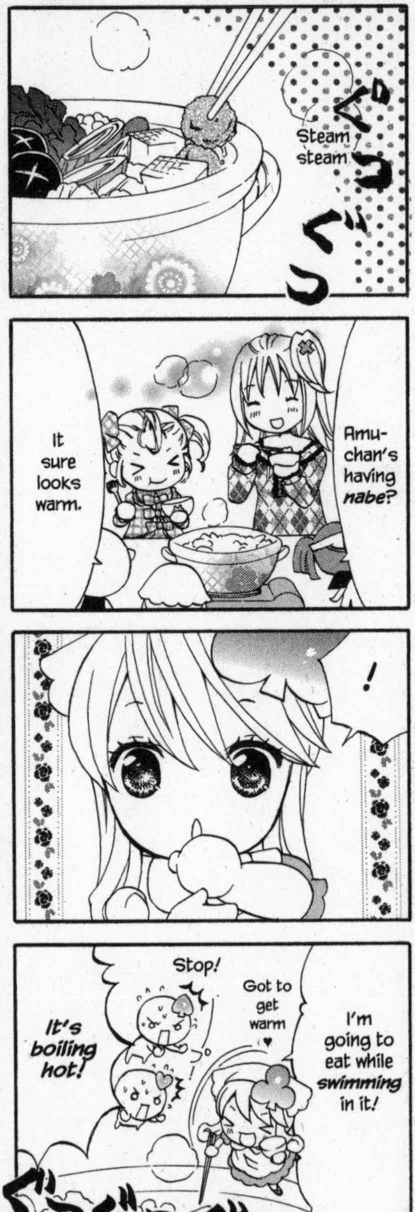
Steam steam
Amu-chan's having *nabe*?
It sure looks warm.
!
I'm going to eat while **swimming** in it!
Got to get warm ♥
Stop!
It's boiling hot!
Bubble bubble bubble

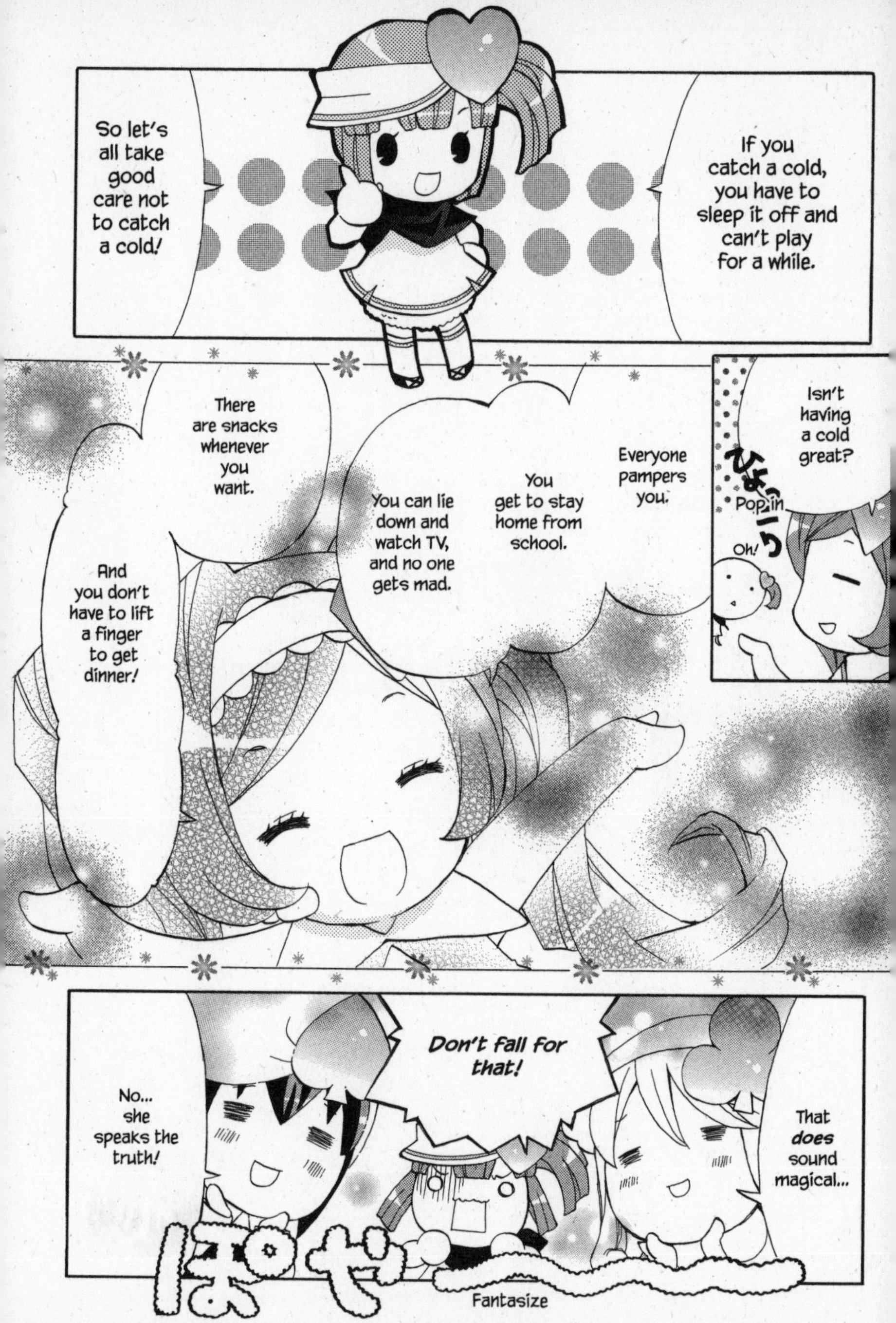

If you catch a cold, you have to sleep it off and can't play for a while.
So let's all take good care not to catch a cold!
Isn't having a cold great?
Pop in
Oh!
Everyone pampers you.
You get to stay home from school.
You can lie down and watch TV, and no one gets mad.
There are snacks whenever you want.
And you don't have to lift a finger to get dinner!
That *does* sound magical...
Don't fall for that!
No... she speaks the truth!
Fantasize

Shugo Chara Chan!

ONE PANEL MANGA.

This is the last of the one panel manga.

Please enjoy the rest of the issue ♥

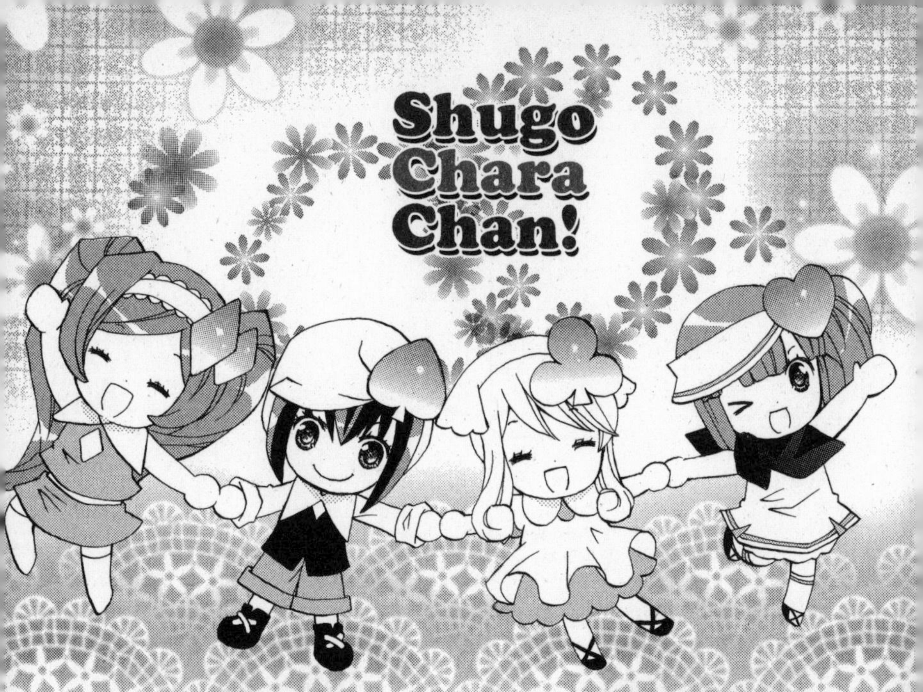
Shugo Chara Chan!

CHRISTMAS PARTY FINALE!

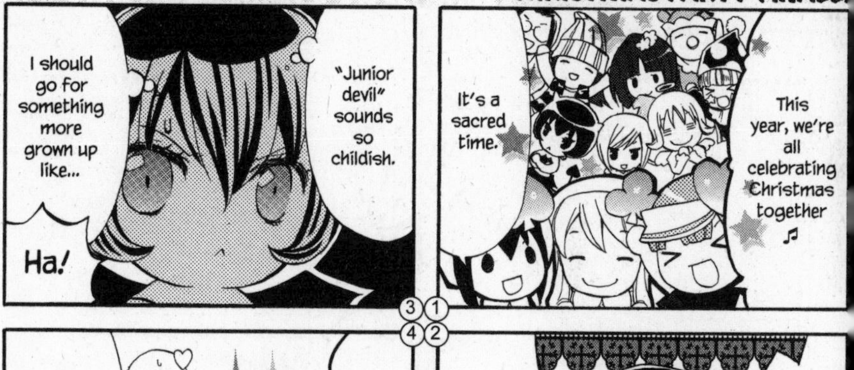
This year, we're all celebrating Christmas together ♫
It's a sacred time.
A sacred time? You expect me to celebrate that?
I'm a junior devil character, after all.
"Junior devil" sounds so childish.
I should go for something more grown up like...
Ha!
Devil Woman!
It's gotta have "Devil" in it, huh?

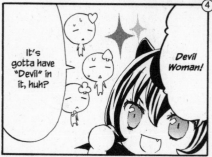

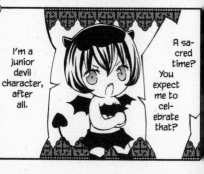

Fits the mood

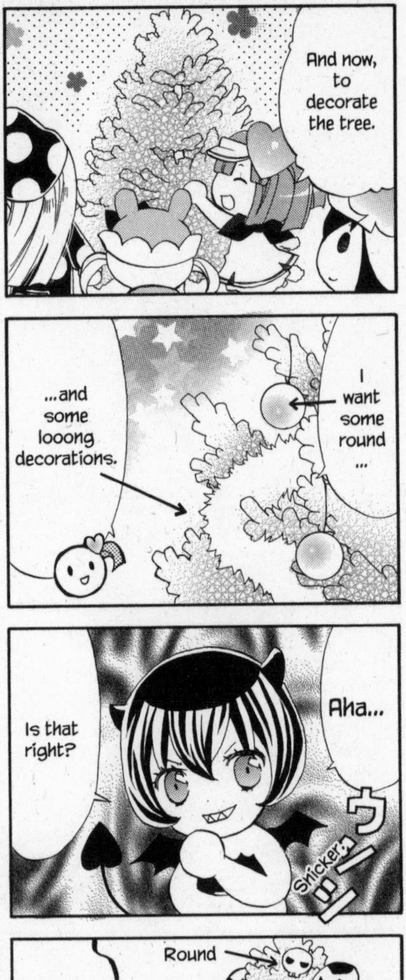
And now, to decorate the tree.
I want some round ...
...and some looong decorations.
Aha...
Is that right?
Shicker
Round
Long
Ahhh! What kind of holiday is this?

Sparkles just as bright

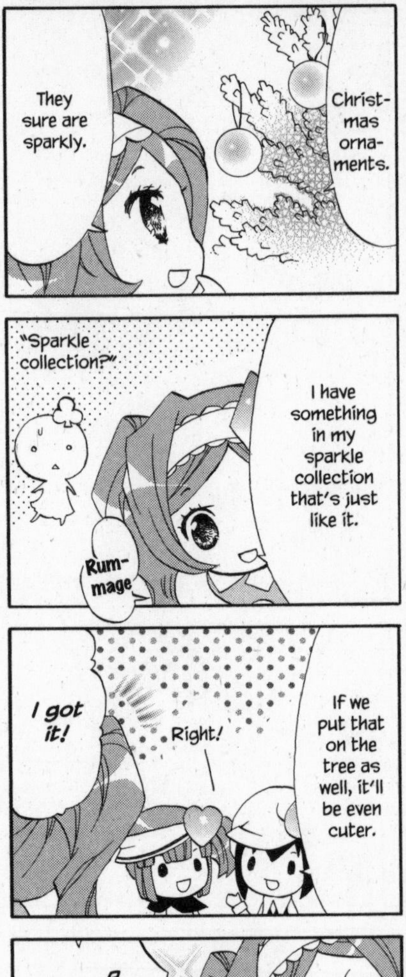
Christmas ornaments.
They sure are sparkly.
I have something in my sparkle collection that's just like it.
"Sparkle collection?"
Rummage
If we put that on the tree as well, it'll be even cuter.
Right!
I got it!
A pachinko ball!
It's like she's an old grandpa!

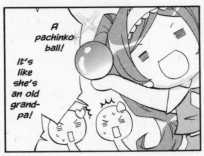

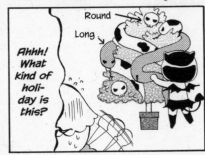

You said it yourself

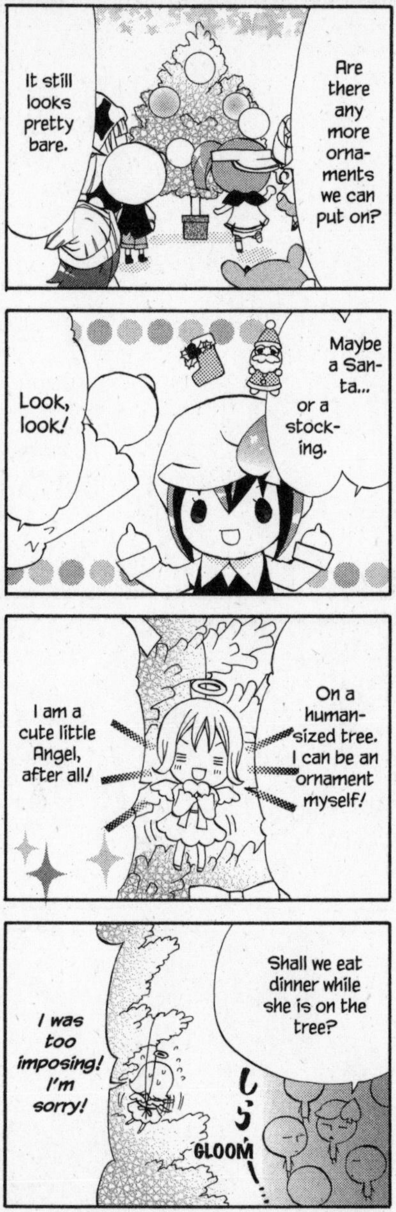
Are there any more ornaments we can put on?
It still looks pretty bare.
Maybe a Santa... or a stocking.
Look, look!
On a human-sized tree. I can be an ornament myself!
I am a cute little Angel, after all!
Shall we eat dinner while she is on the tree?
しら〜
GLOOM
I was too imposing! I'm sorry!

Prank protection

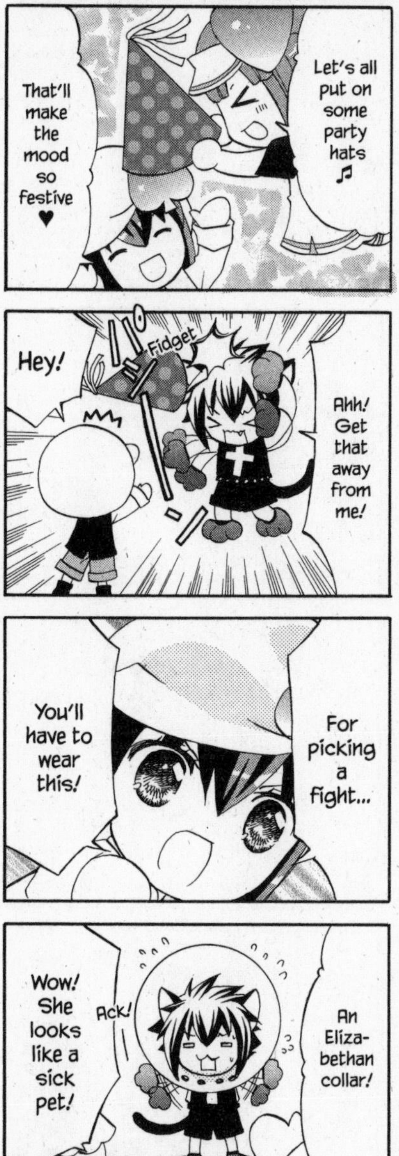
Let's all put on some party hats ♫
That'll make the mood so festive ♥
Ahh! Get that away from me!
Fidget
Hey!
For picking a fight...
You'll have to wear this!
An Elizabethan collar!
Ack!
Wow! She looks like a sick pet!

Shape memory

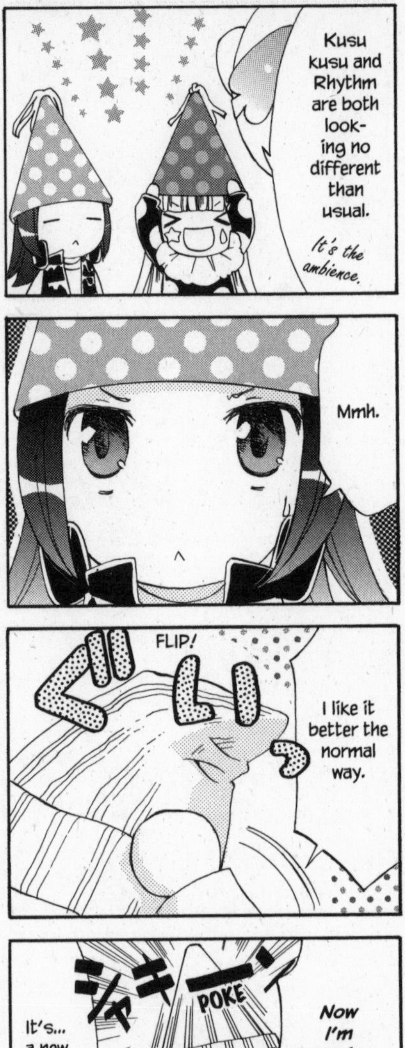
Kusu kusu and Rhythm are both looking no different than usual.
It's the ambience.
Mmh.
FLIP!
I like it better the normal way.
POKE
Now I'm wearing my cap over my party hat!
It's... a new look, that's for sure.

An honest mistake

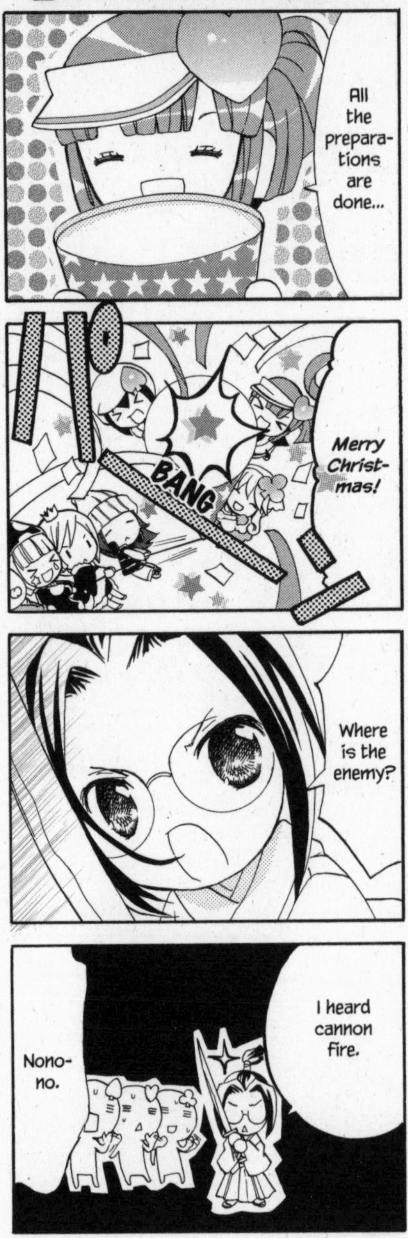
All the preparations are done...
Merry Christmas!
BANG
Where is the enemy?
I heard cannon fire.
Nonono.

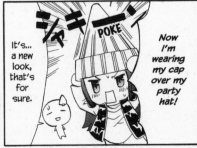

Celebration!

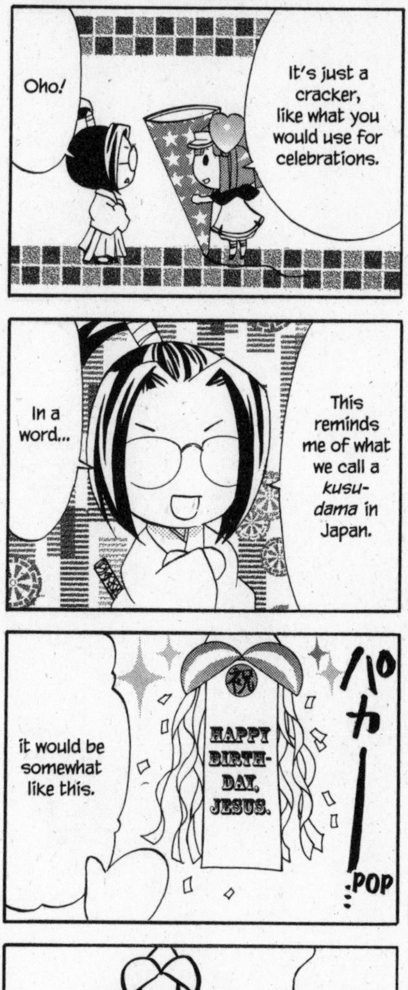
It's just a cracker, like what you would use for celebrations.
Oho!
This reminds me of what we call a *kusu-dama* in Japan.
In a word...
パカー
POP
祝
HAPPY BIRTH-DAY, JESUS.
it would be somewhat like this.
This turned into a new kind of Christ-mas...

Mood altering

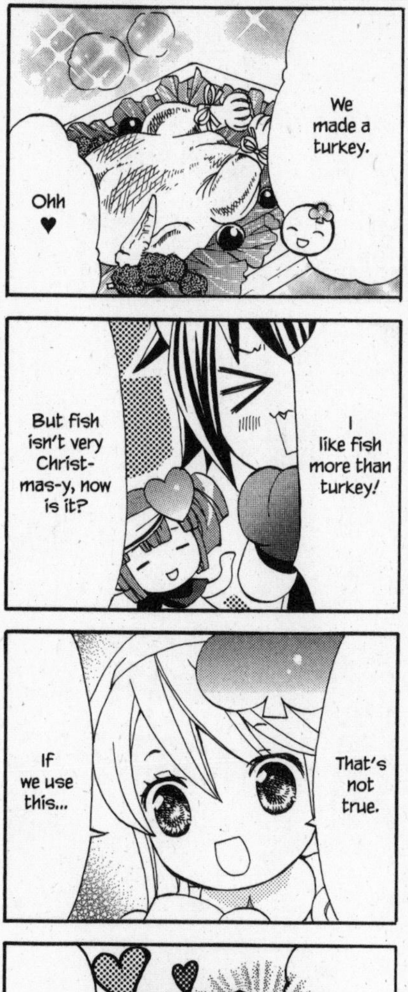
We made a turkey.
Ohh ♥
I like fish more than turkey!
But fish isn't very Christ-mas-y, now is it?
That's not true.
If we use this...
It's super Christ-mas-y ♥♥
Is it?

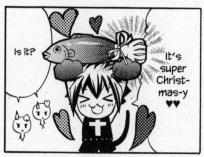

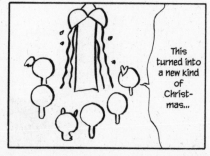

Trouble

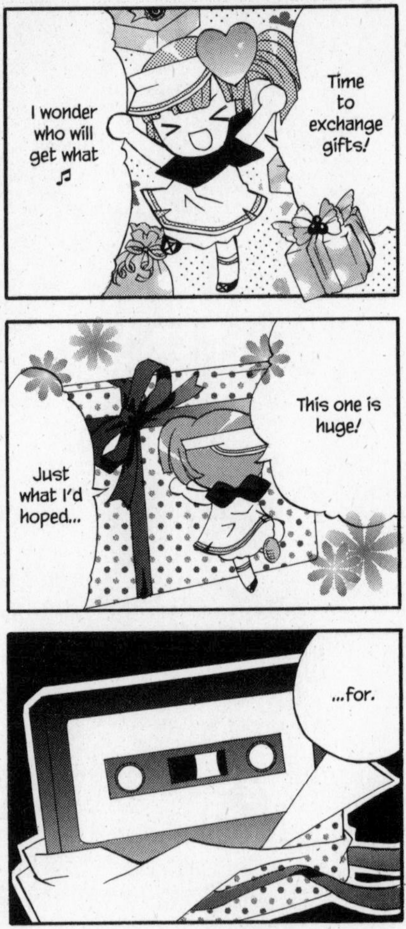
Time to exchange gifts!
I wonder who will get what ♫
This one is huge!
Just what I'd hoped...
...for.
It's an original recording of El's album ♥
Ugh. This is gonna be trouble-some...
Cas-sette tapes are so old-timey...

Don't need it

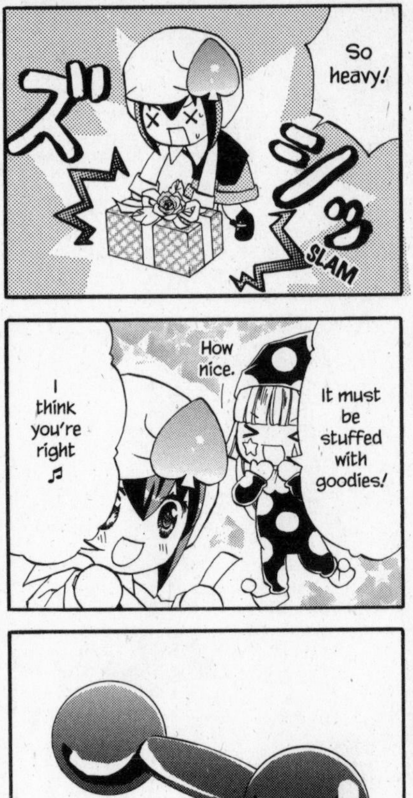
So heavy!
SLAM
It must be stuffed with goodies!
How nice.
I think you're right ♫
Iron weight
That's from me!
I could've guessed that...

Published in "Nakayoshi" July 2010 - December 2010, "Nakayoshi July Special Edition Nakayoshi Lovely", "Nakayoshi September Special Edition Nakayoshi Lovely", "Nakayoshi December Special Edition Nakayoshi Lovely, "Nakayoshi" January 2011, "Nakayoshi February Special Edition, Nakayoshi Lovely."

Kusu kusu is evil

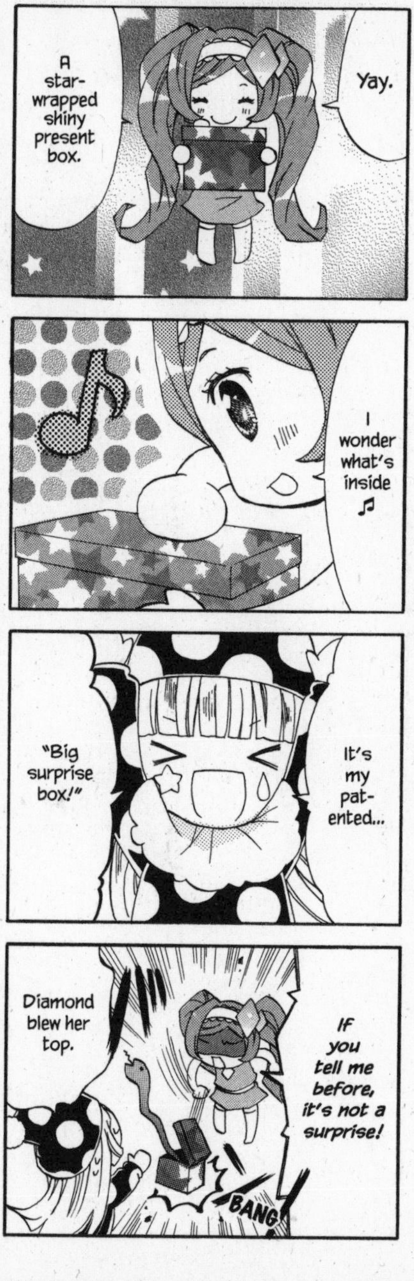
Yay.
A star-wrapped shiny present box.
I wonder what's inside ♫
It's my patented...
"Big surprise box!"
If you tell me before, it's not a surprise!
Diamond blew her top.
BANG

Cute?

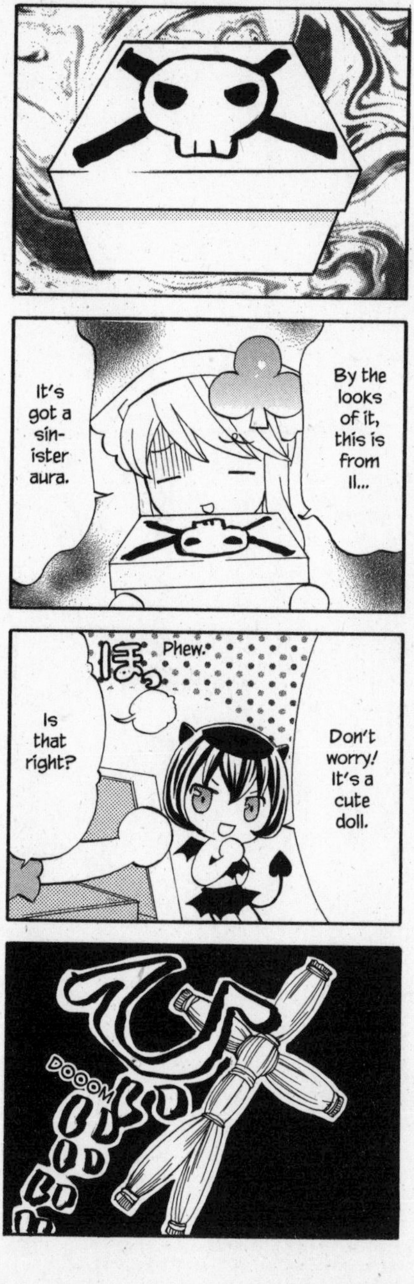
By the looks of it, this is from Il...
It's got a sinister aura.
ほっ
Phew.
Don't worry! It's a cute doll.
Is that right?
DOOOM

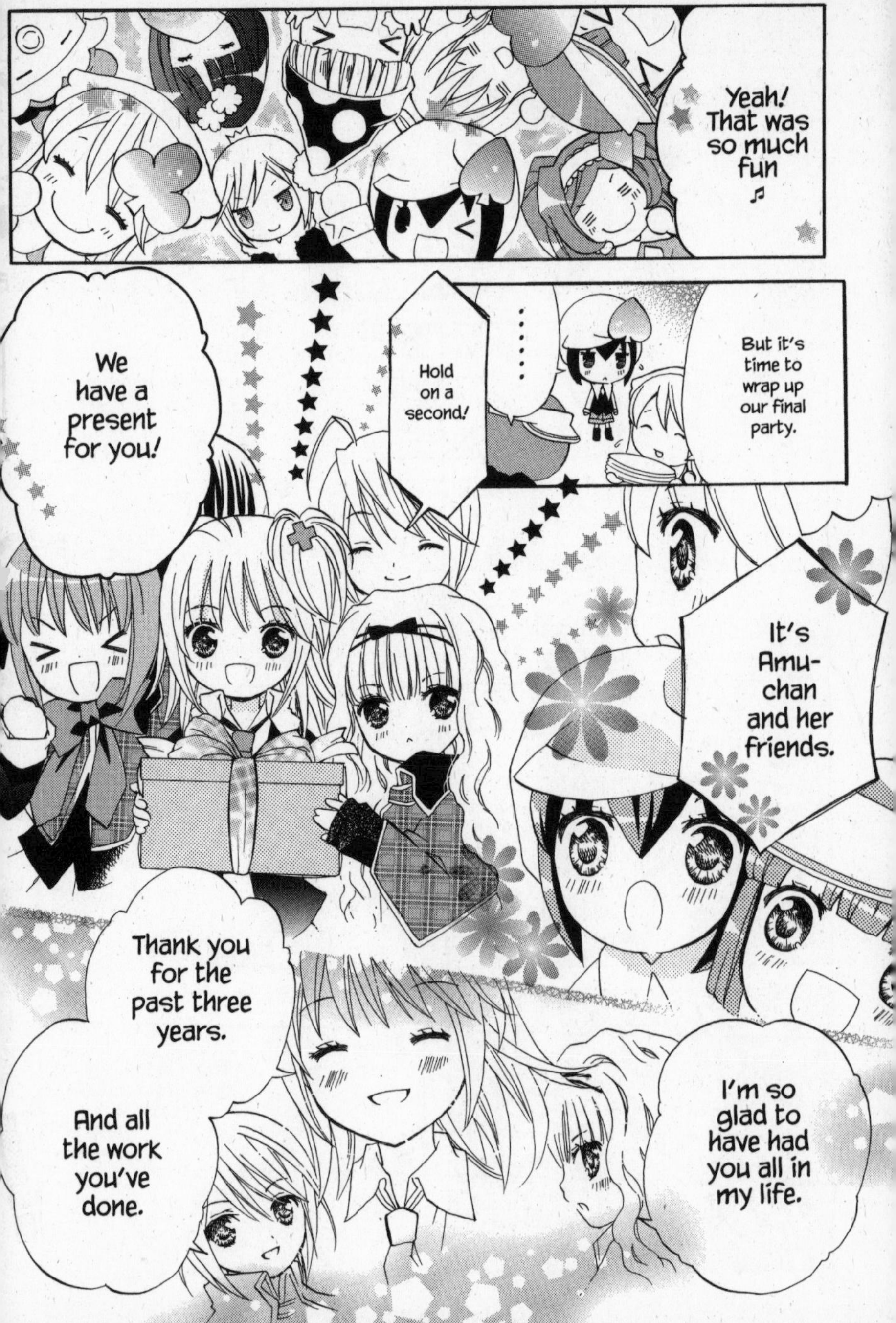
Yeah! That was so much fun ♪
But it's time to wrap up our final party.
......
Hold on a second!
It's Amu-chan and her friends.
We have a present for you!
Thank you for the past three years.
And all the work you've done.
I'm so glad to have had you all in my life.

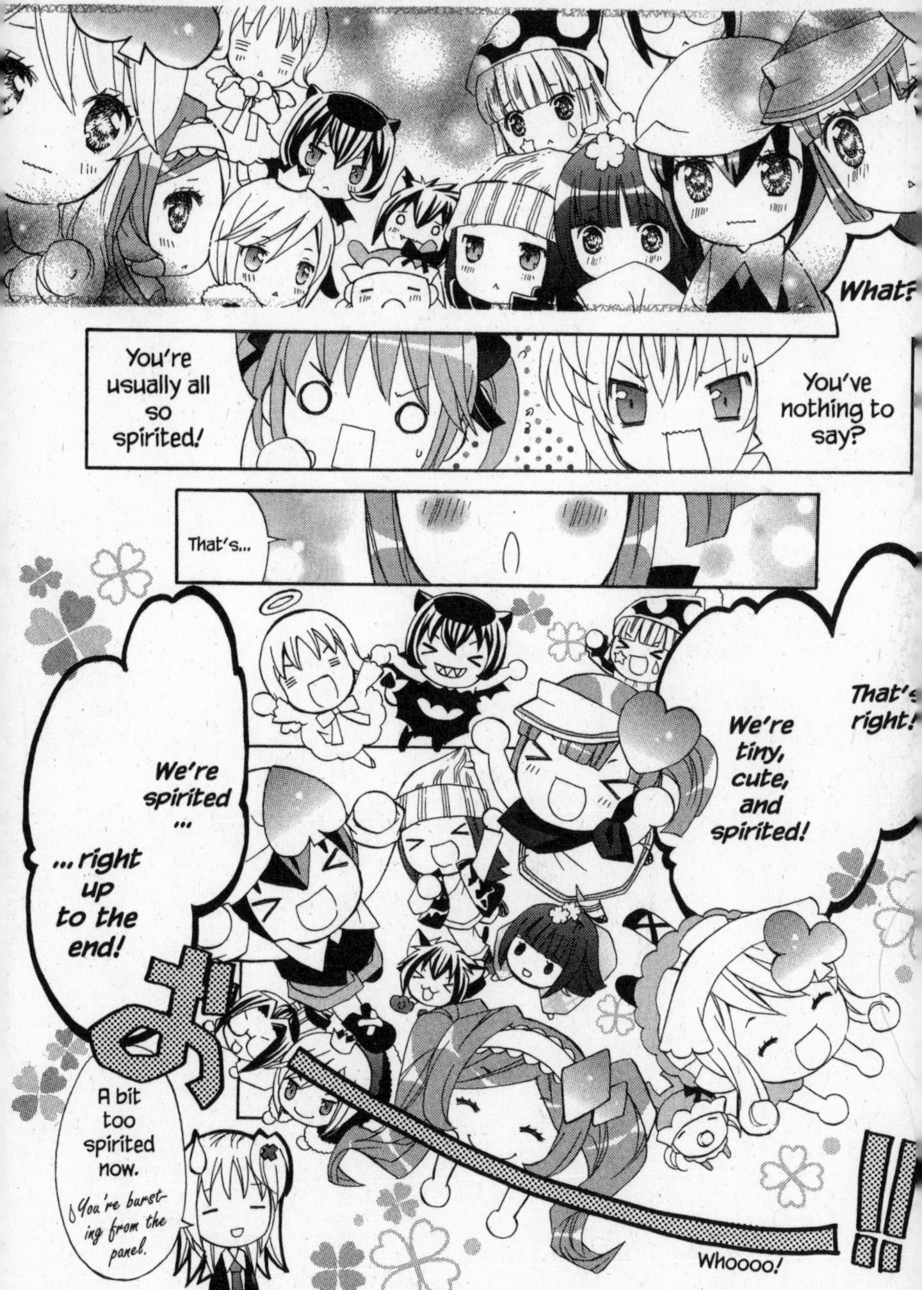
What?
You've nothing to say?
You're usually all so spirited!
That's...
That's right!
We're tiny, cute, and spirited!
We're spirited ...
... right up to the end!
Whoooo!
A bit too spirited now.
You're bursting from the panel.

THE END.

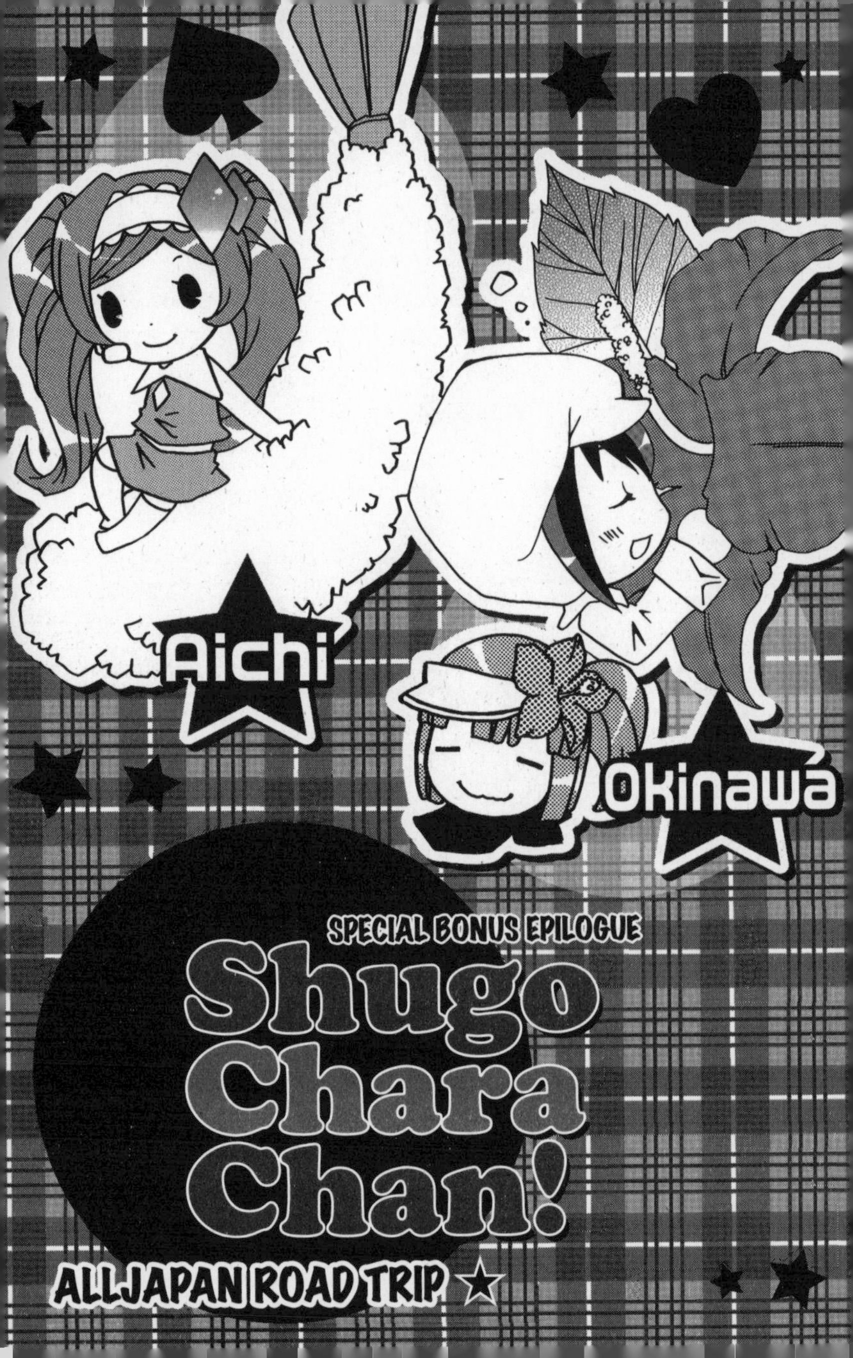
Aichi
Okinawa
SPECIAL BONUS EPILOGUE
Shugo Chara Chan!
ALLJAPAN ROAD TRIP ★

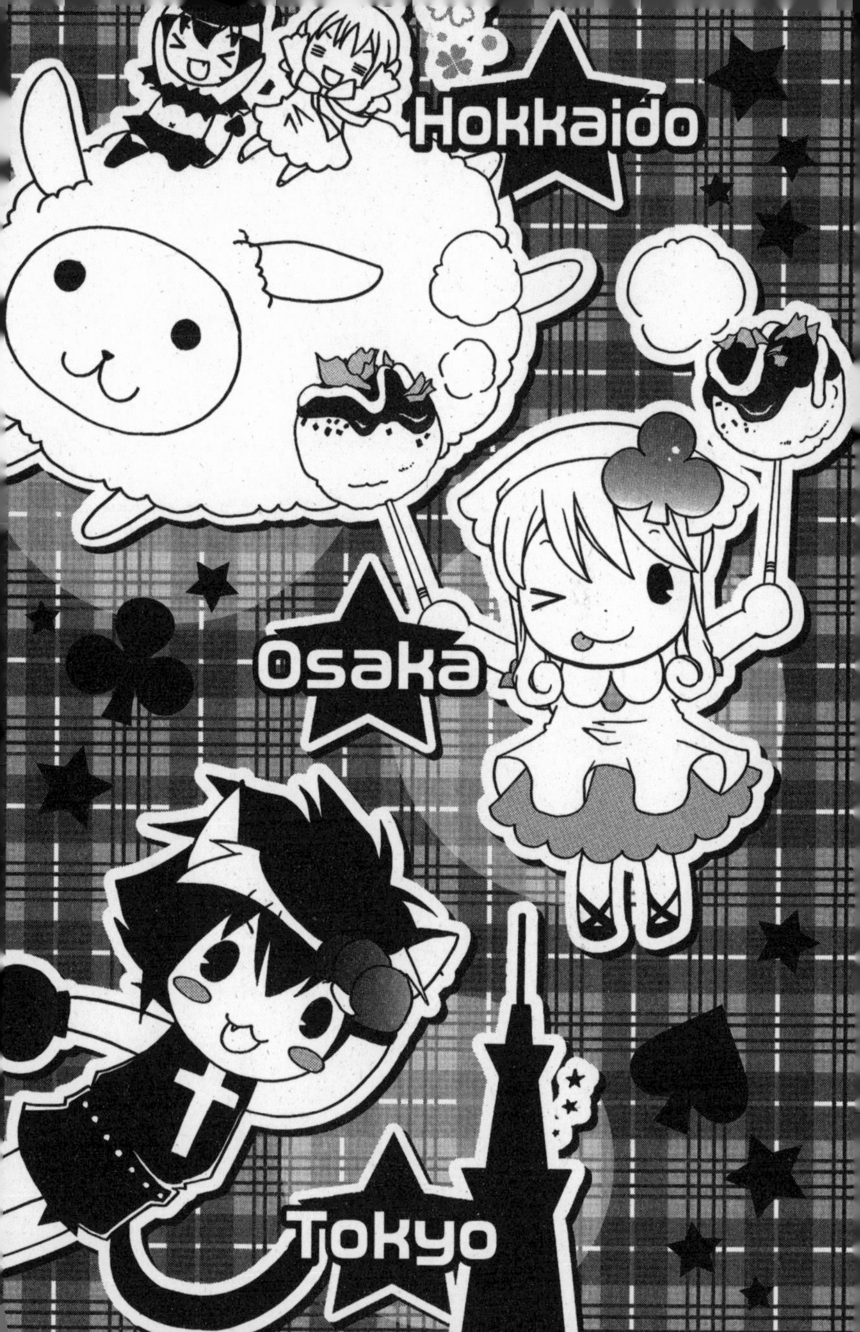
Hokkaido
Osaka
Tokyo

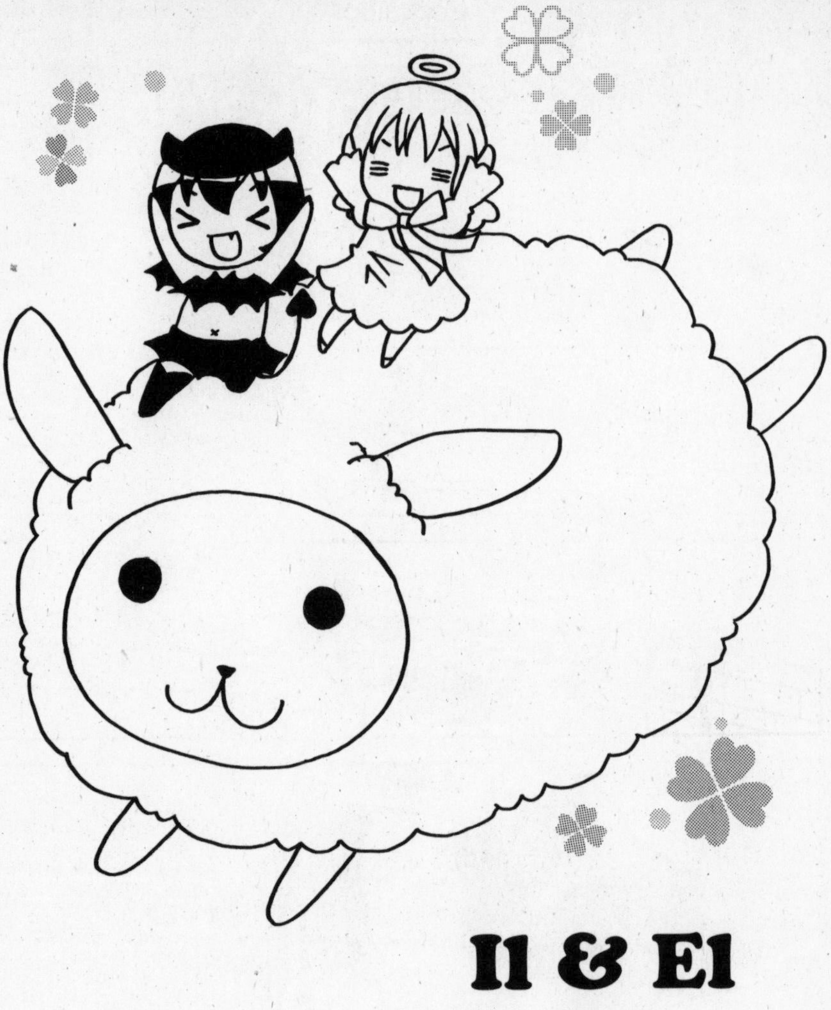

Il & El in Hokkaido

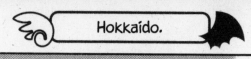

Hokkaido.

Hokkaido is all about...
...the great outdoors!
And also the dairy farms.
Moo
Huh? Where did we go?
Moo
Moo
N...
Right here!
We're camouflaged ★

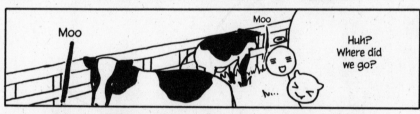

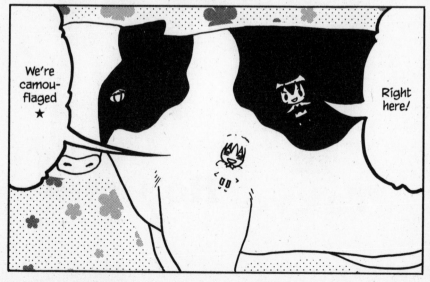

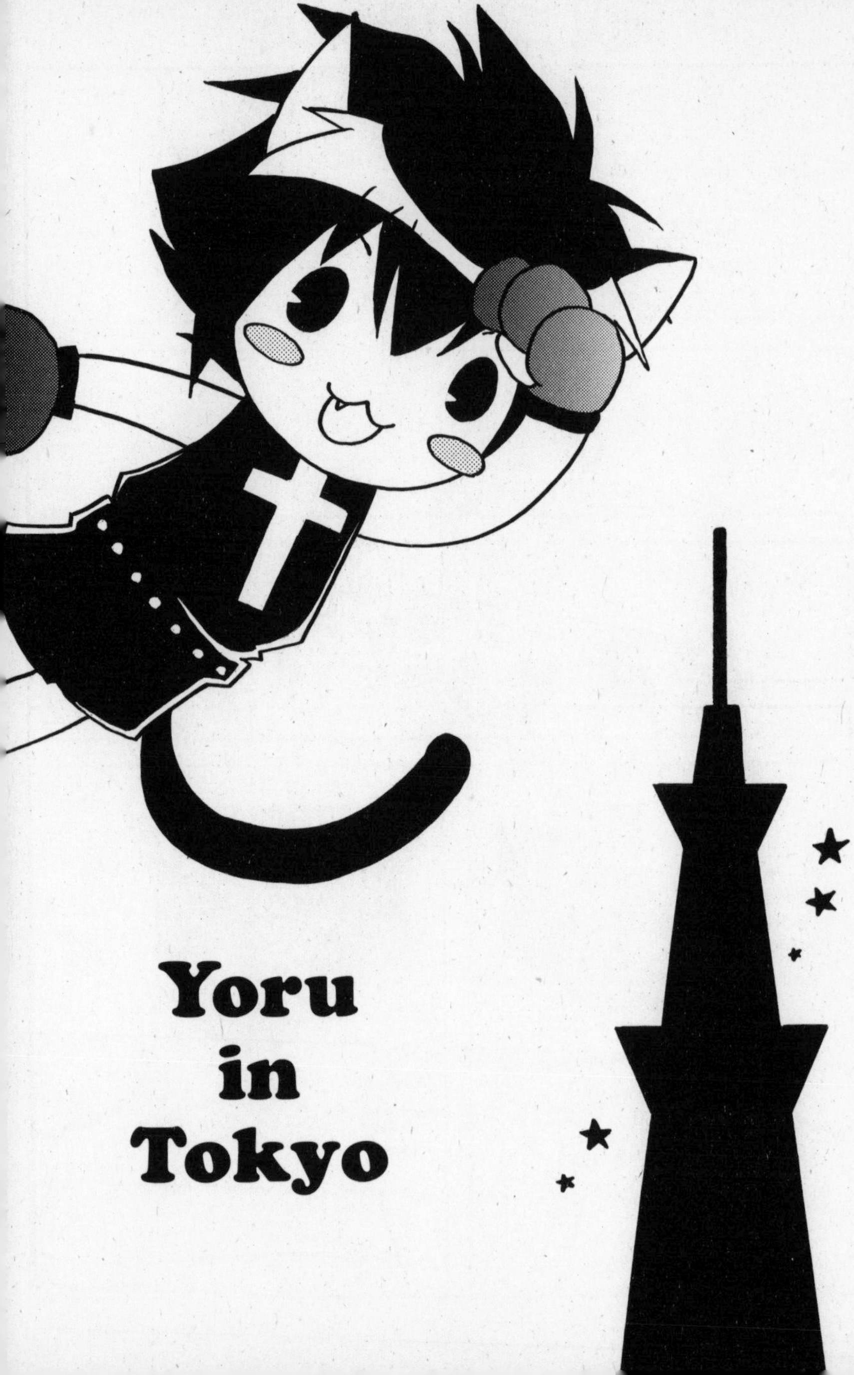
Yoru
in
Tokyo

Tokyo

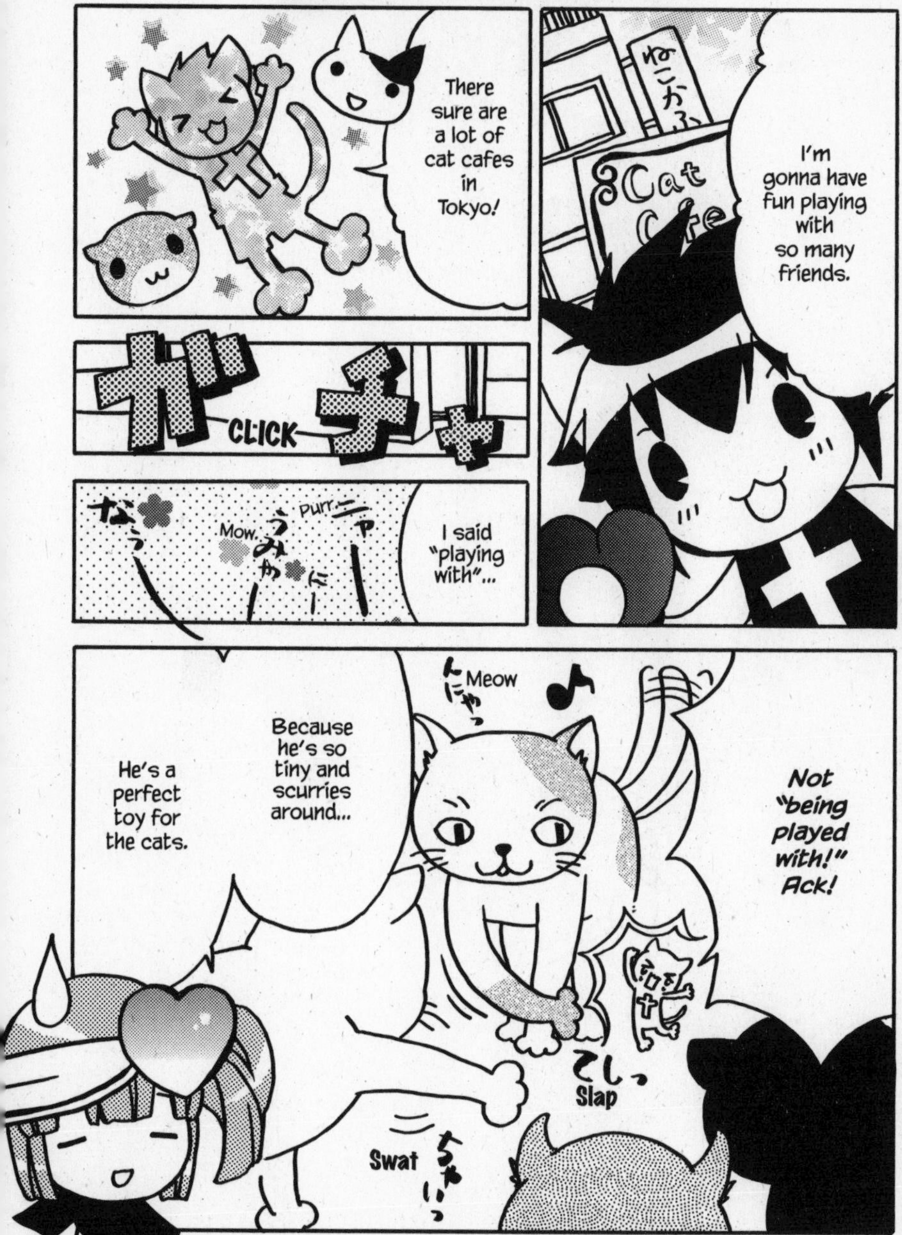

ねこかふ
Cat Cafe
I'm gonna have fun playing with so many friends.
There sure are a lot of cat cafes in Tokyo!
ガチャ
CLICK
ニャー
Purr.
にー
うみゃ
Mow.
なぁ
I said "playing with"...
Not "being played with!" Ack!
んにゃっ
Meow
Because he's so tiny and scurries around...
He's a perfect toy for the cats.
てしっ
Slap
ちゃいっ
Swat

Diamond in Aichi

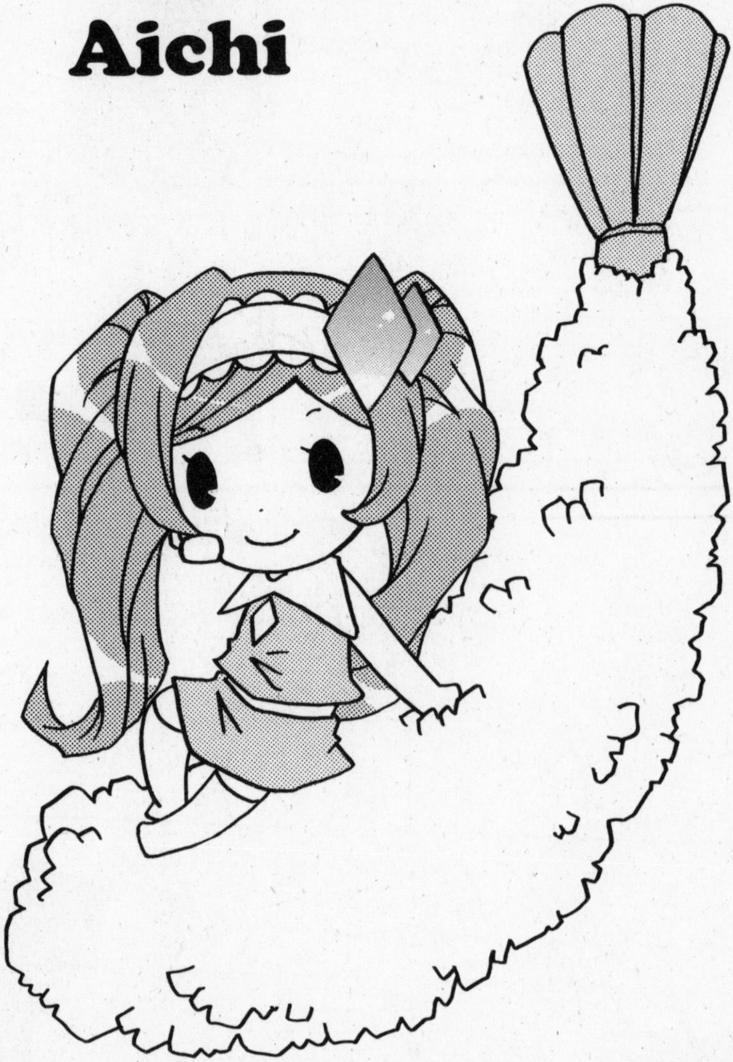

Aichi (Nagoya City)

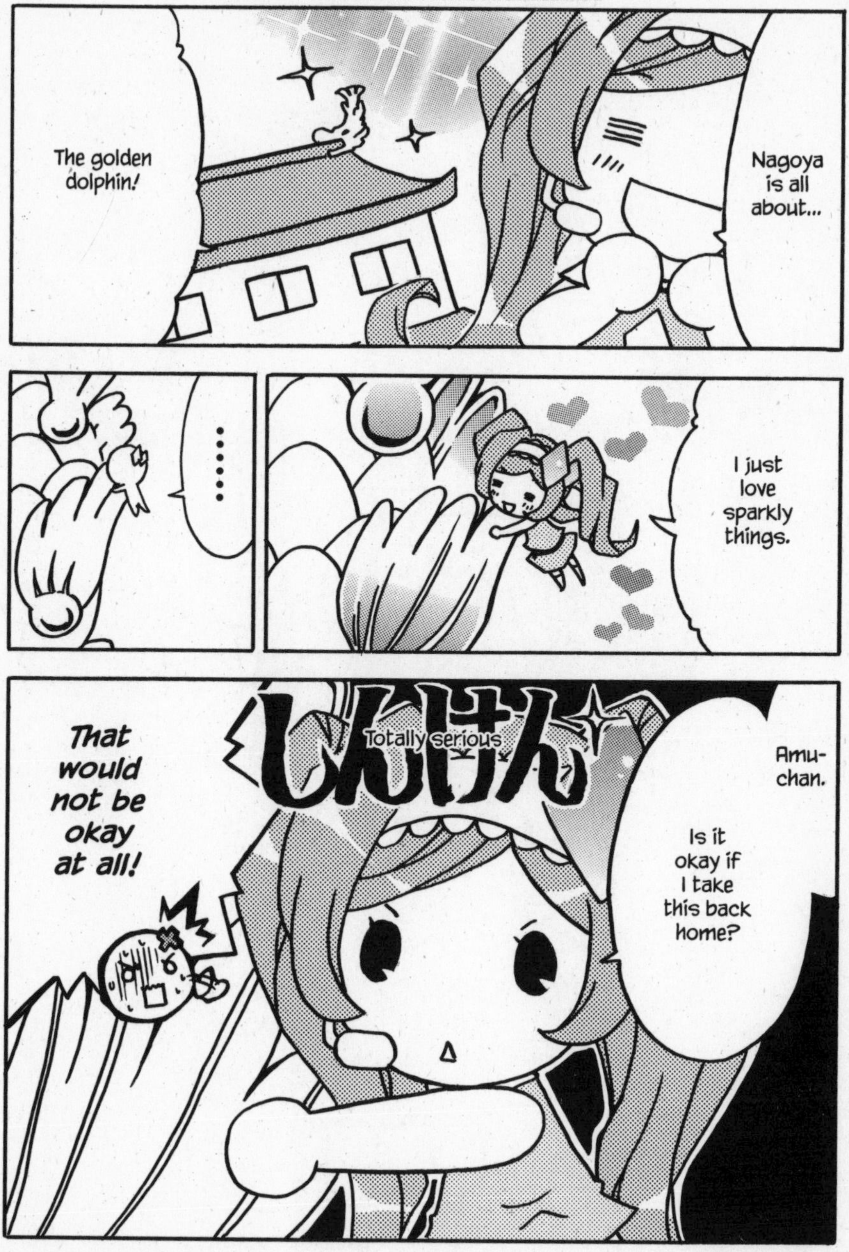
Nagoya is all about...
The golden dolphin!
I just love sparkly things.
....
Amu-chan.
Is it okay if I take this back home?
しんけん
Totally serious
That would not be okay at all!

Su in Osaka

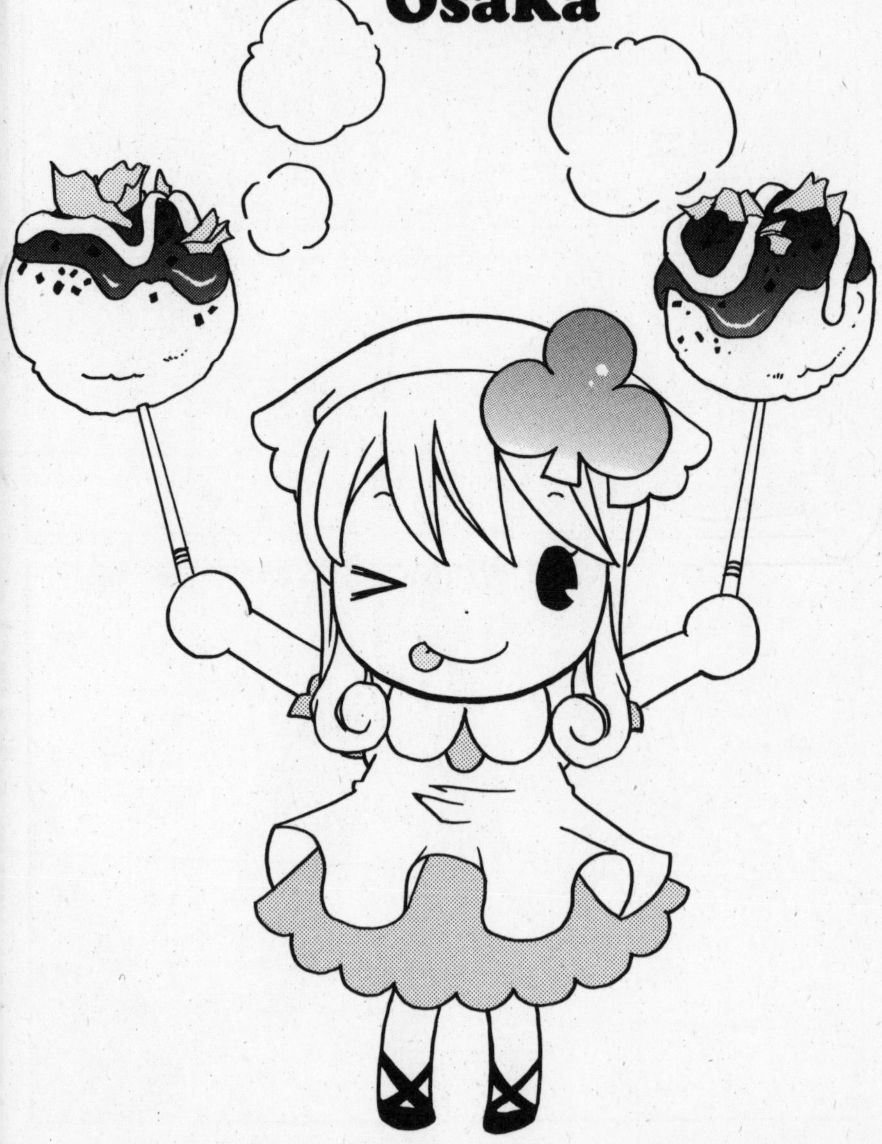

Osaka

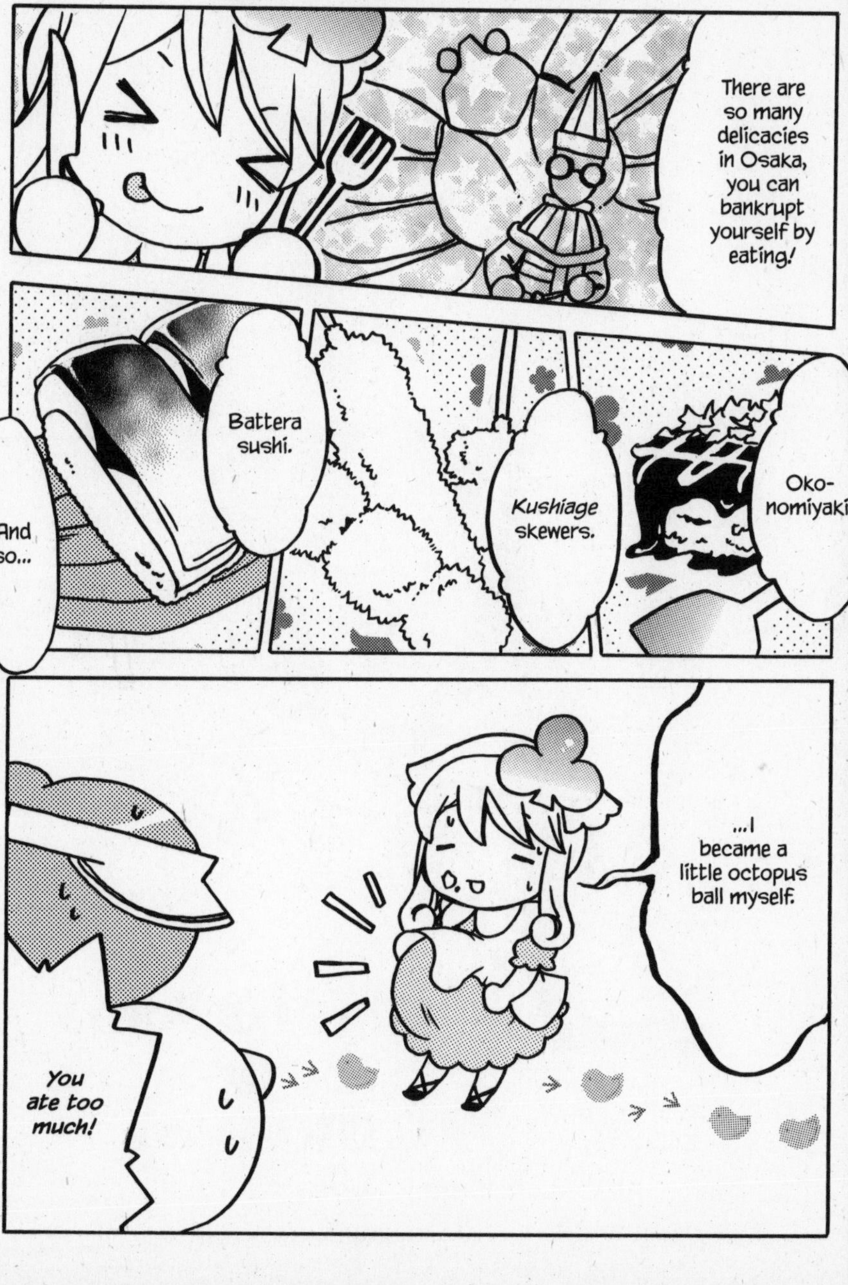

There are so many delicacies in Osaka, you can bankrupt yourself by eating!
Oko-nomiyaki.
Kushiage skewers.
Battera sushi.
And so...
...I became a little octopus ball myself.
You ate too much!

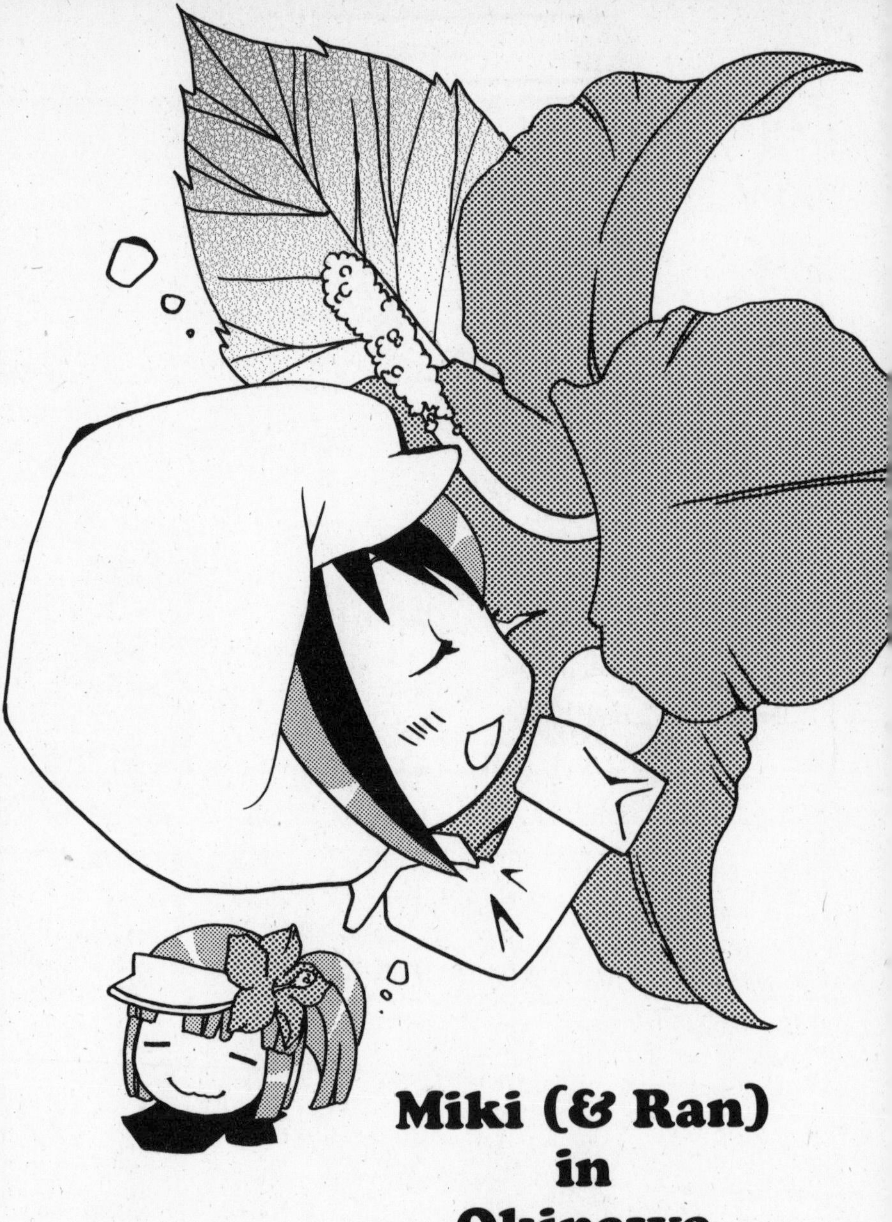

Miki (& Ran) in Okinawa

Okinawa

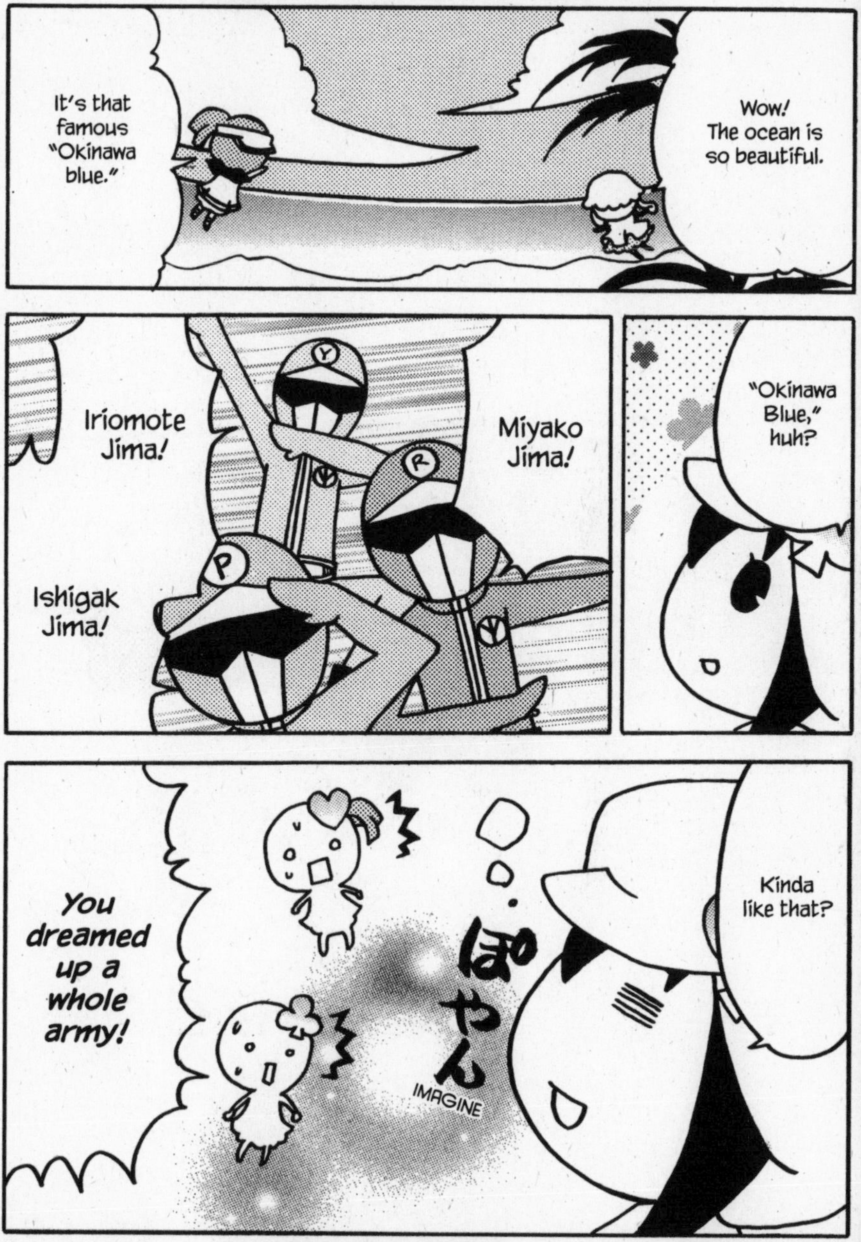
Wow! The ocean is so beautiful.
It's that famous "Okinawa blue."
"Okinawa Blue," huh?
Miyako Jima!
Iriomote Jima!
Ishigak Jima!
Kinda like that?
ぽやん
IMAGINE
You dreamed up a whole army!

EPILOGUE THE END.

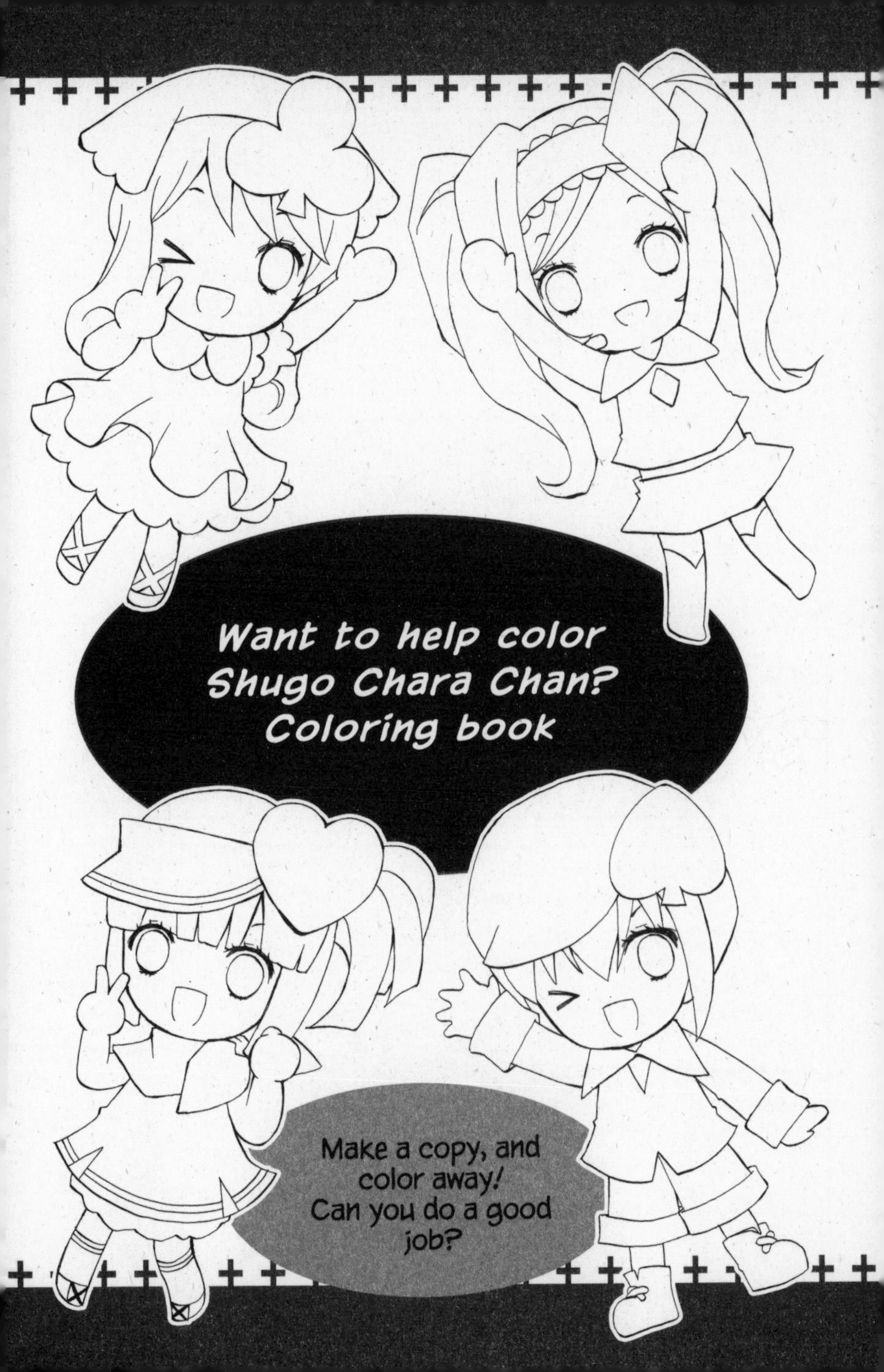
Want to help color
Shugo Chara Chan?
Coloring book
Make a copy, and
color away!
Can you do a good
job?

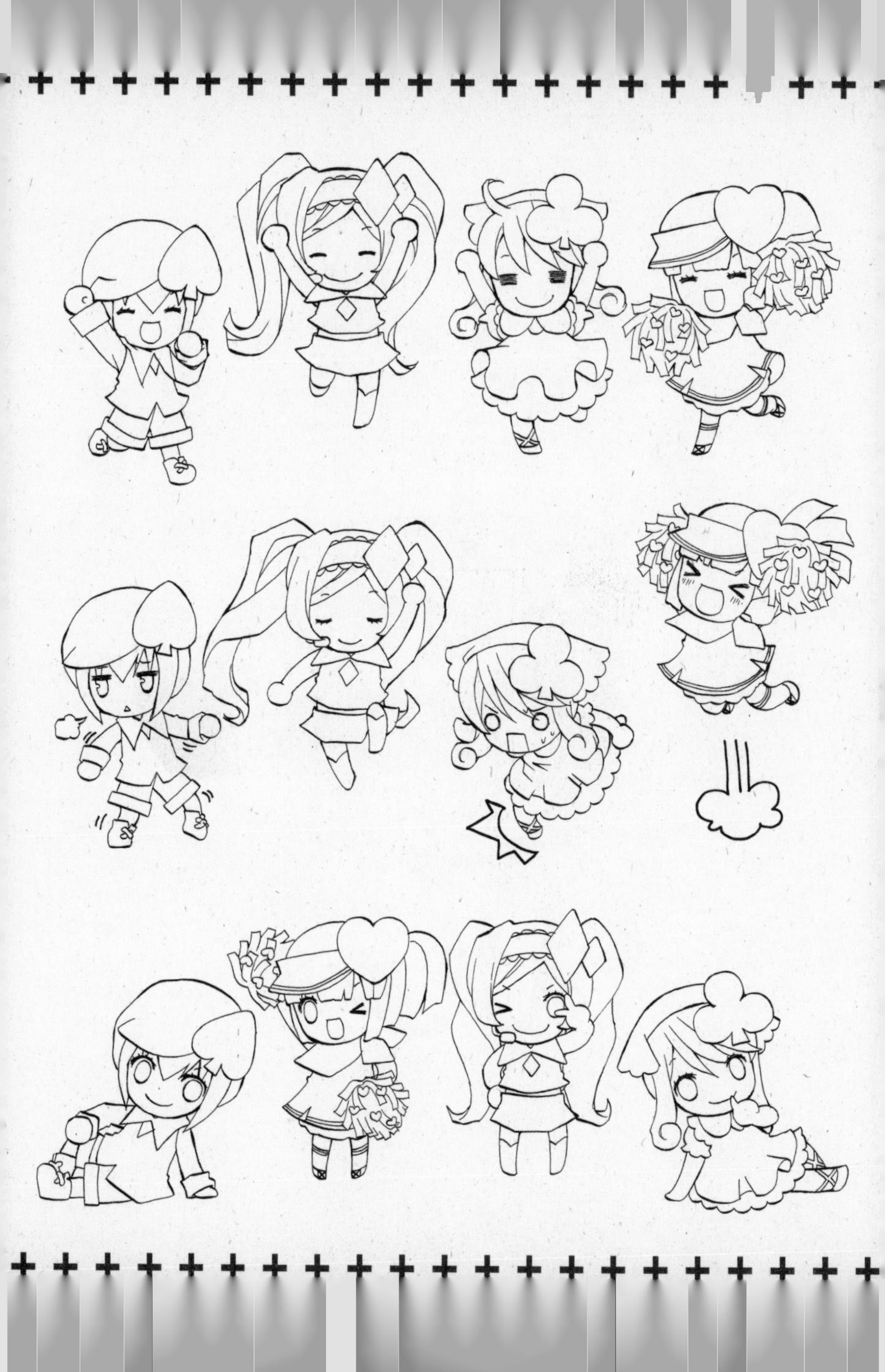

Afterword

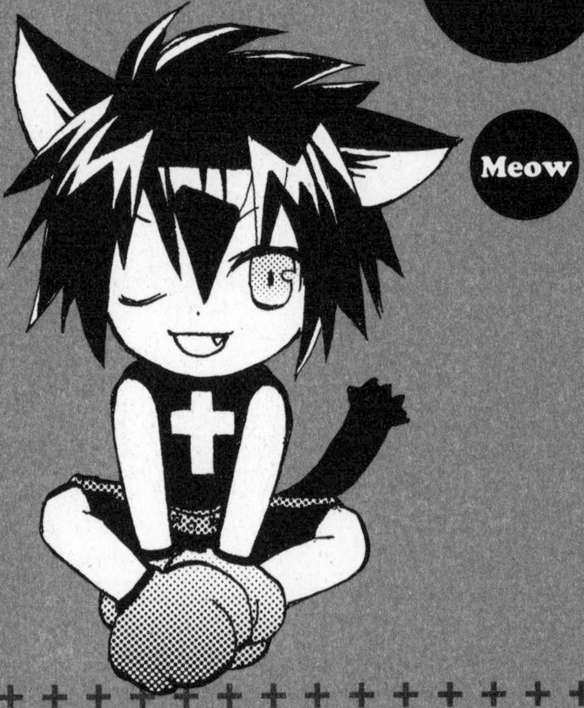
Meow

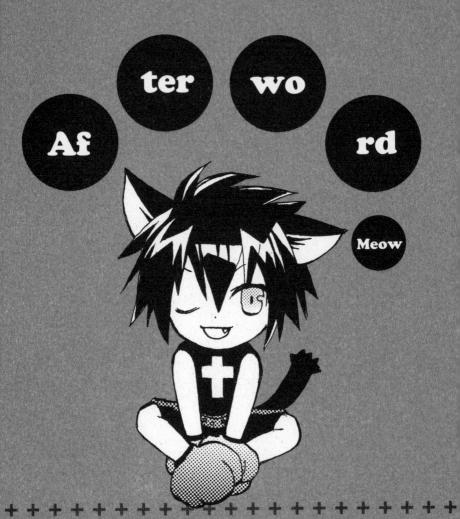

And so we've reached the final volume.

Thanks to the efforts of many talented authors, this cute spin-off world of "Shugo Chara!" has come to an end as well. From now on, anytime you want a smile on your face, please open a copy of "Shugo Chara Chan!"

Many thanks to
Naphthalene Mizushima Sensei
for seeing it through
to the end.

PEACH-PIT

Afterword

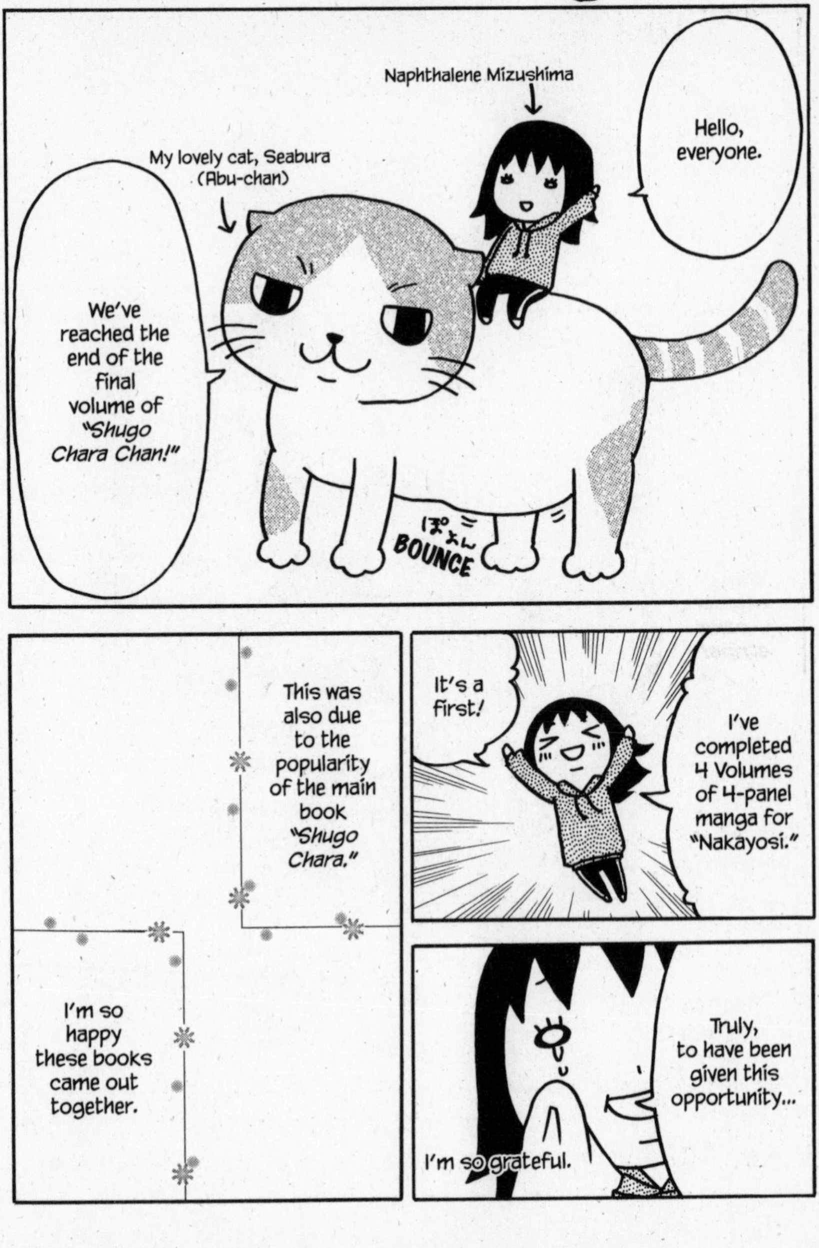
Hello, everyone.
Naphthalene Mizushima
My lovely cat, Seabura (Abu-chan)
We've reached the end of the final volume of "Shugo Chara Chan!"
ぽよん
BOUNCE
I've completed 4 Volumes of 4-panel manga for "Nakayosi."
It's a first!
Truly, to have been given this opportunity...
I'm so grateful.
This was also due to the popularity of the main book "Shugo Chara."
I'm so happy these books came out together.

Phew...
What shall I do now?
I'm out of work.
Well then, what do you think she does when she is out of work?
Eat.
Drink.
Sleep.
...it's an endless loop.
Heh heh.
That's so typical of you!
Despite being the author of these magical 4-panel strips!
Don't shatter the children's dreams.
Kids, make sure you don't grow up to be like this, okay?
May your lives be full of sparkles!
So long!
Hey... don't be so strict with me all of a sudden.
Farewell! Until next time we all can be together again! ♥

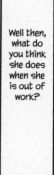

Translation Notes

Momotaro, Page 9
[9.1]
Momotaro is a famous hero of Japanese folklore. In it, a friendly, old farmer and his wife find a baby, floating in a giant peach on a river. For this reason, they name him 'Momotaro,' which means "Peach Boy." Momotaro grows up big and strong and one day sets out to an island of ogres that are terrorizing the area. On his travels. he meets a dog, a monkey. and a pheasant. He gives them each a dumpling to eat. and they join him. Momotaro and his companions sail to Ogre Island and defeat all the evil Ogres there, taking their chief captive. They return home with all the treasures the Ogres had stolen.
The story of Momotaro has been the subject of many manga, cartoons, and movies in Japan throughout the years. He is often depicted wearing a flag on his back with the characters Nippon Ichi, which means "the strongest in Japan".

Glasses character, Page 9
[9.5]
A megane kyara, or "glasses character." is a term for a manga character whose defining characteristic is his or her glasses. There are many characters in manga who have glasses, simply because it makes them look smarter and more fashionable--unlike our poor Musashi, who really has bad eyesight, so without his glasses. he's helpless. That's why Ran calls him a "classic glasses character."

Mountain Yam, Page 18
[18.4]
Nagaimo, meaning "long yam" is a vegetable often used in Japanese cuisine. It is often grated and eaten as a kind of paste, which is very refreshing and restoring. When preparing nagaimo, many people get an allergic reaction that causes their hands to itch.

Mozuku, Megabu, Junsai, Page 19
[19.2]
Mozuku is a type of edible seaweed. Megabu is the sprout of the sea vegetable wakame. Junsai is another type of aquatic plant of the same family as the water lily. All three of these plants are eaten seasonally in Japan.

Daruma otoshi, Page 19
[19.8]
Daruma otoshi, meaning "Daruma Drop" is a Japanese children's game. It is played with a daruma doll in five pieces, each piece being a different color, so it looks almost like a hamburger! The game is played using a small hammer to knock out each colored piece without toppling the whole doll. So Su is trying to knock out the meat patty of the burger without making the burger fall over.

Nagashi somen, Page 20
[20.5]
Nagashi somen, or "flowing somen" is a way of eating noodles, often done during the summer months. The thin somen noodles are placed in a bamboo flume across the length of the restaurant. The noodles flow down the bamboo on ice-cold water. Customers catch the noodles with chopsticks and dip them in cold sauce. It's a fun and delicious way to have a summer meal.

Katori buta, Page 24
[24.8]
Katori-buta, or "mosquito/repellant pig" are small ceramic pigs that one burns mosquito coils in. The odors of the burnt coils keeps mosquitoes away, so katori-buta are often used during the hot summer months.

Tsukkomi, Page 26
[26.8]
In Japan, comedy duos are often split into the role of tsukkomi and boke. A boke is the person who says something silly or nonsensical. and the tsukkomi reacts to the comment, usually by letting the boke know how dumb he's being.

Split the Watermelon, Page 30
[30.2]
Suika-wari, or "Split the Watermelon" is a game played in summer, usually on a beach.
A watermelon is laid out. Players are blindfolded and spun around three times. Then they are given a bat and have to try and split the melon in one hit! Once it's been split, the watermelon is eaten.

Kabuto beetle, Page 32
[32.7]
Kabuto beetle, or "Japanese horned beetle" is an insect that is very common in Japan. Many children, especially boys, catch and breed these beetles as a hobby. They are often depicted in manga and anime, as every child in Japan knows about kabuto.

Golden Week, Page 41
[41]
Golden Week is the period from April 29th to May 5th. During this time, several national holidays occur right after another so almost all Japanese end up with an entire week off. Golden Week is one of the most popular times for the Japanese to travel, with millions of people taking trips around the country or overseas.

String of 1000 Cranes. Page 44
[44.1]
A Senbazuru, or "1000 Cranes" is a large number, traditionally one thousand, of folded origami cranes held together by strings. Legend promises that whoever folds one thousand cranes will be granted a wish. Senbazuru remain popular gifts to this day, especially for newly wed couples.

Baumkuchen, Page 50
[50.2]
Baumkuchen is a layered cake served primarily in Germany. When it is cut, the layers look a bit like the rings of a tree. This gave the cake its German name, "Tree Cake". Baumkuchen was introduced to Japan by a German baker, and it remains one of the most popular deserts to this day.

Yuzuyu, Page 53
[53.1]
Yuzuyu is the practice of placing a yuzu, which is a kind of Japanese lemon, into hot bath water. This bathwater is said to prevent colds and has other health benefits. It is customary to have a yuzuyu bath around the Winter Solstice in Japan.

Oden, Page 66
[66.8]
Oden is a Japanese winter dish that involves lightly stewing vegetables, fish, and tofu in a dashi broth. Usually, oden is prepared in a large pot in which all the ingredients are stewed together. Customers can pick whichever items they want from the boiling broth with wooden skewers.

Oyakodon, Page 67
[67.8]
Oyakodon is a dish, in which chicken, egg, and scallions are simmered together and served on a bowl of rice. The name, meaning literally "parent and child bowl," is a reflection on the fact that both chicken (parent) and egg (child) are used in the dish.

Dovetail. page 68
Japanese word for dove is hato, which sounds like the Japnese word for hat, which is hatto. (Pulling a hato(dove) out of a hatto (hat)) Then later the person gasps ecause the dove's got an announcement/ flier. Japanese SFX for gasp is Ha. Then the magician person says "You're gasping ("ha tto") because of the dove ("hato"), aren't you!"

Haramaki, Page 76
[76.3]
Haramaki are belly warmers that are worn in Japan during the colder seasons. They were popular in the early 20th Century before falling out of style.

Kairo, Page 77
[77.1]
Kairo are disposable pouches filled with a powder that heat up when exposed to oxygen. You can put one in each coat pocket and keep your hands warm in the winter.

X-Mark, Page 77
[77.8]
In Japan, "X" does not mark the spot so much as indicate a wrong or an incorrect answer. A circle is used to mark a correct answer.

Kamakura, Page 78
[78.2]
A festival held annually on February 15th in the city of Yokote. It involves children building many small igloo-like structures, called kamakura, sitting inside, and cooking over small campfires.

Nabe, Page 80
[80.2]
Nabe, which is short for nabemono, is a Japanese dish often eaten in the winter. The nabe is a pot, in which all kinds of ingredients are steamed and eaten together. In Japan, eating from one pot is said to tighten relationships so eating nabe together makes for warm hearts as well as warm stomachs.

Pachinko, Page 84
[84.8]
Pachinko is a kind of slot machine where the player must guide many metal balls through a series of traps and levers to win even more balls, which can be traded for prizes. Though Pachinko is tremendously popular all across Japan, the image it often garners is that only old men play this game.

Kusudama, Page 87
[87.2]
Kusudama, meaning "medicine ball." is an origami ball made of paper that in Japan is used as festival decorations or gifts. Kusudama used to refer to a bunch of healing herbs tied together to form a ball but has since taken on this modern meaning.

Kushiage, Page 101
[101.3]
Kushiage is a Japanese skewer dish consisting of pork, vegetables, or seafood deep-fried in oil. It is a specialty of Osaka.

Battera, Page 101
[101.4]
Another specialty of Osaka, Battera is a special type of sushi, made by compressing mackerel fish with rice in a small box. This gives the sushi its unique square shape.

A Kodansha Comics Trade Paperback Original

Shugo Chara Chan! volume 4 copyright © 2010 PEACH-PIT and Naphthalene Mizushima
English translation copyright © 2012 PEACH-PIT and Naphthalene Mizushima

Published in the United States by Kodansha Comics, an imprint of Kodansha USA Publishing, LLC, New York.

Publication rights for this English edition arranged through Kodansha Ltd., Tokyo.

First published in Japan in 2010 by Kodansha Ltd., Tokyo.

ISBN 978-1-61262-233-0

Printed in the United States of America.

www.kodanshacomics.com

9 8 7 6 5 4 3 2 1

Translator: Sebastian Girner
Lettering: Drew Rausch